"Their argument has intuitive appeal . . . [and] is made more attractive by their clear prose and by their many helpful descriptions and historical explanations of US health care policy."
—Arnold Relman, *New York Review of Books*

"[A] crucial addition to public deliberations on what is wrong with the American health care system. . . . Bradley and Taylor walk the reader through the historical, political, and institutional contours of the problem . . . [and] offer a way of looking at [it] that is at once eminently intuitive and completely radical. . . . *The American Health Care Paradox* has as much to offer religious leaders and scholars of religion as it does to those crafting health care policy." —*Harvard Divinity Bulletin*

"It seems like there are daily stories of skyrocketing medical costs here in the US coupled with our bad health outcomes compared with other developed countries. This book argues compellingly that we may have been looking for solutions in the wrong places. It is time we started to get serious about building a culture of health and making it easier for people to live that kind of life than merely paying the costs to repair the damages from injury and disease."
—James S. Marks, MD, MPH, president and director of Health Group at the Robert Wood Johnson Foundation

"*The American Health Care Paradox* has enough intellectual heft to bring an opera house to its feet. Drawing on data from dozens of international and domestic site visits, wide-ranging scholarly studies and in-depth interviews with patients, practitioners, health care administrators and social service staff from all over the world, the authors tackle the unenviable task of explaining why we think of health care the way we do—to the near total exclusion of social services. And they manage to do it with astonishing clarity, conciseness and narrative ease."
—Pauline Chen, *New York Times*

"*The American Health Care Paradox* is a paradigm shifter . . . Completely reframes the usual (and by now tedious) discussion. . . . Looking at other countries' approaches to health care is just one of the ways Bradley and Taylor hammer home their message that an effective health-care system requires social even more than medical services." —*The Christian Century*

"This remarkably well-written, lucid work is highly appropriate for public and academic libraries. —*Library Journal*, STARRED review

"Makes[s] a sober, well-reasoned case that, in more ways than one, we focus too much on symptoms and too little on root causes. . . . For starters, our definition of 'health care' needs some work."
—*Washington Independent Review of Books*

"The book's central argument is that we spend too much on health care . . . while spending too little on the social, behavioral, and environmental factors that account for 60–70 percent of premature deaths. . . . Bradley and Taylor's well-written book provides vivid examples of the problems resulting from this imbalance." —HealthAffairs.org

"Bradley and Taylor have identified social services as the unnamed culprit behind high health care costs and poor outcomes. Highlighting the non-medical determinants of patients' health may not only make physicians' jobs easier but also prove to be a prudent strategy for payers. This book offers an important reality check about what actually creates health in the United States."
—William Gillespie, MD, Chief Medical Officer of Emblem Health, and president of AdvantageCare Physicians

"Using an array of data, historical context, and research, Bradley and Taylor make the case that the idea that medical care is a substitute for whole-body health is at the heart of our health care paradox. . . . [A] clear and concise argument for how America's obsession with individualism contributes to our lack of consistent and evenly distributed health care." —*Spirituality & Health*

"An important attempt to shift the discussion on health in the United States." —*Kirkus Reviews*

"The challenge of addressing social as well as health needs is daunting. One could become 'paralyzed by the complexity inherent in the relationships among health, social services, and health outcomes, and . . . consider strategic action all but impossible.' The book provides a counterweight to such pessimism. The authors examine four case studies of successful 'home grown innovations' that provide evidence that it is, in fact, feasible to integrate social and medical services." —*Health Affairs*

"These authors offer us a comprehensive view of our healthcare system. I enthusiastically recommend this book for all nurses."
—American Holistic Nurses Association

"The US has worse health outcomes than other wealthy countries not only because of a deeply flawed insurance system, but also because it spends less than other countries on the fundamentals of life that affect people's health, including education, housing, good jobs, nutrition, and environmental protection." —World Wide Work bulletin

"Admirably presented as an apolitical examination of an urgent situation, Bradley and Taylor's carefully researched and lucidly reported findings . . . offer what appears to be an easily rendered fix, but their equally striking depiction of uniquely American hostility to government involvement in private matters, exposes a daunting uphill battle."
—Publishers Weekly

"If we're so rich, why aren't we healthier? I'd wondered about that for years, always assuming it was a medical question with a medical answer. I now know the answer lies not in what happens in our hospitals but what happens (or fails to happen) in our social services. This compelling, groundbreaking, and utterly persuasive book has opened my eyes."
—Anne Fadiman, author of The Spirit Catches You and You Fall Down

"The authors' iteration of the fundamental cause of the system's root paradox—it rewards a person who waits until they're so sick they require expensive care while at the same time shaming the expensive-care provider for, well, charging for the expensive care—is not new. What is new here is their call for a holistic approach, integrating social and medical services into a cohesive cross-disciplinary system with the goal of supporting good health. Health-care systems fail because they don't address the life circumstances (education, housing, employment) required to sustain wellness. To be clear, the authors don't endorse a nanny state that becomes all things to all people but, rather, a government that is a catalyst for holistic innovation, nurturing good health at all socioeconomic levels. —Donna Chavez, Booklist

"This book provides new insight on why it is the United States is spending so much on medicine without seeing commensurate health outcomes. Bradley and Taylor provide a clear account of life in the chasm between health and social services, where so much of our health care investment is lost, and put forth concrete ideas on how we can do better."

—Dr. Paul Farmer, MD, PhD, Harvard Medical School, Brigham and Women's Hospital, Partners In Health, and author of *To Repair the World* and *Haiti After the Earthquake*

"Crisp, clear, and easily digestible . . . their message is that health eludes all socioeconomic sectors (rich and poor) who are not living in safe, secure homes with environments that offer opportunities for education and work as well as protections against life's misfortunes (like unemployment insurance and family benefits). Of course, the poor and minorities are disproportionately impacted since the social dimensions of their lives are far more deprived than those of the 'one percent.'"

—Lloyd I. Sederer, MD, medical director, NYS Office of Mental Health, *Huffington Post*

THE AMERICAN HEALTH CARE PARADOX

THE **AMERICAN HEALTH CARE PARADOX**

· · · · · · · · · · · · · · ·

WHY SPENDING MORE IS GETTING US LESS

ELIZABETH H. BRADLEY AND
LAUREN A. TAYLOR

FOREWORD BY HARVEY V. FINEBERG,
President, Institute of Medicine

PublicAffairs

NEW YORK

For our most energetic supporters, John Bradley and Lynn Jennings Taylor, whose dedicated careers as front-line providers in the social service and health care sectors have inspired and informed this work.

Book design by Pauline Brown

The Library of Congress has cataloged the hardcover as follows:

Bradley, Elizabeth H., 1962–
    The American health care paradox : why spending more is getting us less /
Elizabeth H. Bradley and Lauren A. Taylor ; foreword by Harvey V. Fineberg.—First edition.
        p. cm.
    Includes bibliographical references and index.
    ISBN 978-1-61039-209-9 (hbk. : alk. paper)—ISBN 978-1-61039-210-5
    (e-book)
    I. Taylor, Lauren A., author. II. Title.
[DNLM: 1. Delivery of Health Care—United States. 2. Health Care
Reform—United States. 3. Health Expenditures—United States. 4. Social
Conditions—United States. 5. Social Work—United States. W 84 AA1]
RA410.53
362.10973—dc23
                                                                2013030237

ISBN: 978-1-61039-548-9 (paperback)

LSC-C

10 9 8 7 6 5 4

CONTENTS

A NOTE ON QUOTATIONS

WE CONDUCTED INTERVIEWS WITH MORE than eighty health and social policy experts, researchers, practitioners, and consumers for the purpose of creating this book. We audio-recorded and transcribed the majority, resulting in thousands of pages of data and many more pages of interpretive and reflective notes. Wherever possible, we used direct quotations from our interviewees in the pages that follow. We adapted language at times to improve clarity without altering its meaning, and in some cases, we changed places and details to maintain anonymity.

FOREWORD

"How often have I said to you that when you have eliminated
the impossible, whatever remains, however improbable, must be
the truth?"

—Sir Arthur Conan Doyle, *The Sign of the Four*

OVER THE COURSE of the twentieth century, life expectancy at birth
in the United States increased by more than twenty-five years, and
continued to rise gradually in the first decade of the twenty-first
century. However, a recent assessment of health status among thirty-
four member states in the Organization for Economic Co-operation
and Development (OECD) found that US health standing compared to the other countries declined between 1990 and 2010.[1]
Even relatively advantaged Americans—college-educated, Cauca-
sian, insured, upper-income—fared worse than their peers in many
comparison countries.[2] The relatively lackluster health standing of
the United States is a paradox, as the title of this book conveys,
when you consider that the US per capita expenditures on health are
nearly double the average of other OECD countries. Like the foot-
ball player who may not be big but is slow, the United States seems
both to spend more on health and get less.

How can this paradox be explained? Elizabeth Bradley and Lauren
Taylor explore some important clues in this book. They begin with
the recognition that the health status of a population depends on

much more than health care. In particular, they stress the powerful direct and indirect effects that social factors exert. These determinants range widely: across income, education, housing, stress, social relationships, and more. Their influence has been well documented,[3] but national expenditures that promote socioeconomic benefits and meet social needs are not included in national accounts for health. When the authors combine national expenditures in these social domains with the traditional health accounts, a dozen countries spend in aggregate a higher proportion of their gross domestic product than this nation does This brings the United States into a middling position in both overall expenditures that bear on health and in overall health results.

This insight may help resolve the results-expenditure paradox, but it hardly leaves the United States in an enviable position on health. The authors describe the experience of Scandinavian countries, which invest much more than the United States in social services and income equity and achieve better health results. They examine American programs that successfully provide medical care and meet social needs. Although the authors recognize that the United States will need to forge its own path to affordable expenditures and better health, this book holds out the prospect that we can learn from the experience of others, and from our own. One lesson is abundantly clear: we cannot attain superior health results by continuing to outspend others on medical care. We have already tried that option, and it doesn't work.

Even if everyone agrees that we are spending too much on medical care and getting too little in return, there will be as many solutions as there are political persuasions. The Bill of Rights, the first ten amendments to the US Constitution, delineate a set of individual rights and freedoms that are a cornerstone of American democracy. We treasure its guarantees of freedom of speech and of the press, freedom from unreasonable searches and seizure, the right to assemble peaceably and to petition the government, the right to bear arms and to practice the religion of our choice, and all many more. These enumerated rights of the people are all civil and political rights. The US Constitution is silent on social and economic rights: there is no Constitutional guarantee of a right to education, or to old-age pensions, or to work, or to health care. These have always, in the American context, been matters of political choice rather than of natural right, and future choices for the United States will be decided through its political process.

In a democracy, an informed and engaged electorate is the strongest foundation for sound decision making. Finding our way to an affordable, sustainable, and healthier future is a quintessential American dilemma. This book will enlighten and enliven the discourse.

Harvey V. Fineberg, MD, PhD
President, Institute of Medicine

PREFACE

IN DECEMBER 2011, WE AWOKE early to check the *New York Times* for the opinion piece that we had worked on for months. The piece commented on a set of empirical findings we had published in the academic literature earlier that year, and the opportunity to discuss its implications on such a grand stage was thrilling.

Our research had presented the surprising finding that the health spending in the United States, as compared with other industrialized countries, was not as inflated as we had long thought it to be, when social services, which also contribute to individuals' health, were taken into account. If we add together health care spending and social service spending, the nation's investment in services that foster health is actually moderate compared with peer countries. Thus, the average ratings that the United States had been receiving in measures comparing international health outcomes seemed more deserved.

From our homes in two different US cities, we typed the *New York Times* web address into our web browsers, hit Return, and found our piece under the banner headline, "To Fix Health Care, Help the Poor." That headline concerned us. We wondered if it left readers with an incomplete picture.

Neither that opinion piece, nor this book, has been about help-ing "the poor." We are not aiming to advance a political agenda, advocate on behalf of social justice, or discuss health as a human right. Rather, our work for the past two years has been about reconceptualizing the way Americans think about health so as to uncover opportunities to increase the effectiveness of American health care. The investigation was motivated in large part by a concern central to Americans of all ideological persuasions: maximizing the return on investment of our national expenditures. Throughout the book, we use the term "American" to refer to the United States, recognizing that in other venues, the broad term "American" may include people from North and South America, outside the United States. We hope readers will understand the need for such shorthand in an undertaking of this size and scope.

The exposure that the *New York Times* gave to our research ended up having a profound impact. We never intended to write a book, but amid the hundreds of e-mails we received in the wake of that publication came a generous offer encouraging us to do just that. Although initially hesitant, we ultimately decided that the outpouring of enthusiastic responses was evidence that we were on to something, and that the message had resonated among certain health care and social service providers, if among no one else. Readers had written from all over the country and world, affirming for us that our research reflected their experiences on the front lines of care delivery. For the rest of the year and into the next, our inboxes were receptacles for any number of qualitative data points—and the book, in some ways, began to sketch itself.

More precisely, the original empirical research, conducted in collaboration with Brian Elbel, Benjamin Elkins, and Jeph Herrin at the Yale School of Public Health in 2009 and 2010, showed that the central paradox faced by the US health care system—exorbitantly high spending and relatively poor health outcomes—could be explained by examining a broader set of national expenditures. We demonstrated that when both social services and health services were taken into account, the United States was *not* a high spender. The country had moderate levels of spending and moderate health outcomes. Paradox unraveled. The credo of public health schools everywhere was made manifest: the health of a nation is created by more than the money spent in the health care sector. Investments in larger systems of economic, environmental, and social support produce health and support individuals' quest for well-being.

Since its publication, our message has been enthusiastically received by a diverse set of communities. The Institute of Medicine and our peers in academe have cited the work frequently, practitioners have affirmed our findings with their own experience, and the general public has taken an interest in what the findings mean for future health care reform. Each opportunity to write about the findings has seemed to beget another opportunity to share them more widely—culminating in the *New York Times* column and now this book.

We hope here to extend our discussion of these findings beyond what an academic article or short newspaper column permits. Keeping Americans at or above a certain baseline of good health requires collective action to assure the availability of such necessities as food, housing, and transportation. Furthermore, making such social assurances is likely to save the nation health care dollars in the long run. In this way, our research supports the view that health care and social service investments may best be thought of as operating on a continuum, or perhaps even as two sides of the same coin. In direct contrast to the " . . . Help the Poor" headline, we argue that this reorienting of our health investments is relevant for Americans across the socioeconomic spectrum.

It seems important at this early stage to make clear that we are not necessarily experts in all areas of this work; nor do we have prescriptive answers to the health care issues that plague us. Although we have command of the original and new findings presented herein, contextualizing this research has necessitated that we learn as we go. Our learning curve in the history of social services, for instance, has been particularly steep. We regularly received e-mails from students, front-line workers, and fellow academicians pointing us to new lines of research, new pieces of history, or field practices that we had not previously considered. As a result, we make no claims to mastery. The question of how to reform the American health care system is an enduring one requiring any number of bright minds and enthusiastic actors. We guarantee only a deep interest in continuing to wrestle with the data and explore the implications.

Thankfully, we have found help at every turn. In particular, we have to extend thanks to our team of student researchers over the course of two years, who included Lisa Hansmann, Kristin Horneffer, Kevin Li, Maya Major, and Caroline Wentworth. Boyd Jackson, in particular, sustained this effort from start to finish, patiently helping us to interpret, fact check, cite, and note innumerable revisions of each chapter. We are also grateful for the contributions of Kristina Talbert-Slagle, who edited the text and reflected with us throughout. We are similarly indebted to our international interviewees who warmly greeted us and generously explained their systems' nuances. Other critical readers who have contributed significantly to the strength of the text included Shane Bannon, Ole Berg, Alice Bradley, Deanna Caplan, Sam Chauncey, Emily Cherlin, Leslie Curry, Howard Forman, Jan Frich, Luke Hansen, Jessica Holzer, Leora Horwitz, Jon Howe, Marcia Inhorn, Helen Jack, Marty Klein, Sanjeev Kumar, Georgina Lucas, Lydia Maurer, Aly Moore, Ingrid Nembhard, Martha Radford, Naomi Rogers, Lily Roh, Robert Rosenheck, Heather Sipsma, Fred Strebeigh, and Cornelia Valdejuli. We have been inspired by your understanding of the phenomena and energized by your commitment to our message.

Science generally values research that is contrarian. The researcher who uses evidence to upend a commonly held belief or widely endorsed approach is hailed as an innovator, whereas those who merely support what is already known are dismissed as followers. In some ways, this research has probably garnered attention because it runs counter to many of the popular messages about American health care. For many people, we are providing a new look at an issue that has already received quite a bit of attention in recent years. In this way, we like to think our work has the potential to create a watershed change in how Americans understand and think about health.

At the same time, we have welcomed the realization that the underlying premise of the book is also deeply intuitive. As we have traveled the country (and parts of the world) explaining the implications of our research, we have been met more often by knowing nods than by puzzled looks. People of all professional and political persuasions know what we are saying to be true in their daily lives. The evidence confirms their instinct—health is built by much more than the doctors we see, the radiology scans we get, and the medications we take. We hope that readers will find our message to be as intuitive as it has been to those with whom we have preliminarily shared it.

Within these pages are nuggets of experience and data that may inspire readers to change how they steward their own health. In that sense, we hope the book will have deep personal impact. The implications of our research for larger action are also many. In the face of widespread acknowledgment that current American investment practices have failed to produce the population health we assumed they would, we present an alternative strategy for how to invest in the health of the nation. Whether or not this strategy finds a warm welcome in the current cultural and political climate remains to be seen, but, at the very least, we hope it will prompt new lines of public discourse regarding health care reform in America.

CHAPTER 1

THE PARADOX

Joe is a twenty-eight-year-old man with type 1 diabetes, living in the United States. He lacks permanent housing and has been staying in a friend's condemned, boarded-up house. To avoid being seen there, Joe enters through the marshlands behind the house. His shoes are full of holes, but he cannot afford to replace them. Joe's diet has similarly suffered from his lack of income; he sometimes goes several days without fresh food, which negatively affects his diabetes. Also, after a lifetime of poor insulin control, he is starting to lose circulation in his feet. Last year, Joe had two toes removed on his right foot to save his life (hospital cost: $7,132). Still, neuropathy continues to cause him decreased sensitivity in and increased risk of trauma to his feet. The doctor he last saw emphasized the importance of keeping his feet dry, getting proper nutrition, and taking his costly insulin as prescribed, all of which Joe is eager to do. Since that appointment, Joe has been diligent in taking his insulin, but dry feet and proper nutrition remain difficult to achieve due to his living conditions and unemployment. His doctor has already raised the issue of having to have more toes removed on his left foot (cost: $14,430), and without immediate changes, Joe will need to have a below-the-knee amputation in the years ahead (cost: $17,347) and will likely need a wheelchair (cost: $1,042). The estimated cost of his medical expenses will top $30,000, paid by a state medical assistance program that is funded by taxpayers. Amid a system marked by the most advanced medical treatment in the world, Joe is dying a slow, painful, and expensive death. A decent pair of shoes costs $50.

WE BEGIN WITH THE TRUE STORY of a young man living in the United States. While that story may sound like the basis of a Hollywood plot, we encountered similar stories throughout our research on the American health care system. It goes without saying that Joe needs more than a good pair of shoes to improve his health; he also needs accessible shelter and nutritious food. But the cost of these interventions still pale compared with $30,000 in medical treatment he is currently on track to accrue in the coming years. Furthermore, shelter, food, and shoes might enable him to return to work and not suffer a lifetime dependent on a wheelchair. Joe, and many others like him, whose diverse stories we share in the coming chapters, illustrate how inadequate attention to social services and supports can lead to exorbitant health care expenses. We confront the consequences of this imbalance experienced by people across the income spectrum. Joe's is one story, which, replicated across the country, begins to unravel the paradox that has perplexed policymakers for decades: How is it that the United States spends more per capita than any other nation on health care, while Americans fare worse in many measures of health?

According to the 2013 Institute of Medicine report *Shorter Lives, Poorer Health*, Americans have lower life expectancy and higher rates of infant mortality, low birth weight, injuries and homicides, adolescent pregnancy and sexually transmitted diseases, HIV/AIDS, drug-related deaths, obesity, diabetes, heart disease, chronic lung disease, and disability than people in other industrialized countries. Furthermore, racial and economic disparities fail to explain this national health disadvantage in the United States. Americans who are white, insured, college educated, and upper income have poorer health than do their counterparts in other industrialized countries.[1]

Although the Institute of Medicine report was circulated as news,[2] the "spend more, get less" paradox it documented has been recognized for decades. As early as 1971, Nathan Glazer, a sociologist at Harvard University who worked on President Lyndon Johnson's

Model Cities Program, used the term *paradox* to describe American health care. In his article published in *The Public Interest*, Glazer pointed out that while the American population increased 17 percent between 1955 and 1965, medical personnel increased 63 percent with no improvement in general health of the population.[3] More recently, Dartmouth economist Jonathan Skinner used the term to demonstrate that between 1986 and 2005, the geographic regions with the largest increases in Medicare spending were not the ones with the largest survival gains.[4]

Researchers, policymakers, and practitioners have offered a number of rationales for this paradox mostly related to the design and financing of the health care system. Pundits of various political views have laid blame on greedy insurance companies, inefficient and wasteful hospitals and government programs, and skyrocketing costs of pharmaceutical drugs. These assertions can be supported with data but do not fully explain why spending more on health care is getting Americans less health.

We propose a different explanation, based on compelling data gathered over years of research. Inadequate attention to and investment in services that address the broader determinants of health is the unnamed culprit behind why the United States spends so much on health care but continues to lag behind in health outcomes.

THE IDEA THAT AMERICANS SPEND more and get less when it comes to health care is frustrating to a populace long steeped in the virtues and benefits of capitalism. The American spirit resists the thought that the nation may not be getting value for money. The situation is upsetting not only because it connotes waste in the system, but because it provides evidence of the United States' falling behind its peer, industrialized countries—spending more but not being any healthier for it. The United States ranks top out of thirty-four nations in national spending on health care as a percentage of GDP. Data from countries in the Organisation for Economic Co-operation and Development (OECD) from 2009 puts US health care spending at $7,960 per person, while most others spend less than $4,000 per capita (see Figure 1.1) and rank above the United States in multiple measures of health.

Most of the health care spending finances hospitals, physicians, and clinics. According to 2010 data from the Centers for Medicare & Medicaid Services, it is allocated as follows: approximately 31 percent is for hospital care; 20 percent, for physician and clinic services; 10 percent, for prescription drugs; 7 percent, for dental and other professionals; 7 percent, for government administration; 6 percent is for investment (structures, equipment, and noncommercial research); 6 percent is for nursing home and other long-term care; and 14 percent is for other medical costs including home health care (3 percent), government public health activities (3 percent), other medical products (3 percent), and other health, residential, and personal care (5 percent).[5]

FIGURE 1.1.   TOTAL HEALTH EXPENDITURE PER CAPITA, PUBLIC AND PRIVATE, 2009

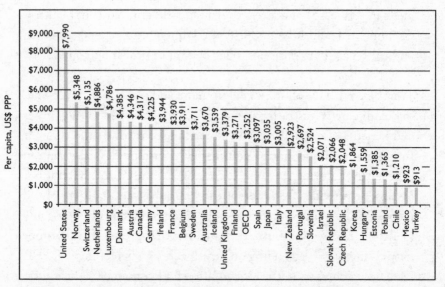

"US$ PPP" means US dollars adjusted for purchasing power parity across countries; 2009 data.
Source: OECD, *Health at a Glance 2011* (Paris, France: OECD Publishing, 2011).

And who pays for these services? Government programs cover about 45 percent of total spending in the United States, primarily through Medicare and Medicaid, implemented in the mid-1960s. Medicare commonly insures older people with acute care needs and accounts for 22.9 percent of all health care spending in the United States. (Acute care is short-term treatment for a severe injury or episode of illness, including medical and surgical treatments.) Medicaid commonly insures people with lower incomes and disabilities, and people receiving nursing home care, and accounts for 16.4 percent of health care spending. Private insurance and private resources cover 34.5 and 13.5 percent of health care spending, respectively. The remaining spending is for the Veterans Administration and other third-party payers and programs (including worksite health care, other private revenues, Indian Health Service, workers' compensation, general assistance, maternal and child health, vocational rehabilitation, the Substance Abuse and Mental Health Services Administration, school health, and other federal and state local programs, and other investments).[6]

In some ways, America's massive investment in this area has conferred important benefits. When one measures the quantity of medical interventions undertaken or available, the United States does quite well in comparison with its peers. A higher proportion of women aged twenty to sixty-nine are screened for cervical cancer in the United States than in any other nation, and the United States leads the world in the number of knee replacements performed per year and the number of people living with a kidney transplant.[7] Furthermore, when it comes to the speed at which health care is delivered, the United States has no equal. The United States is number one in the percentage of people who receive diabetes treatment within six months, the percentage of seniors needing hip replacement who receive one within six months, and the percentage of people referred to a medical specialist who see him or her within one month. Americans are treated with more catheterizations, more

FIGURE 1.2. US HEALTH OUTCOMES RANKINGS ACROSS 34 OECD
COUNTRIES, 2007

Population Health Outcome	US Ranking
Maternal mortality	25th
Life expectancy	26th
Low birth weight	28th
Infant mortality	31st

Source: OECD, *Health at a Glance 2009* (Paris, France: OECD Publishing, 2007).

angioplasties, and more bypass surgeries than in any European country,[8] and the United States enjoys 26 magnetic resonance imaging (MRI) scanners per million people, while England and Canada report 5.6 and 8, respectively.[9] Nevertheless, despite this leadership in the application of medical care, the United States continues to fall behind other industrialized countries in many important health outcomes (see Figure 1.2).[10]

ON ACCOUNT OF THESE MANY strengths, Americans sometimes dismiss the less inspiring population-level health outcomes, in part because they do not always see themselves in the data. These are, after all, *national* figures, meaning they may not reflect the experience of population subgroups, which may fare considerably better or worse than the average. The challenge of interpreting national data for a diverse population is similar in the realm of education. Although one can attain the best education possible in America, educational performance of the population as a whole is less stellar. Nationally representative statistics pertaining to math and science test scores, literacy rates, and college graduation rates flag in comparison to industrialized peer countries, according to the US National Center for Education Statistics,[11] the United Nations,[12] and the US Census.[13]

Additionally, some Americans have criticized international comparisons of infant mortality, as record-keeping practices for preterm babies may differ across countries, artificially inflating or deflating infant mortality rates.[14] Some of this may be true, although considerable efforts have been undertaken to harmonize measurement across the international community of the OECD. Moreover, the data reveal that infant mortality rates in the United States are double those of Western Europe, and even without consideration of infant mortality, the pattern of poor health outcomes in the United States compared with peer countries persists in many other measures of health.

Why else do Americans dislike hearing about these numbers? These figures show that the United States is not necessarily on top. Look at any political speech or piece of public discourse, and the fact that the United States expects to lead the world in virtually every indicator of development and progress becomes abundantly clear. French writer Alexis de Tocqueville captured this sentiment, from a foreigner's perspective, writing in 1831 after a tour of the nascent country that "The position of the Americans is therefore quite exceptional, and it may be believed that no democratic people will ever be placed in a similar one . . . Let us cease, then, to view all democratic nations under the example of the American people."[15]

The idea took hold. One hundred and thirty years later, President Dwight Eisenhower added a sense of superiority to the already entrenched sense of exceptionalism. Following the 1961 conclusion of the Korean War, he declared, "We now stand ten years past the midpoint of a century that has witnessed four major wars among great nations. Three of these involved our own country. Despite these holocausts, America is today the strongest, the most influential, and most productive nation in the world."[16]

As recently as President Barack Obama's 2012 State of the Union Speech, Americans heard a proposal for a new defense strategy that would "ensure [the United States] maintained the finest military in the world."[17] A month earlier, the president had offered similarly boisterous rhetoric in discussing Americans' propensity for innovation: "The world is shifting to an innovation economy and nobody does innovation better than America. Nobody does it better.

No one has better colleges. Nobody has better universities. Nobody has a greater diversity of talent and ingenuity. No one's workers or entrepreneurs are more driven or more daring."[18]

Belief in American exceptionalism is just as fervent on the other side of the political aisle, as Mitt Romney indicated at a November 2011 Republican Party Debate at Wofford College in South Carolina. There, he stated, "We have a president right now who thinks America is just another nation. America is an exceptional nation."[19]

Given this political and cultural backdrop, it seems reasonable to think that Americans might be proud to spend more than any other nation on health care—if the health outcomes measured up. They do not. Americans are hence left wondering why, and how to improve the situation.

Historians, health services researchers, health policy scholars, and political leaders have devised a number of rationalizations for America's mediocre-to-poor performance, usually linked with proposed reforms intended to provide people with greater access or have people pay less for care. Many have attributed the failures of health care in delivering better outcomes at lower costs to several facets of the current approach. First, some have suggested that underinsurance has resulted in poor prevention and inadequate adherence to medical recommendations.[20] Second, blame has been placed on fragmentation between public and private payers and inadequate primary care with fee-for-service arrangements that can result in unnecessary duplication and inefficiencies. (Fewer than 15 percent of all physicians practicing in the United States are primary care physicians and the remainder are specialists of some kind,[21] despite evidence that areas with more primary care resources per capita have better health on many measures, including lower premature mortality.[22]) Third, many have suggested that fears of medical malpractice compel physicians to screen for every conceivable disease and use the most aggressive treatment available, lest they be sued for not doing everything.[23] Fourth, experts have cited cultural demands for the most sophisticated medical technology as the main driver of cost.[24] For the last twenty years, policymakers and practitioners have sought to address these problematic features in the health care system, but without success in delivering the same level of health per dollar found in other industrialized countries.

Those who believe the fundamental problem reflected in Americans' poor health outcomes is underinsurance highlight the fact that about 15 percent of the American population lacked health insurance as of 2011. This camp has argued that the answer is to insure everyone so as to promote better access to preventive and acute care and ideally improve outcomes. Although providing insurance does improve access to needed care, the cost of such access can be substantial,[25] and data suggests that American health outcomes among insured populations still lag substantially behind those of other countries.[26] Thus, such reforms in isolation are unlikely to resolve the spend more, get less paradox.

Others, who believe the nation's health problems are rooted in the fragmented financing system and the lack of primary care physicians to coordinate care, have called for medical homes. Conceptually, medical homes are designed to reduce fragmentation and duplication and help individuals navigate the health care sector. These are physician-led, team-based health care delivery models that seek to provide comprehensive, continuous, and well-coordinated medical care to patients to maximize health outcomes. Medical homes typically implement care coordination services and limit fee-for-service reimbursement in favor of various managed care payment schemes, which reduce financial incentives for physicians to provide unnecessary services.

Unfortunately, evidence indicates that the potential value of medical homes has been mixed, although rigorous evaluation of these initiatives is limited.[27] Case studies have documented modest financial savings, but findings are inconsistent.[28] Efforts at the Geisinger Health System in Pennsylvania[29] and in urban hospitals in Texas[30] have shown some savings. In contrast, however, a larger experiment—the Medicare Coordinated Care Demonstration

Project—initiated at fifteen sites not only failed to reduce costs but also resulted in increased costs in ten of these sites (for a total cost increase of 11 percent).[31] A second evaluation of eleven Medicare Coordinated Care Demonstration sites found that savings were largely eliminated by the coordination fees paid to the program.[32] The central issue associated with medical home proposals, however, is the lack of practical methods by which such a model would be implemented, replicated, and scaled up nationally.

Those who believe that medical malpractice is the source of the high costs and mediocre outcomes have called for tort reform; however, in states that have made efforts to reduce medical malpractice, the overall impact has been unimpressive. Recent experience in Texas informs this debate. In 2004, Texas conducted what is now referred to as "a failed experiment."[33] The state capped medical liability expenses as a part of medical malpractice reform. In the six years after malpractice reform was inaugurated in Texas, the state's health spending per Medicare enrollee rose from seventh to second highest in the United States. Private health insurance premiums also rose faster than the national average over this time. At the same time, the percentage of Texans who were uninsured rose.[34] The number of medical malpractice payments did decrease considerably, but the clear beneficiaries of the liability caps were the insurance companies, whose payouts in medical malpractice damages were 65 percent lower in 2010 than in 2003, while the premiums paid by physicians decreased by only 50 percent. Thus, this initiative failed to promote financial savings broadly, and the impact on health outcomes is unclear.

Last, robust evidence supports those who believe that Americans' high utilization of advanced medical technology is the main reason for high costs and relatively poor outcomes, but recent efforts to restrain this use are weak. Evidence has shown dramatic increases in the use of certain technologies following approval for federal reimbursement via Medicare. Recent examples of this tendency include the tenfold increase in the use of implantable cardiac defibrillators (ICDs) for heart disease between 1987 and 1995 after Medicare approved their reimbursement;[35] as well as the overuse of intensity-modulated radiotherapy (IMRT)[36] for prostate cancer, which has been described as lucrative for providers who are paid as much as $40,000 per treatment. IMRT has more recently been approved to treat additional cancers, accounting for upward of $1 billion annually in Medicare expenses.[37] Although during the last ten years, examples exist of medical technologies that have allowed care to be delivered in fewer hospital days or in less expensive outpatient settings (as in cardiac catheterization, cataract surgery, or hernia repair), overall medical technology has added to national health care spending. In light of this pattern, the federal government has tried to control overuse by establishing various offices of technology assessment over several decades,[38] but these efforts have done little to reduce the spend more, get less paradox—largely because Americans are not comfortable rationing anything that even one American might be able to afford. Furthermore, the use of technology often benefits medical professionals amid a population that believes the greater use of technology may improve their health outcomes, particularly if that technology is paid for by insurance plans.

The most recent reform proposals call for more National Institutes of Health research funding on "comparative effectiveness," an emerging field for studying the relative cost effectiveness of new technologies and pharmaceuticals prior to their large-scale use. Although such research may be helpful, reducing the use of high-technology advances remains an unlikely solution to high costs and poor health outcomes, given the current economic, political, and cultural landscape of American health care.

WE PROPOSE ANOTHER APPROACH TO understanding the American failure to achieve top-rated health outcomes despite its enormous investment in health care. We agree that the United States is failing to achieve the population health outcomes that other industrialized nations enjoy, but to unravel the spend more, get less paradox, we need to look more closely at what is (and is not) commonly being measured.

For the purpose of comparing spending and outcomes across member countries, the OECD defines *health expenditure* to mean all spending on the final consumption of health goods and services plus capital investment in health care infrastructure. Therefore, these expenditures include public and private spending on curative care, rehabilitative care, long-term care, mental health care, ancillary services (e.g., diagnostic imaging, laboratory tests, and patient transport), outpatient medical goods, prevention and public health services, health administration, public health insurance, new health care building and facilities, health education and training, health research and development, and long-term care services for people with functional limitations.

Not included as health spending are expenditures for social services and economic well-being that contribute to health, such as investments in housing, nutrition, education, the environment and unemployment support. Given the World Health Organization's definition of *health* as "a state of complete physical, mental and social well-being," one can see how health spending limited solely to what the OECD measures might leave a population wanting. The houses and neighborhoods people live in, the food people eat, the air people breathe, the amount of exercise people get, and the jobs people have all influence their health. Yet, none of these inputs is captured by the calculation of national health care expenditure. As a result, what researchers see from health spending data is an incomplete picture of the spending each nation puts forth in pursuit of health on behalf of its population.

The field of public health refers to the conditions that are not medical but that can produce or undermine health as the "social determinants of health." These are the socioeconomic, environmental, and behavioral factors that research over many decades has shown to be strong influences on health.[39] For instance, people from more socioeconomically disadvantaged backgrounds are twice as likely as those from advantaged backgrounds to face serious illness and premature death.[40] Among middle-class office workers, those occupying a lower rank in the organizational hierarchy face more disease and earlier death than do higher ranking staff.[41] Poverty, social isolation, lack of control in one's life and work life, and other psychological stresses, risky lifestyle choices, food insecurity, lack of educational support and housing, and job insecurity have all been shown to compromise health.[42]

Medicine alone cannot prevent or attenuate these risk factors. In a study using data from the Centers for Disease Control/National Center for Health Statistics from 1999 to 2001, Professors Mark Cullen, Clint Cummins, and Victor Fuchs from Stanford University reported that a common set of twenty-two socioeconomic and environmental variables (including education, income, air pollution, and access to healthy food) largely explain geographic and racial differences in premature mortality.[43] Among specific disease groups, the data are similarly striking. Social and behavioral factors contribute to more than 70 percent of colon cancer[44] and stroke,[45] more than 80 percent of coronary heart disease cases,[46] and more than 90 percent of adult-onset (type 2) diabetes cases.[47] Environmental factors drive health in similar fashion. For example, maternal exposure to insecticides has been linked with lower birth weight and length in infants;[48] researchers have shown links between fine particulate air pollution and both lung disease and cardiopulmonary mortality;[49] and, when ingested, heavy metals, such as cadmium, lead, and arsenic (from industrial waste that can seep into soil and groundwater), have been tied to kidney injury and chronic renal failure.[50] The highly publicized case of firefighters and rescue workers' developing cancer and lung disease only a few years after working at the site of the fallen World Trade Center towers underscores the connection between the environment and health.[51]

Despite the strong evidence about social determinants of health,[52] attention devoted to improving health in the United States has been directed largely at reforming the health care industry. Reform efforts have sought to enhance insurance coverage and access to medical care, redesign physician and hospital payment schemes, and improve the quality of medical care. Although it is too early to evaluate the full impact of the Patient Protection and Affordable Care Act (known colloquially as Obamacare), this reform focuses largely on providing access to health care to previously uninsured groups, with little attention on the social determinants of health. Improving access will have positive effects, but by itself is unlikely to address fundamental causes of the American paradox of high costs and poor outcomes. Extensive literature suggests that health care has relatively less impact on health than these social determinants of health,[53] begging the question of whether past health care reforms have been too narrow to have an effect.

If we view the national expenditure data while keeping the social determinants of health in mind, the United States' spend more, get less paradox begins to unravel. The United States is spending an extraordinary amount on health care as narrowly defined by the OECD, and a substantial amount of time, energy, and money reforming the way in which this health care is paid for and delivered. But the United States is not spending as much as other industrialized countries on fortifying crucial social services that help make people healthy. For instance, it spends less than 10 percent of its GDP on social services, while France, Sweden, Austria, Switzerland, Denmark, and Italy all spend about 20 percent of their GDP on social services (see Figure 1.3); the inclusion of the US nonprofit sector in the analysis does not begin to close this gap.[54] When researchers look at how the United States is doing in these other areas—providing reliable housing, ensuring nutritious food sufficiency, and safeguarding against harmful exposures—they find the performance lackluster. Between September 30, 2008, and October 1, 2009, roughly one

FIGURE 1.3. OECD COUNTRIES: AGGREGATE HEALTH AND SOCIAL
SPENDING, 2007

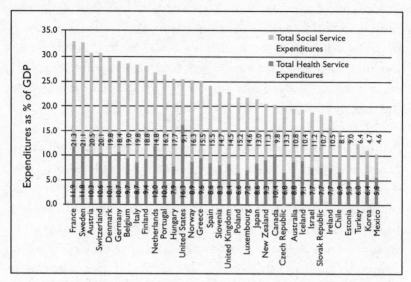

Source: OECD *Health Data 2009*, Social Expenditure Dataset (Paris, France: OECD, 2009).

in two hundred Americans used an emergency shelter.[55] The year 2010 represented an all-time high in the number of households (17.2 million) reporting food insecurity, meaning they did not know where their next meal would come from,[56] and these numbers are not improving.[57] And as recently as 2009, the *New York Times* reported that violations of the Safe Drinking Water Act had potentially contaminated the water delivered to more than 49 million Americans (about 15 percent of the population) with illegal concentrations of chemicals, such as arsenic, or radioactive substances, such as uranium; in addition, dangerous bacteria was often found in sewage.[58]

In spite of the clear and recent data, the United States stumbles when addressing these social determinants of health. Although Americans do not like being mediocre in national health outcomes, they have been even less enthusiastic about facing the complex web of social conditions that produce and reinforce these outcomes.

They continue to pay top dollar for hospitals, physicians, medications, and diagnostic testing yet skimp in broad areas that are central to health, such as housing, clean water, safe food, education, and other social services. It may even be that Americans are spending large sums for health care to compensate for what they are not paying in social services—and the trade-off is not good for the country's health.

Roughly five years ago we started thinking that there might be a connection between soaring health costs and meager social service spending, when we were musing about theoretical roots to the so-called health care paradox in the United States. To explore whether our hypothesis would hold up, we examined ten years of spending and health outcome data from thirty OECD countries that collected data using comparable methodologies. The results confirmed our suspicions.

Our comparative study, published in the academic literature in 2010,[59] broadened the scope of inquiry about health and health spending to include spending on social services as a potential determinant of population-level health outcomes. For the purposes of our study, social services expenditures included public and private spending[60] on old-age pension and support services for older adults, survivors benefits, disability and sickness cash benefits, family supports, employment programs (e.g., public employment services and employment training, unemployment benefits, supportive housing and rent subsidies), and other social services that exclude health expenditures. Health expenditures included public and private spending on curative care, rehabilitative care, long-term care, laboratory and diagnostic services, outpatient and preventive care, and public health services.

The study found that if we counted countries' combined investment in health care *and* in social services, the United States was no longer spending the largest percentage of GDP—far from it. In 2007, for example, the United States devoted only 25 percent of gross domestic product to health and social services combined, while such countries as Sweden, France, Austria, Switzerland, and Denmark dedicated about 30 to 33 percent of their respective GDP to the combination.[61] In 2007, while the United States ranked highest in health spending, it ranked only thirteenth in spending on health services and social services combined (see Figure 1.4).

Moreover, the study revealed that America was one of only three industrialized countries (the other two were Korea and Mexico) to spend the majority of its total health and social services budget on health care. On average in the OECD countries other than the United States, for every dollar spent on health care, an additional two dollars was spent on social services. Yet in the United States, for every dollar spent on health care, less than sixty cents was spent on social services. Most important, we found that less spending on social services relative to spending on health services was statistically

FIGURE 1.4. OECD COUNTRIES: RATIO OF HEALTH TO SOCIAL SERVICE
EXPENDITURES, 2007

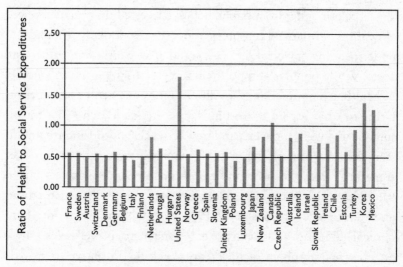

Source: OECD, *Health Data 2009* (Paris, France: OECD Publishing, 2009).

associated with poorer health outcomes in key measures, such as infant mortality and life expectancy, and this result held even when the United States was removed from the analysis.[62]

Our study found that countries with high health care spending relative to social service spending had significantly lower life expectancy and higher rates of infant mortality and low birth weights than did countries that favored social spending.[63] While the life expectancy in the United States remains stagnant at age seventy-eight, it has leapt well over eighty years of age in many European countries, and several countries boast infant mortality rates approximately half of those in the United States.[64]

These findings validated our initial suspicions about the significant impact social service investments have on health outcomes at a national level. But as is the case with any good piece of research, the results left us with more questions than answers. In particular, we were left interested in better understanding this new way in which we had discovered the United States to be an outlier. The United States was not necessarily spending more than everyone else; but it was spending quite differently.

Core principles from public health suggested that such a skewed allocation of financial resources, reflecting what many would deem underspending on social services, could drive exorbitant health care costs. While popular and political discussions about saving money in health care proliferate, they almost uniformly center on issues relating to what is paid to hospitals and physicians, who pays for insurance and what it covers, and how to set diagnostic and treatment standards. Reform proposals have taken different approaches over the years—from the growth of health maintenance organizations in the 1970s and '80s, to the development of managed care organizations and coinsurance schemes in the 1990s, to establishing of more recent clinical guidelines and quality of care campaigns. Nevertheless, these are all proposals about medical care. Even the initiative to provide health care insurance for the currently underinsured expands access only to medical care, not to better housing, nutrition, employment, and other social services.

Our research has forced a reconsideration of whether more effective means of improving health may exist beyond the traditional bounds of health care. Instead of seeing health and social spending as independent entities, should we be considering how what is done in one area may be affecting the other? Perhaps it is time to take a broader view.

THIS BOOK REFLECTS OUR EFFORTS to better understand the relationship between the health and social service sectors in the United States. In concept, the two sectors are intuitively linked. In practice, however, the health care industry and social support systems in this country are rarely coordinated, much less planned together or provided in an integrated way. Should they be? How might Americans gain by thinking differently about the essential elements of health? Is it practical to think these long-divided domains could be addressed simultaneously? If so, how? These were the questions we set off to investigate.

We organized this book as follows. In Chapter 2, we discuss the historical roots of the current bifurcation of American's health and social care sectors to illuminate why they evolved this way and to recognize potential impediments to reform. Chapter 3 takes the readers to the front lines to see the real-life challenges created by the administrative, financial, and cultural boundaries between the two sectors. We profile a set of people who are frequent users of health care services and social services, and we share their perspectives of health care and social service providers who coordinate services on behalf of patients and clients. In Chapter 4, we present examples of national systems that do integrate health and social services, and compare the United States with Scandinavia, which leads the world in achieving superior health outcomes for its people. We examine the values of American and Scandinavian societies as they relate to health and investigate whether Scandinavia's balance between health service and social service sectors provides a potentially instructive model. We consider data from the World Values Survey to investigate how different Americans really are, and are not, from their Scandinavian peers. Chapter 5 highlights a set of small but innovative programs in the United States that offer new models of health and social service integration with strong results. Chapter 6 explores the shortfalls of national efforts to integrate social services and health care delivery and highlights the need for a new conception of health in order for effective approaches to flourish, and Chapter 7 summarizes the key messages and identifies new issues for public dialogue.

In the course of this inquiry, we seek to broaden readers' views about what creates health. We do so in hopes of shifting American discourse about the intersection of the health care sector and social services and opportunities for effective reform. Our goal for readers is that they may recognize the role that social, environmental, and behavioral realities play in the moderation of health—on both personal and societal levels—and incorporate this perspective into meaningful discussions about the United States' efforts to improve health without accelerating costs.

CHAPTER 2

HISTORICAL PERSPECTIVES

DESPITE SHARING THE GOAL OF supporting and sustaining a prosperous American society, the American health care and social service sectors have developed on distinct paths. Remarkably separate financing, management, infrastructure support, and planning processes have therefore emerged. Ad hoc overlap exists, at times, in the form of a social worker based at a hospital, or a nurse who works out of a shelter or school, but structurally, the social service sector and the health care sector rarely intersect. How did this come to be? Many scholars have rendered historical analyses of health services and many others have described historical developments in social services, yet few have analyzed these two narratives together.

A review of the distinct histories in tandem reveals different political and cultural influences that led to their separation, and clarifies the roots of the current bifurcation. This chapter examines the professionalization of medicine and the emergence of insurance models to cover costs of increasingly expensive health care, and profiles the development of public and private social service programs. Taken together, the histories help contextualize the costly chasm that now exists.

FROM THE COLONIAL ERA UNTIL the early nineteenth century, health care in the United States was poorly organized. Medicine was a non-professionalized trade with little prestige. Physicians in the early nineteenth century, trained in medical schools that were typically of low quality, used practices such as bloodletting and mineral cathartics in an effort to restore balance and bring individuals back to their natural state.[1] If there were a poison in the body, physicians would advise its removal by evacuation. Similarly, sweating, urinating, defecating, and vomiting were all believed to be pathways by which a patient could hope to restore balance. Confidence in such therapies led physicians to recommend violent laxatives and other purgatives that sometimes blistered the body but, in theory, improved health.[2]

Physicians had few tools in which to be confident. Effective medicines at this time included mercury for syphilis and ringworm, digitalis to strengthen the heart, amyl nitrate to dilate the arteries, quinine for malaria, and colchicum for gout. Physicians were aware of their own limits and relied on early-form prescriptions to fortify their authority. As one turn-of-the-century American physician put it, "Just plain advice was never productive of revenue unless fortified by a few pills."[3] Practices varied substantially across regions in the United States during the 1800s;[4] however, an influential group of physicians who had studied in France at the Paris Clinical School as named by historians, returned to the United States with newfound faith in their ability to combat disease.[5] The new learning from France conceptualized diseases not as a general state of malaise, but rather as a set of specific entities with predictable courses and symptoms, the source of which could be identified at autopsy.[6] Still, with only a handful of effective medical treatments available, even prominent physicians, such as Jacob Bigelow from the Harvard Medical School who had studied in Paris, were skeptical of physicians' ability to influence the course of disease. His view, reported by Paul Starr in his seminal book, *The Social Transformation of American Medicine*, was captured by Bigelow's words in 1835: "[It is] the unbiased opinion of most medical men of sound judgment and long experience [that] the amount of death and disaster in the world would be less, if all disease were left to itself."[7]

Throughout the early 1900s, hospitals were regarded poorly. They were rightly considered dangerous, and people with illnesses who could receive care at home would. Those who used hospitals were generally estranged or isolated from their families—travelers, paupers, outcasts, or runaways.[8] The major hospitals were in major urban centers, including Boston, New Orleans, Philadelphia, New York, and St. Louis. In lieu of health insurance, people drew on personal savings to pay for medical care often delivered at home, and for those who could not pay, patron-supported almshouses took in patients to provide care for them. Almshouses were populated most commonly by people who were destitute, in many cases those who were elderly, had mental illness, or were otherwise unable to work.

The latter half of the nineteenth century brought about several discoveries that would enable science to unravel the biologic causes and consequences of disease (see Figure 2.1). Among the most notable of these advances was Louis Pasteur's development of the germ theory of disease, beginning in 1862. Prior to his work, popular thinking had held that it was miasma, or noxious air from decomposition and filth, that ominously carried disease from one neighborhood to another. While scientifically incorrect, the miasma model of disease spread had motivated public health efforts to clean the streets, encourage people to find fresh air to breathe, and remove those who were ill from the community by means of quarantine. Although the disciplines of urban design, sanitation, and recreation science grew in importance during this time, miasma theory offered only methods to prevent disease, without providing insight into how to address disease once it had befallen a person. With the acceptance of Pasteur's germ theory came an era of greater precision in medicine, wherein both practitioners and the public would recognize that microbe-size life-forms were to blame for illness, rather than evil spirits or an imbalance of bodily humors. With germs now correctly identified as the culpable parties, progress in defeating disease came more quickly.

FIGURE 2.1. TIMELINE OF SELECTED EVENTS IN HEALTH CARE AND
SOCIAL SERVICE SECTOR DEVELOPMENT

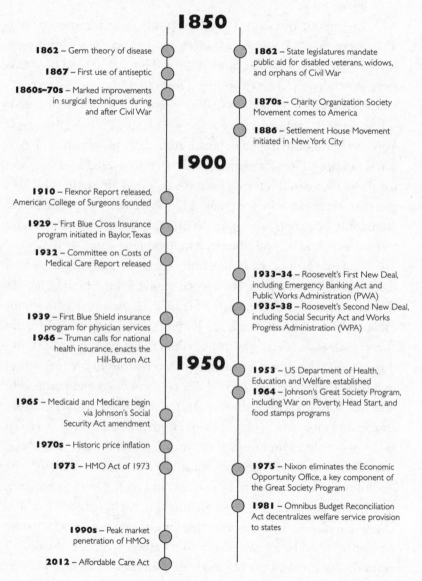

Concurrent technological advances and major educational reforms also elevated the prestige and impact of both medical doctors
and surgeons. Just as Pasteur's discoveries would revolutionize medicine, the demonstration of ether anesthesia at Massachusetts General Hospital in 1846, Joseph Lister's work on antisepsis in 1865, and
the development of X-rays in 1895 would recast surgery. Whereas
surgery had formerly been undertaken only as a last-ditch effort to
remove disease, the surgical profession matured rapidly during the
Civil War. Surgery as a profession became increasingly respected by
the 1860s and '70s, bringing enormous creativity and accomplish-
ment to the medical profession, as well as substantial expense.[9]

Until the late nineteenth century, however, medical education
remained poorly organized and without a standard curriculum. Physician education relied on an apprenticeship model, which provided
clinical training to aspiring doctors who would shadow and observe
a practicing physician. Medical schools were not required to be affiliated with hospitals, nor were physicians required to seek licensure
before beginning their own practices. Many students undergoing such
apprenticeships to become physicians had not completed high school.

Large-scale medical reform efforts in the late 1880s and early
1900s would prove a harbinger for the future professionalization of
health care. Medical schools began affiliating with larger hospitals
for their clinical training. In 1893, Johns Hopkins became a pioneer
in medical education by requiring a college degree prior to admission, thereby setting the new standard that being a physician would
require a graduate-level degree. Even so, lack of standard curricula
and faculty persisted throughout the rest of medical education in the
United States. A 1910 report by Abraham Flexner, commissioned
by the Carnegie Foundation for the Advancement of Teaching, cat-
alyzed critical changes to medical education in the United States.
The Flexner Report revealed what medical professionals already
knew: marked inconsistencies pervaded medical schools' admissions
criteria, curriculum, length of time to complete medical training,

and quality of instruction. The response to the report, however, was historic. Multiple proprietary, relatively small medical schools were forced to close, and sentiments of concern over the state of American medicine gave rise to a marked influx of philanthropy to medical education across the country, particularly from the Carnegie Corporation and the General Electric Board, where Flexner worked, but also from private philanthropists and state governments.[10]

Efforts to elevate the quality and consistency of medical education resulted in more rigorous science requirements and the creation of an academic degree in medicine. Importantly, the academic degree of medical doctorate (MD) was separated from apprenticeship experience, which would now follow academic preparation. With more stringent standards, the number of medical schools dropped precipitously from 160 in 1904 to only 66 by 1935.[11] Under the reforms, medical education included four years of postbaccalaureate study of didactic material plus one to two years of apprenticeship. Postbaccalaureate practical training (medical residencies) occurred at hospitals affiliated with the new and improved medical schools, deemed acceptable by accrediting agencies and state licensure laws.[12]

The early twentieth century brought similar scrutiny to the quality and standardization of surgical procedures, with the founding of the American College of Surgeons in Chicago by surgeon Franklin Martin in 1910.[13] Its committee on standardization led by Professor Edward Martin in Philadelphia and E. A. Codman of Boston developed and implemented a new "end results" system, a precursor to modern methods of hospital quality assurance.[14] The American College of Surgeons launched criteria for training programs and successfully advocated for a system of certifying surgeons, created a fellowship supported by the American College of Surgeons, and established criteria by which hospital staffs could monitor their own performance.

Soon after the end of the Civil War, the Gilded Age ushered in an era of economic prosperity that coincided with tremendous scientific progress. By the 1920s, Americans' faith in and demand for physician service had increased, just as the supply of such services was being restricted by education reforms that reduced the number of legitimate medical schools. Over the course of half a century, medicine went from being a poor, unappreciated craft to being a lucrative, prestigious profession.

The scientific discoveries of the preceding decades had become widespread in the time leading up to World War II. The discovery of penicillin in 1928 and the rise of sulfa drugs in the 1930s proved to be seminal developments that further bolstered the ability to manage disease. Armed with novel tools to address illness and injury, physicians continued to enjoy increasing demand in the interwar years and beyond.[15] People who were once thought to be doomed to death were resurrected through newly discovered medical interventions, including antibiotics, sterile surgeries, and mended bones. As Charles Rosenberg, an expert on the history of the hospital, documents in his book *The Care of Strangers*, whereas hospitals had been a place of filth, danger, and poverty half a century earlier, they had been transformed to places of cleanliness, order, and optimism.[16]

By the late 1920s, hospitals became places where members of the middle class would receive their health care, with a heavy focus on three of the most successful types of surgery—obstetrical deliveries, appendectomies, and tonsillectomies and adenoidectomies. Rosemary Stevens traces the development of the modern hospital in her book *In Sickness and in Wealth*, indicating that these three surgeries, as well as accidents, accounted for about 60 percent of all admissions in the late 1920s.[17] The dramatic results produced by these procedures brought physicians a reasonable compensation from a middle-class clientele that now recognized the value of modern medical care, and American medicine emerged as a successful and effective, even profitable, industry. Public relations films, a new monthly hospital management journal, and even a National Hospital Day celebrated the swift entrance of hospitals into the mainstream of American life and thought.[18]

The role that hospitals play in Americans' lives has continued to grow ever since. The century between the end of the Civil War and the beginning of the civil rights movement saw hospital use increase two hundredfold during a time when the population increased only fivefold. Even during the Great Depression, the number of hospital admissions generally increased annually. With the exception of a minor 3 percent dip from 1929 to 1931, admissions to general hospitals increased from fifty-one per one thousand people in 1931 to seventy per one thousand in 1940.[19] The dominant form of hospitals at the time remained private, nonprofit entities with primary responsibility to serve individual patients who sought medical care, rather than the public at large. Health care infrastructure and utilization expanded markedly throughout the 1900s.[20] The Hill-Burton Act of 1946 provided major expansion money from the federal government to increase the number of hospital beds, and by the 1960s, the number of people admitted to a hospital each year was more than 29 million.[21] The number of visits to physicians also grew substantially. By 2010, 80 percent of adults in the United States had seen a doctor or health professional in the past year. The average adult made 3.8 medical visits per year.[22] Fueled by increasing demand for valued services, the United States' health care industry—including medical treatment, mental health care, life sciences and pharmaceuticals, and nursing homes—is now the largest industry in the world, occupying more than 17 percent of the nation's GDP. Health care expenditures are expected to increase to more than 19 percent of GDP by 2019,[23] although history fails to provide clear insight as to who will finance this projected growth.

THE FIRST MODERN AMERICAN HEALTH insurance plan was developed in 1929 by Justin Ford Kimball, vice president at Baylor University, for teachers in the university system in Dallas, Texas.

Noting that the Baylor University hospital had many unpaid bills, particularly from Dallas educators, and faced with revenue downturns due to the Depression, Kimball developed a payment scheme to bolster the financial stability of the university.[24] The plan built upon strategies of prepayment plans, such as the Franklin Health Assurance Company (established in Massachusetts in 1850), which covered employee work-related accidents and disability for workers in the railroad and steamboat travel industries. The Kimball plan made history by extending its reach beyond coverage for work-related accidents and disability to cover, more generally, any hospitalization expenses incurred at Baylor Hospital. The plan guaranteed payment for up to twenty-one days of hospital care for Baylor teachers at Baylor Hospital for a prepaid premium of six dollars per year. Kimball's plan was a success with 75 percent of teachers in the university system enrolling, followed quickly by employees of the *Dallas Morning News* and the Republic National Bank, both notable employers in the area.[25] As the plan grew, it attracted national attention. Several similar plans emerged and became known as Blue Cross plans, many of which extended the original Baylor concept by financing care at multiple hospitals. In 1937, the American Hospital Association (AHA) consolidated those nonprofit plans that met certain standards, and by the following year, thirty-eight plans covering more than one million Americans joined the newly formed Blue Cross network, each displaying the blue-colored cross marked with the AHA seal.[26]

The concept of insurance for physician services (as opposed to hospital care) first appeared in the lumber and mining camps of the Pacific Northwest operating at the turn of the twentieth century. Employers wanted to provide medical care for their workers, so they paid monthly fees to "medical service bureaus" that comprised groups of physicians. These pioneer programs led to the first Blue Shield Plan, which was established in California in 1939 to cover physician services. In 1982, the Blue Cross Association and the National Association of Blue Shield Plans merged, forming the modern Blue Cross and Blue Shield Association.

While Americans were demonstrating characteristic entrepreneurship in providing insurance on a local level throughout the early twentieth century, multiple European countries were developing or had already developed national, compulsory insurance plans that would be governmentally planned and managed. Germany led the way in 1883 with national, compulsory sickness insurance, organizing this effort through government subsidized sickness funds. Although the program was originally designed for low-income workers and certain government workers, by the 1950s it had been expanded to cover nearly the entire population. Other nations soon followed the German example of providing national, publicly funded health insurance, including Austria in 1888, Hungary in 1891, Denmark in 1892, Norway in 1909, Britain in 1911, and the Netherlands in 1913.[27] Each country arrived at universal health insurance schemes after several decades of incremental benefit expansion, usually beginning with compulsory industrial accident insurance. By the 1970s, Germany, the United Kingdom, Sweden, Canada, France, and Italy all had compulsory public insurance programs for industrial accidents, pension insurance, unemployment insurance, family allowances, and health insurance.

Perhaps unsurprisingly, the history of national insurance programs was quite different in the United States. Although industrial accident, pension, and unemployment insurance programs were secured by federal requirements in the first half of the twentieth century, efforts to create universal health insurance have never been widely endorsed. In 1906, the American Association for Labor Legislation (AALL) began advocating for comprehensive public insurance, including compulsory health insurance, peaking in support from the Progressive movement in 1917. Founder of the movement, President Theodore Roosevelt supported such reform out of a belief that the country could not be strong if people who fell ill were made poor on account of growing medical liabilities. Nevertheless, compulsory health insurance would not be afforded the same political support in the United States that it had in Europe during this time,[28] and Roosevelt was defeated as a third-party candidate in 1912.

The United States' entry into World War I in 1917 further quelled attempts to develop a national health insurance scheme for the country. Anti-socialist sentiment increased, and as Paul Starr records in his sociological history of American health care, opponents now assaulted national health insurance as a "Prussian menace inconsistent with American values."[29] The war distracted attention from efforts to expand the reach of health insurance, and postwar fears of communism stemmed any remaining interest in compulsory insurance by hopeful Progressive Party members.

Just as the discovery of penicillin and sulfa drugs increased the desirability of health care, the grave financial stresses of the Depression reignited heated debate in the 1930s about how America should organize and pay for medicine. Americans shifted their hospital utilization patterns during the Depression, increasingly forgoing care at private, nonprofit hospitals to seek less expensive and often free services at state-owned hospitals. As private, nonprofit hospitals watched their revenues plummet, government hospitals were overwhelmed with burgeoning demand from families strapped for income. Increasing demand for what were, by this time, viewed as valuable commodities—medical care, hospital treatments, surgical procedures—coupled with precipitous declines in middle-class incomes proved fertile ground for renewed questions about who should pay how much for health care.

It was against this backdrop that an independent and prominent body of economists, physicians, and public health specialists adjourned themselves to review the state of health care in the United States. They cataloged their findings in the final report of the Committee on the Costs of Medical Care in 1932, which argued for universal health insurance, with varying degrees of compulsory requirements for citizens. The American Medical Association firmly opposed any government control of medical care, particularly through financing of physicians' work. Opposition from the AMA was based on both economic and social concerns, with the latter being more persistently vocalized. The AMA voiced its disagreement through the elocution of Morris Fishbein, editor of the *Journal of the American Medical Association*, who in 1932 articulated the sentiment in cold war terms, describing the choice to endorse a universal health insurance scheme as being one of "Americanism versus Sovietism for the American people."[30] Fishbein featured oppositions that had been published in newspapers across the land. One 1932 commentary on the Committee on the Costs of Medical Care's report published that same year epitomizes the AMA's stance:

> [The prospect of universal health insurance] is dangerous from the standpoint of the patient. It creates malingerers. It makes self-pitying hypochondriacs out of people who are free to go to a physician at any time without extra cost. Secondly, it is bad for the physician. The best physician has been the highly "individualistic" "old country doctor." The worst has been the "company doctor." Secretary [of the Interior] Wilbur's socialization plan seeks to turn the first into the second. At a time when we are trying to analyze just how far we can afford our present "socialization" expense, Secretary Wilbur comes along and claps another change upon us.[31]

The outcome of the debate on universal insurance during this time now seems predictable; the AMA and its supporters were successful in appealing both to the national ideology of individualism and to concerns that expanded government involvement in health care would ultimately be unaffordable. These concerns were magnified by the financial pressures of the Depression.

The New Deal, a set of economic initiatives promulgated by President Franklin D. Roosevelt's administration from 1933 to 1938, represented a unique instance in which certain models of health insurance fell under the auspices of federal social welfare programming. Such programs as the Federal Emergency Relief Administration, Civil Works Administration, and Public Works Administration featured not only employment and income support but also public health and medical care financing programs. The Farm Security Administration (FSA), in particular, focused its attention on rural farmers, who were left destitute in the Depression. The FSA, while working to put rural families back on their feet, recognized the centrality of medical care in achieving economic stability.

The FSA underlined the economic rationale for their involvement in medicine and collaborated with the United States Public Health Service to enroll 650,000 people into prepaid medical cooperative plans by 1942. Support for the program was remarkable, and according to Michael Grey, physician, historian, and author of *New Deal Medicine*, can be attributed to several factors. First, the program was circumscribed at the beginning to rural, very-low-income areas. Second, rural physicians saw the value of the FSA plans insomuch as they guaranteed them payment and kept their communities healthier. Third, only licensed physicians were eligible for reimbursement under these plans, a requirement that promoted the professionalization of rural physicians and guaranteed them a patient base.[32]

Despite the success of the FSA, early tolerance for this government intrusion into medical care eventually gave way, and by the late 1930s, the schism between the AMA physicians that supported an expanded government role in medical care and those who opposed such a move widened. *The Nation* reported that "Civil War has broken out at last in the AMA—a very civil and respectable war," and the fault lines grew with the US Public Health Service on one side and the AMA on the other.[33] President Roosevelt's reelection in 1936 strengthened his commitment to the domestic agenda, including the nation's health.[34] The president asked the Interdepartmental Committee to Coordinate Health and Welfare Activities to oversee an assessment of the nation's health needs and to consider a national health program. These tasks were delegated to the Technical Committee on Medical Care, which was chaired by US Public Health Service officer Edgar Sydenstricker, and whose members had been associated with the FSA. The resulting report reiterated the findings of the 1932 Committee on the Costs of Medical Care. The group proposed federal expansion of financing for provision of public health services, hospital construction, and medical care for the indigent. The report also recommended the creation of state-based insurance programs, similar to those created by the FSA, and the consideration of compulsory national health insurance, which was the most controversial of the recommendations.

Although President Roosevelt received the report with enthusiasm, much of the AMA persisted in its opposition. Quietly, the AMA negotiated with the Interdepartmental Committee to Coordinate Health and Welfare Activities, offering to agree with their recommendations if all mention of compulsory health insurance were dropped. The committee refused, and in 1938, the AMA compromised by rescinding its opposition to voluntary third-party insurance, apparently seeing this as the lesser of two evils. By the time Senator Robert F. Wagner of New York introduced his bill to implement the recommendations of the report in 1939, an influx of newly elected conservatives had shifted the balance of power in the Senate and, with the AMA, led a full-on attack of the bill. President Roosevelt had failed to mobilize the political support necessary for passage of the bill, and it died without reaching the floor of Congress.[35]

Seven years later, President Harry Truman became the first US president to call formally for the creation of a federal health insurance fund that would be open to all Americans. His plan did not require individuals to participate in the federal insurance program, but those who did participate would pay monthly fees into the plan, which would then cover all medical expenses. He asked Congress to view access to adequate medical care and protection from the financial fears of sickness as "economic rights" to which all Americans should be entitled. It was on this platform that Truman was reelected in 1948.[36] By 1950, however, lobbying efforts from the AMA, which had published an editorial forecasting that national health insurance would make doctors "slaves," linked national health insurance programs to communism.[37] The Senate hearings on the topic exposed continued fears of socialism, marked by Ohio senator Robert Taft's suggestion that universal health insurance came right out of the Soviet constitution and his announcement that Republicans would boycott further hearings.[38] Objectors maintained that government money should fund science rather than socialized medicine. Curtis Bok, a Pennsylvania philanthropist and writer, embodied this type of conservatism when he explained that he and his peers were "convinced that the only genuine medical insurance for this country lies in making the benefits of *science* available to all practitioners and to all patients."[39] A series of unpopular union strikes, as well as the nation's entry into the Korean War further undermined Truman's original plan.

Although President Truman's legacy on American health care would not be what he had hoped, his political contributions have had lasting impact. His signature health legislation, the Hill-Burton Act (known formally as the Hospital Survey and Reconstruction Act of 1946), provided federal funds to massively scale up the number of hospital beds from 3.2 to 4.5 beds per one thousand people.[40] Although this large investment greatly accelerated health care utilization and spending, it did little to expand a uniformly accessible financing system for the American public. Ironically, Truman's well-intended initiative to increase access to health care ultimately served to escalate costs by making hospitals the centerpiece of the health care landscape. World War II and the subsequent cold war era pushed the country even further away from federal provision of health insurance. Fears of socialism fueled Americans' skepticism of a government expansion, thus allowing the now common employer-based insurance schemes to emerge as viable, privatized alternatives.

For employers, the offer of medical insurance to workers began as an innovative and effective means to create a competitive advantage for their businesses during the wartime wage freezes. Given the rising expenses of medical care, employees gladly accepted employer-paid health insurance in lieu of salary increases. Congress amended the Internal Revenue Code to make employer-sponsored health insurance tax-exempt, and the US Supreme Court ruled that employee benefits, including health insurance, could be bargained as part of the union-employer contracting. Employer-based insurance quickly took root in the wake of these developments, with private health insurance companies largely administering the financing and payment of health care services. The private health insurance market has since grown exponentially, from a $1 billion industry in 1950, to an $8.7 billion industry in 1965, and to an $848.7 billion industry in 2010. With an eight-hundredfold increase in private insurance in just sixty years, the notion that health insurance is employer-based has become increasingly entrenched in American society.[41]

The largest government-run health insurance programs in the United States thus far, Medicare and Medicaid, were signed into law by President Johnson in 1965. The Medicare program was a federal, government-funded and government-administered program to provide health insurance (partly financed by Social Security) for older adults, who conservatives and liberals alike agreed had earned such a benefit after a lifetime of honest work. Although the federal program would later be extended to cover people with disabilities and people with end-stage renal disease,[42] it began as a way to protect older adults, whose employment-based insurance coverage often ceased with retirement, from shouldering high medical expenses.

Medicaid, funded that same year, partly by the federal government and partly by the states and administered by the states, was designed to protect people with low income who met state-specific categories (e.g., pregnant women, blind, disabled). Like the stimulus of the Hill-Burton Act, the funding of Medicare and Medicaid

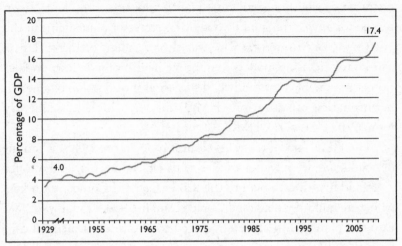

FIGURE 2.2. NATIONAL HEALTH EXPENDITURES IN THE UNITED STATES
AS A PERCENTAGE OF GDP, 1929–2009

Source: Adapted from Christopher Conover, *The American Health Economy Illustrated* (Washington, DC: AEI Press, 2012), Table 1.1.

inadvertently fueled the largest increases in health care spending ever seen in the world. Whereas health care spending increased 42.5 percent (from 4.0 to 5.7 percent of GDP) in the thirty years before Medicare and Medicaid (1935 to 1965), spending ballooned by 140.4 percent (5.7 to 13.7 percent of GDP) in the thirty years following Medicare and Medicaid (1965 to 1995) (see Figure 2.2), topping what many OECD countries would be spending even forty years later. This growth was fueled first by the improvement in medical education, then by an enormous expansion of hospital beds, and finally by major funding for the Medicare and Medicaid programs.

Politically, the explosion in health care expenses, coupled with general inflationary concerns in the 1970s, confronted President Richard Nixon with a difficult proposition. Whereas price controls were controversial in all sectors, their use in medical care seemed untenable after the entitlement expansion of Medicare and Medicaid less than ten years earlier. Desperate to find an innovative way to restrain costs without reducing quality or access, President Nixon turned for advice to Paul Ellwood, MD, professor of medicine at the University of Minnesota, who was the president of InterStudy, a think tank devising models to improve health of a defined population at reasonable cost.[43] Ellwood suggested the adoption of a health maintenance organization (HMO) model, which subsequently formed the basis of the HMO Act of 1973.[44]

The HMO model traces its earliest roots in the 1940s, when industrialist Henry J. Kaiser worked with Dr. Sidney Garfield to offer a prepaid health care plan to the Kaiser Cement Company workers who were building the Grand Coulee Dam in 1938.[45] Employees paid into the plan and then were required to obtain their medical care from the physicians that the Kaiser Cement Company employed. Thus was born the earliest staff-model HMO (in which physicians are employed by the health plan) in the United States. The experiment was successful, demonstrating the value of the prepaid HMO model to confer health benefits at reasonable cost. The federal HMO Act of 1973 was a trial program that included enabling legislation for HMOs (by removing state-level restrictions if the HMO met standards to be federally qualified) and contributed capital to initiate new HMOs, as long as they, too, met the standards for federal qualification. Although the HMO Act did not require employers to offer health insurance, employers with at least twenty-five employees that elected to offer health insurance were required to also offer a federally qualified HMO as an alternative. A core principle of HMOs was the plan's role in medical decision-making, meaning that the HMO would oversee and approve physicians' decisions such as whether to admit a patient, how long to keep the patient in the hospital, and whether to order expensive diagnostic tests for the patient, all of which heretofore had been made autonomously by physicians. The HMO in effect "managed" care, with the goal of limiting high costs due to overutilization, without compromising patient outcomes.

During the three decades that followed, efforts to manage care proliferated beyond the traditional HMO model. Health insurance plans generally adopted tactics introduced by HMOs to limit expenditures and health care use. In time, managed care grew to encompass 97 percent of the employer-sponsored health insurance market (which represented approximately half of all insured Americans), reaching its peak in 2005 (see Figure 2.3).[46] Furthermore, early data indicating that managed care might save costs attracted the attention of federal and state-financed programs. In the mid-1990s, both Medicare and Medicaid programs expanded their use of managed care tactics, instituting greater control over physician and hospital decision-making, again to rationalize spending. In the mid-1990s, managed care efforts briefly slowed the acceleration in health care costs (see Figure 2.2); however, this attenuation would not sustain, as

FIGURE 2.3. MANAGED CARE AS A PERCENTAGE OF THE EMPLOYER-BASED INSURANCE MARKET OVER TIME (1988–2010)

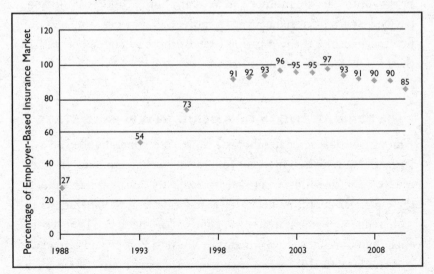

Source: Adapted from G. Claxton et al., *Employer Health Benefits: 2012 Annual Survey* (Menlo Park, CA: The Kaiser Family Foundation and Health Research & Educational Trust, 2012), 5, 65–70.

public outcries of overly harsh rationing by managed care companies reduced their popularity in the employer insurance market by the late 1990s, and cost acceleration then resumed.

IN CONTRAST, THE DEVELOPMENT OF the social service sector would take a different tack. Relegated largely to the domain of government or nonprofit agencies, social welfare efforts, such as the provision of housing subsidies, old-age assistance, unemployment benefits, and childcare support have been directed primarily at Americans who are poor or otherwise live at the fringes of society. Historically, these efforts have been stigmatized as ineffective, unprofitable, and in some instances, even immoral. The result has been a fragmented series of federal, state, and locally run programs administered according to differing qualification standards and provided at a litany of diffuse sites. The complicated history of the United States' social service sector reveals the challenge of coordinating among its own enterprises, let alone with health care or other related sectors. The United States, unlike its counterparts in Western Europe and Scandinavia, pursued a path of "residual" versus "universal" services, aimed at defined segments of the population (usually those who are poor) rather than a fully inclusive constituency.[47]

HISTORICAL ROOTS OF AMERICAN WELFARE STATE

Among political science scholars, America is generally viewed as a laggard country when it comes to its social welfare policies. In addition to being unwilling to provide federally funded health insurance, the US government has been slower to fund social welfare programs, such as unemployment insurance, family allowances, and health benefits, than have most governments in Western Europe and Canada.[48]

The historical reasons for this reticence are many. Some have argued that the United States is missing the primary historical root of the welfare state—feudalism.[49] This argument asserts that by the eleventh century, feudalism had created a system of government in which those who possessed land sought to safeguard their serfs, who were constrained in individual freedom but protected by their lords or masters against such hazards as sickness, unemployment, and old age. Whether or not one accepts this argument, the Pilgrims' escape from religious persecution and their desire for freedom certainly laid a foundation of resistance to an overly prescriptive government in their new home. The first coastal winters of brutal survival and subsequent westward expansion, achieved by pioneers and governed by cowboys, has left a historical legacy that glorifies rugged individualism. In addition, the Protestant work ethic coupled with Calvinist views of sinful idleness underlay the American belief that hard work is fundamental to the good life and that handouts should be provided sparingly. Deep fears about the potential of public aid to weaken individuals' work ethic overcame religion's emphasis on the virtues of mercy and charity, when it came to carving out the role of government in early American life. Charitable tendencies were relegated to voluntary and private religious entities. Finally, widespread poverty, which existed in the Old World, was less pervasive in the New World of colonial America, and unemployment was not viewed as a major social problem. America was viewed by its people as the land of plenty, with a frontier of endless opportunities for those who were willing to work for them.[50]

Even so, American history is not entirely without its own brand of social welfare, which has often taken the form of localized generosity for vulnerable community members. Beginning in the colonial era, poor laws, fashioned after Elizabethan legislation in England, directed municipal funds to needy neighbors.[51] Town meetings, often held in collaboration with churches, were the sites of decision-making regarding both raising and allocating charitable funds. The system seemed sufficient for towns that were stable and knew their residents; however, cities with room to sprawl and wealthier seaport towns drew impoverished refugees from frontier settlements, particularly during skirmishes with Native American tribes and in King Philip's War in 1675–1677. People fleeing from and displaced by the wars entered Newport, Boston, and New York in what residents of those cities perceived to be droves. These coastal cities, suffering as a result of their locations and unable to accommodate "the unsettled poor," appealed to the General Court for support from the colonial treasury in an attempt to avoid draining funds from their own townships.

The decentralized nature of early American social relief was apt for the disparate colonies, which were still a long way from consolidating forces in opposition to the British crown. In 1701, still ninety years before the establishment of the first Bank of the United States, local communities began receiving reimbursement from a colonial treasury and "state aid" was born, albeit only for relief of people who were "unsettled" and who, if forced to moved, might harm other communities.[52] Meanwhile, the demand for public expenditure to support people who were poor grew exponentially during the era of the American Revolution. Towns strove to manage the mounting burdens through local redistributive practices. In Boston, residents contributed £500 to help people who were destitute in 1700, £2,000 by 1715, and £10,000 by 1753, even though the population growth was almost level during this time.[53]

After the colonies unified and began pursuing an expansionist vision of manifest destiny, the decentralized approach to social welfare continued. The prospect that a single (government) entity could cater to such a large terrain seemed unlikely, and the perpetual tension between the autonomy of the states and the authority of the new federal government limited efforts to expand the latter. As a result, the United States would not construct a unifying national code for social welfare, thereby distinguishing itself from Germany, Great Britain, and other Western European countries. Instead, it accorded the state and local governments flexibility in developing programs that suited their populations.

The accordance of responsibility for social welfare to local entities was undermined in the early nineteenth century, when new waves of immigration made clear the inadequacy of the emerging American social welfare system. Many newcomers arrived on American shores suffering from malnutrition, exploitation, and brutal travels across the sea. Their needs would quickly outstrip the local capacity to provide relief. The first comprehensive survey of poor relief in the United States, the 1824 *Yates Report* (commissioned by the legislature to the New York secretary of state, John Van Ness Yates), and the New York State County Poorhouse Act enacted that same year highlighted the extensive need for poverty relief. Together, these gave rise to a series of poorhouses that would shelter and care for people in hardship.[54] These poorhouses, described by some as "living tombs" and "social cemeteries," were marked by foul conditions including overcrowding, inadequate food, and very limited medical care.[55] Social reformer Dorothea Dix worked on legislation by which the federal government would make land grants to states to improve the treatment of people who were poor, mentally ill, deaf, or blind. Although her Bill for the Benefit of the Indigent Insane was passed in both House and Senate, it was vetoed by President Franklin Pierce in 1854. In justifying his decision, President Pierce stated, "I cannot find any authority in the Constitution for making the Federal Government the great almoner of public charity throughout the United States. To do so would, in my judgment, be contrary to the letter and spirit of the Constitution, and subversive of the whole theory upon which the Union of these States is founded."[56]

In the wake of Pierce's veto, federal involvement in social welfare was restricted to certain categories of deprived people—such as Native Americans, former slaves, and indigent merchant seamen. While many Western European nations were rolling out universal schemes of social insurance, the United States refrained from offering social welfare programs to broader segments of the populace. As a result, leading up to the Civil War, social welfare programs remained the domain of local government or voluntarism, largely outside the scope of federal government responsibility.[57]

American reliance on voluntary organizations to meet community needs became well established by the mid 1800s, supported by traditional American values, such as individualism, hostility to centralized power, and separation of church and state. The strengthening on the nonprofit social sector coincided with the aggressive reforms in medical education at this time, resulting in firmer boundaries around both industries. Nonprofit organizations flourished and picked up the slack for a limited welfare state; their presence and effectiveness became a rallying cry for those who sought to stymie further expansions of government programs. In the view of Lester Salamon, director of Johns Hopkins University Institute for Policy Studies, "The historic American practice of relying on voluntary organizations was transformed from pragmatic necessity into a high moral principle, and ultimately political ideology."[58] This ideology would later fuel a uniquely American perception of the nonprofit sector as an alternative, rather than a supplement, to state activities.[59]

The devastation wrought by the Civil War created a generation of needy Americans that the country could not ignore. Beginning in 1862, state legislatures in the North and then the South mandated public aid to be directed to disabled veterans, widows, and orphans caused by the war. The newly elected federal government of President Abraham Lincoln established a pension fund for veterans on both sides of the conflict, aiming to "care for him who shall have borne the battle, and for his widow, and his orphan."[60] At the same time, the industrialization hastened by the war gave rise to oil, steel, railroad, and meatpacking sectors that conferred large fortunes on the auspicious few, highlighting the misery of poverty in the contrast.[61] Most of the support for people who were poor and unable to work, however, was relegated to private or voluntary entities. These entities would soon find themselves overwhelmed, as the early years of the twentieth century brought rapid urbanization, industrialization, and immigration—and with these changes, increased inequality, and economic deprivation.

Even within the evolving private, nonprofit sector, distinct approaches to providing for people who were poor crystallized opposing views about the root causes of poverty. The charity organization movement, which ascribed to the notion of social Darwinism, believed poverty was often the result of individuals' debauchery and weakness and advocated for a paid agent to visit community members and assess their "worthiness" before distributing aid. Although its earliest roots are in England, the movement was pioneered in the United States in the late 1870s by leadership at St. Mary's Episcopal Church in Buffalo, New York. Supporters of this kind of "scientific charity" found little to fault in the economy at large and viewed their mission as identifying and sustaining virtuous families who had fallen on hard times. In contrast, the settlement house movement, initiated by Stanton Coit and Charles Bunstein Stover's Neighborhood Guild of New York City in 1886 and Jane Addams's Hull House in Chicago in 1889, argued that poverty arose from a malfunctioning society, which limited certain families' and individuals' flourishing. With this mental model, the movement designed settlement houses to shelter both highly and poorly educated people. Program activities included neighborhood clubs, recreation and educational activities, and advocacy efforts for political change. These two service philosophies— one that attributed poverty to individual weakness and dysfunction and one that attributed poverty to social dysfunction—contributed to the development of the social work profession as dually focused on individual and family support as well as legislative action to improve social welfare.[62]

Large corporations also made efforts to address social welfare issues pertinent to their workforces, termed "welfare capitalism."[63] Baylor Hospital's move to provide a basic form of medical health insurance to its employees is exemplary of this movement. Some companies even created what was called "industrial villages," offering workers affordable housing, schools, churches, and entertainment.[64] Although these company towns did not survive past the bloody Pullman strikes of 1894, the broader strategy of welfare capitalism continued on and reached its peak in the 1920s. Through World War I, the speed at which large corporations developed welfare programs for their laborers accelerated in part to deflect potential labor disputes and disruption of profitable business, although they were never intended to be a true alternative to a welfare state. This embrace of welfare capitalism paralleled the rise in demand for physician services throughout this decade; businesses were thriving financially and could afford to give back, and employees had money in their pockets with which to seek medical care.

Just as the Great Depression proved to be a crux in the narrative of American health care, so, too, was it a turning point in the history of American social politics, challenging the corporate strategy of welfare capitalism. In some states, more than 20 percent of the citizens were unemployed, and corporate America was hard pressed to provide salaries, let alone unemployment insurance, housing, and other safety net programs. The economic pressures faced by the nation allowed an opportunity for Democratic ideals of government expansion to take hold in the form of the New Deal. Between 1933 and 1938, Franklin D. Roosevelt (FDR) built government relief programs to assist people who were unemployed and poor, including the Works Progress Administration (WPA) and the United States Housing Authorities (USHA). These federal interventions have been viewed as a major victory for the liberal agenda in the United States, the effects of which would remain at the forefront of political minds for decades to come.[65] Nevertheless, the extent to which the New Deal signaled a decisive turning point in the relationship between American government and its people remains less clear. Even in 1932, at the height of the nation's enthusiasm for Roosevelt's progressive agenda, the AMA was publicly expressing its disdain by condemning suggestions of universal health insurance. For many other Americans, the expansion of government's role that FDR was able to achieve was appropriate only in response to a crisis, if at all, and only for people who were deemed to have earned such government support through years of employment and taxation.

On a more limited scale, President Johnson's 1964 Great Society program, and specifically, his War on Poverty echoed ideals embodied by FDR's New Deal and expanded government's involvement in combating social ills. With more than 15 percent of Americans living in poverty at the time, Johnson led Congress to pass the Economic Opportunity Act, allocating federal funds to combat poverty and creating programs such as Head Start, Food Stamps, and Federal Work Study in addition to Medicaid and Medicare. Programs like these would help lessen the need for the Servicemen's Readjustment Act (GI Bill), begun in 1944 and re-upped in 1952, 1959, and 1966, which provided funding for the social supports for more than 2.2 million American service members from World War II, Korea, and Vietnam. Although Johnson's Great Society was initially well received, its popularity waned precipitously with the election of Republican President Nixon in the early 1970s. In 1975, just two years after unveiling his new HMO Act, Nixon eliminated the Office of Economic Opportunity, which had been a cornerstone of the Great Society program.

Today, social welfare programs remain highly decentralized with substantial variation in benefit levels across the states. Even while financing may pull from public taxpayer dollars, benefits and services are administered primarily through a plethora of private nonprofit agencies and employers rather than government agencies. Since the end of the Second World War, American fears of continued government expansion and the relative prosperity of the nation have kept the initiation of long-term, large-scale social programs at bay. America has no national family financial allowance and allows more children to remain in poverty than does any other industrialized nation.

It offers unmarried mothers less help with daily needs, it provides fewer citizens with public housing, and it spends less on job training and job creation than do its European counterparts. These facts have earned the United States the title of a "semiwelfare state" among some political scientists.[66]

WHAT IS THE IMPACT OF this semi-welfare state on how people in the United States experience health care? We know from Chapter 1 that countries that spend proportionally more on social services attain better health, illustrating that the work of the social and health service sectors are intertwined and suggesting that structural disintegration may be imprudent. The history of the health and social service sectors in the United States elucidates the roots of their separateness. Spurred by private sector confidence in a growing and profitable health care market, the United States has favored investments in health care over social services. According to the numbers, this inequity may result in poorer health than might be attained by recalibrating the balance of health and social spending.

CHAPTER 3

FRONT-LINE INSIGHTS

To BETTER UNDERSTAND THE DYNAMICS of the interaction between health and social services, we conducted interviews with
a diverse set of people who played different roles in one or both
sectors in an array of organizations. We spoke with patients, physicians, nurses, social workers, hospital administrators, and social
service agency staff and administrators. We selected people and organizations from varying types of care facilities, system designs, and
geographic regions of the United States. Some organizations were
quite high performing, whereas others were average or struggling,
either financially or in terms of key performance metrics. We continued interviews until no new themes emerged—standard practice
in qualitative research[1]—which occurred after about sixty interviews in the United States (Appendix A details the ID numbers of
interviewees). The research generated three illustrative cases and
four recurrent themes that characterize the human experience of
the "spend more, get less" paradox.

We begin by presenting three true narratives, selected from many
others like them, that represent some of the paths by which health
and social service needs become entwined in Americans' lives. The

first is the story of a boy growing up in an environment of social challenges—violence, drugs, high unemployment—and costly health care consequences. The case illustrates how people with high health and social need, who lack financial and family resources, can accumulate enormous medical bills without much improvement in health or well-being. The second case demonstrates the experience of people at the opposite end of the socioeconomic spectrum: a wealthy, middle-aged couple challenged by job instability, leading to depression and obesity, and portending a future of unaffordable health care bills. The third case depicts the challenges faced by an increasing number of older adults, many of whom face social isolation and loneliness and turn to the medical care system for help. These cases, in which the names have been changed, help to create a nuanced narrative about why we spend so much in health care but fail to produce the anticipated outcomes.

CASE #1: THE URBAN LANDSCAPE

Dwane grew up in an inner city. His father died of AIDS when Dwane was seven years old. His mother had nine other children and only temporary work outside the home. The house was big enough but falling apart, with a cracked cement yard. Dwane was the third eldest, but after his older siblings moved out of the house, he had become the most useful child for bringing in some extra cash. He suffered from asthma and had been husky since he could remember. At the age of nine, he learned how to cut cocaine in his palm and transport drugs on behalf of his brothers. He was paid fairly well and gave the money to his mother, who was happy to have some extra change to make ends meet. Eighteen months later, the drug dealer in the area promoted Dwane to "lookout" status. At eleven years old, he did his first "hand-to-hand," physically meeting the buyer to sell the drugs directly. His older brothers told Dwane he should have waited until his twelfth birthday to do hand-to-hands, and as punishment, they beat him up. When he was thirteen years old, one of his brothers gave him his first bundle of crack, and Dwane sold it in two hours. His mother used the money he brought in to put new clothes on their backs and more food on the table. Dwane did not care much about school, but he felt good about his work, especially when people complimented him by likening him to his father, a successful drug dealer. In Dwane's view, he was doing the right thing for his family.

Most of what Dwane's family ate was fast food: KFC, McDonald's, and his favorite—Popeye's. None of his siblings went to school regularly, and when they did, they had few books and mostly ignored the teachers. After school, there was little to do, few parents at home, and easy access to firearms in the neighborhood. His rite of passage (as it was called in the neighborhood), at fourteen years old, was to intimidate someone older with guns. He did not have to kill anyone, just show he could intimidate someone. So he targeted his twenty-eight-year-old cousin, who was just out of prison after serving a ten-year sentence for manslaughter. His cousin, feeling disrespected by a fourteen-year-old, beat Dwane to a pulp in front of his brothers, his friends, and even his mother, who watched but said nothing. No one intervened. Afterward, Dwane ran to get two guns from the house to kill his cousin. His mother stopped him and locked him in his room until the next morning. He remembers her scolding him, "You need to grow up, young man." Dwane was growing up but in a violent and economically deprived neighborhood with an abundance of drugs, little affordable fresh food, and no stable home or family on which to rely.

Dwane's response to the chaos in his life was to begin using the drugs he sold. At the age of sixteen, with limited literacy and no upper-level math skills, he dropped out of school. He could not get a driver's license because he had not paid the fine for a previous bicycle violation. Without a driver's license, he was ineligible for most job training programs. He made money in the drug trade despite having been shot twice before his seventeenth birthday. Now twenty-five years old, Dwane has developed a drug habit of his own, and his asthma has worsened. Dwane is busy with a carousel of part-time jobs but feels depressed about the neighborhood and the friends who have died. His future promises only sporadic employment, poor housing, and shortened life expectancy, and most likely high medical costs related to potential illnesses at which he is now at high risk, including HIV, chronic pulmonary disease, obesity, and clinical depression.

CASE #2: DOWN ON HIS LUCK

Barry is a fifty-six-year-old, heavy-set man with a hearty laugh. Hailing from an upper-middle-class family of European descent, Barry attended a prep school in New Jersey before attending a prestigious university, where he earned his undergraduate degree in business and economics. After graduating with a grade point average of 3.4, Barry landed an entry-level position in sales with IBM. After three years, his bosses viewed him to be on the fast track to success and suggested he get an MBA, which he completed at a top business school. He then followed his passion for business by accepting positions in marketing for a large pharmaceutical firm and later on Wall Street for a financial consulting firm, where he helped companies develop business strategies and design markets globally.

In midlife, Barry grew restless. The extensive global travel required by his job grew burdensome; the lights of Hong Kong, pubs of London, and noise of New York began to lose their thrill. Barry began to struggle uncharacteristically with a feeling that he had lost his sense of direction and his passion. Worry about his wife, who was diagnosed at this time with thyroid cancer, also made him recalibrate his time on the road. He started to spend more time browsing the web and fantasizing about alternative careers, but nothing sparked his interest. Always heavy but never obese, Barry started to gain weight rapidly. In one twelve-month stretch, he put on fifty pounds, stopped being able to fit into the business suits needed for his professional roles and became chronically exhausted.

Still flush with cash from more than twenty years as a top business executive, Barry decided to try his hand at entrepreneurship, thinking it would bring back his passion for business. With $1 million he had accrued, Barry invested in various ventures over a decade, but none was successful. Over time, he sunk more and more savings into what became failed start-up companies and schemes. He sold his house during this time as he and his wife moved to be closer to the investment properties and businesses. The first project fell through due to his business partner's illegal tax-withholding activity; the second was a little better but never came to fruition; and the third ended tragically when his partner and close friend died of advanced cancer with less than six weeks' notice. His fourth and last business project failed in the recession following the crash of 2008, when the primary investor, a longtime friend, committed suicide. As this business closed its doors in the same year it opened, Barry found himself financially and emotionally depleted. He was without a permanent home, unable to pay rent, and feeling like a failure. His friend's suicide hurt and depressed him but did not surprise him; by then, Barry had contemplated suicide several times himself.

Barry is now morbidly obese, at six feet tall and 320 pounds, a binge eater, and prediabetic. He is uninsured and lives in temporary housing. He suffers from frequent leg cramps, periodic chest pain and despondency, and is in the early stages of developing some of the costliest diseases to treat, including clinical depression, heart disease, and diabetes. He and his wife, whose thyroid cancer is in remission, are living one day at a time without insurance and facing medical bills they cannot afford. Barry says he is trying to figure out how to get bariatric surgery, thinking it might help him lose weight, but he has had difficulty finding doctors who will take his case. Barry and his wife each have multiple prescriptions that place additional strain on household finances, and they express uncertainty over how they will make ends meet in the future.

CASE #3: AGING ALONE

Martha is a seventy-two-year-old Irish American woman with high blood pressure and the beginnings of dementia. She had worked in the business office of an insurance company for four decades and had been married for forty-five years. She never had children and was the primary caretaker for both her parents. Twenty years ago, she lost both her parents and her husband within a two-year time span. At that time, Martha moved in with her older brother at his suggestion, but developed severe anxiety in the new home. Her brother, who was ten years older than Martha, struggled to take care of her after she started to develop more symptomatic forms of dementia. Neither she nor her brother had a driver's license, but they lived close enough to the center of town to pick up staples from the corner store. As Martha aged, walking became more difficult. Money was tight, and the food they bought was increasingly boxed or canned.

Because Martha has anxiety, she frequently feels something is wrong with her health. When her anxiety turns to panic, she calls an ambulance to take her to the emergency room. In a typical year of living with her brother, she made twenty-six such calls; Medicare reimbursed the hospital approximately $1,300 per emergency room visit, and Martha paid about $650 out of her pocket for each ambulance trip. Each time, the physicians found nothing wrong and discharged her, usually the same day, or sometimes the next day after running some diagnostic tests. Once, the hospital social worker took special interest in Martha and sent her to a residential psychiatric facility, where she stayed for thirty days and was treated with shock therapy to no avail, leaving her with substantial medical expenses. When Martha was discharged, she returned to her brother's house, again grew anxious, and resumed her pattern of biweekly visits to the emergency room. Between the emergency room and residential psychiatric care, Martha had racked up medical expenses of nearly $60,000 in one year with virtually no improvement to her health.

THESE CASES REPRESENT CONCRETE WAYS in which a litany of inadequate social supports, environmental and community risks, and economic instability can manifest themselves as health care costs over time. For each of these individuals, ample opportunities existed for intervention with low-cost social services. These could have taken a number of forms, including after-school programs, nutritional support, employment support groups or counseling, and adult daycare programs. These social services could have functioned either preventively to keep Dwane, Barry, and Martha from landing in the expensive health care sector, or in coordination with the medical care they received to enhance the health care sector's impact. These cases demonstrate how neglecting the social, environmental, and behavioral causes of poor health can result in increased health care costs without comparable increased health. They also remind us about the dangers when one scapegoats socioeconomically disadvantaged Americans for the high costs of health care. The pernicious results of relying solely on health care were here felt by rich and poor, educated and uneducated, and younger and older people alike.

PROVIDERS IN ALL PARTS OF the health care system recognize that troublesome social conditions drive much of their work and costs. Major challenges in people's social circumstances—layoffs, foreclosures, accidents, violence—can create horrific health care needs, many of which become chronic and carry high price tags. These extreme needs are omnipresent in the nation's hospitals, which care for about 37 million admissions at a medical expense of $750 billion per year.[2]

Hospital staff are palpably frustrated as they face the dual challenges of treating their patients' heart disease, cancer, diabetes, depression, or other chronic and debilitating illnesses while also attending to the social needs that often drive those conditions. The medical workforce—physicians, nurses, pharmacists, and paraprofessionals—are quick to highlight these social factors as central to many patients' well-being. Without formal training in housing, nutritional education or social work, physicians routinely assess medical histories and make medical diagnoses, knowing they are addressing only the most immediate issues their patients face. Nurses, who are perhaps closest to patients' day-to-day issues, hear about the realities of people's social circumstances and recognize that medical care is just one small input to health and well-being. For hospital administrators, the disadvantaged social conditions faced by many of their patients result in longer than average lengths of hospital stay, creating expense to the hospital that is often not fully recouped in the existing health care payment systems. Third-party payers also recognize that covering people living in difficult social conditions often increases the insurer's liability for higher reimbursement payments, which many address by increasing premiums, reducing benefits, or devising tactics to avoid high-risk enrollees altogether.

As social science researchers, we are accustomed to examining diverse data—be they quantitative (numeric), or in this case, qualitative (from conversations and observations)—and trying to make sense out of the variation. Sometimes, qualitative data are diffuse and can seem initially like "white noise," drowning out the coherent theme. In our interviews, we heard very little white noise. The signal was strong, and several key issues emerged continually among people working in diverse settings. Here is what we found.

THE HEALTH CARE SECTOR BEARS THE BRUNT OF AN INADEQUATE SOCIAL SERVICE SECTOR

Gaps in America's social service sector have driven some people to use medical care as substitutes for the social care they really need.

Although the costs of today's medical care may be exceptional, the co-mingling of medical and social needs has been apparent from the early days of poorhouses. Ray Porter, professor of the history of medicine at University College London, wrote of nineteenth-century primary care, "The open secret of general practice, its strength and weakness, has been that many clients do not actually have a disease; they are sick, sad or solitary, they need solace."[3] Providers we interviewed indicated that this statement is as true today as it was in the nineteenth century, and the expectation that health services can address social needs is a key challenge in delivering timely, cost-effective health care.

Physicians are increasingly aware that unmet social needs contribute significantly to worse health for Americans.[4] Findings from a recent national survey of one thousand primary care physicians by the Robert Wood Johnson Foundation, published in their report titled *Health Care's Blind Side*, underscore this reality.[5] A blind side is a portion of people's field of vision in which they have a poor view, typically of approaching danger. More basically, it is the opposite side of where one is looking. The report highlights that the danger of health care's blind side is the raft of unmet social needs that generate substantial costs within the medical care system.

Physicians surveyed for the Robert Wood Johnson Foundation report highlighted the growing, negative influence of the social environment on people's health.[6] Eighty-five percent of surveyed physicians agreed that unmet social needs lead directly to worse health and that patients' social needs are as important to address as their medical conditions. Physicians further reported that had they the power to write prescriptions to address social needs, these prescriptions would represent one out of every seven they write. The top social needs physicians noted were fitness (75 percent of respondents), nutritional food (64 percent), employment assistance (52 percent), education (49 percent), and housing (43 percent). Physicians we interviewed also recognized that their medical treatments were not able to address the most important drivers of poor health. They consistently described the awkwardness of detecting patients' social service needs and wanting to be responsive to their concerns, while knowing that their skills were inadequate to solve the problems and costly to employ. Among those whom we interviewed, one chair of emergency medicine (ID 6) summarized his work:

> We bandage them and send them out, but what they do out there is a black box. Who knows what happens then.[7]

Social service providers note the same challenge from their perspectives. In the words of one community center director and clergyman (ID 17):

> In our present system, social service is the only service looking at the person, not the disease. And the feds right now are focused on, let's be honest, cutting the money. It's all good stuff [that they're trying to do]. Hospitals should be safer and more efficient . . . but nowhere are they asking, "Where does health care deal with *the person?*" And I think eighty percent, ninety percent, even ninety-five percent of the time, that is the least expensive method.[8]

The needs of his patients, another emergency medicine specialist explained, are often outside the bounds of care that he is trained to provide, and he admitted often feeling unable to be effective. The challenges he cited are substantial, and he is not alone. Many physicians reported feeling overtaxed and undertrained to identify and meet the social needs of patients, and patients themselves may prefer to conceal deeper social issues in favor of a seemingly quicker medical fix. One emergency medicine physician (ID 5) recalled patients' arriving early in the morning to request notes from a doctor to explain a work absence the day before. One such patient was hoping to sidestep the larger issue of alcohol dependency that he faced. The physician mimicked the patient, saying,

> "I need a note, Doc. I've been off the wagon for three months, I got a new job, I work at the laundry down there on the Turnpike and, uh, I started drinking heavy over the weekend. I missed Monday. It's Tuesday morning and it's six A.M. I need help. Can I get a note saying I was sick?"[9]

Sometimes the physician would oblige the patient, writing on a prescription pad, "The patient was ill, requiring my attention Tuesday morning, 7:00 A.M." Other times, he would send such patients away.

In another example of how health care has become the landing ground for social problems, a man who was formerly homeless (ID 11) described how he ended up in an emergency department simply because had no place else to go, after taking a cross-country Greyhound bus to California, where his friend refused to house him. Feeling lost, the man remembered saying:

> Where am I gonna go? You know I can't go on the streets.[10]

He recounted that his friend told him to call 911, and soon after, an ambulance arrived and took him to the nearest emergency department.

The emergency room physician we interviewed (ID 5) illustrated the impact of the lack of community institutions on the emergency room, through an account of a middle-aged couple coming to his emergency department seeking respite care for elderly parents:

> A lot of guys bring in their parents, who have become an incredible burden, [looking for relief.] And [they say], "Oh, I think she has a fever." That's very common.[11]

In reality, both he and the middle-aged couple knew that the parent was in no immediate danger—certainly not the type that required emergency intervention. But, according to the physician (ID 5):

> It's all about, "Oh please, take this burden off my back, preferably
> for the entire weekend, because my wife and I have a flight to catch
> [out of town for the weekend]."[12]

The high cost potential of nonmedical issues' showing up in the health care system is obvious in these examples. More subtle, but no less pernicious, is the financial impact of treating simple, routine medical problems on an inpatient or emergency basis. Third-party payers and individuals paying out of pocket can face extremely high prices for basic procedures, often to cross-subsidize costs that are not paid for by others. This emergency room physician (ID 5) described young Latina "Medicaid moms" as a group with whom he sympathized. From his perspective, it seemed an almost cultural imperative among these women to go to the emergency room for any and all health-related concerns. He sighed:

> You look in the information system, you see that this young mother
> has brought the baby in twelve times in the first six months [of the
> child's life] for sniffles and coughs.[13]

In some ways, because the United States does not have a comprehensive social service sector, but does boast an expansive emergency medical system, medical facilities have become a de facto catchall for the care of vulnerable populations, however inadequate that care may be. That emergency rooms have become a shelter of last resort has become increasingly apparent since the 1986 passage of EMTALA, the Emergency Medical Treatment and Active Labor Act (also known as the Patient Anti-Dumping Act), which requires hospitals to stabilize patients who arrive in an emergency condition before transferring them to other hospitals or discharging them. Since EMTALA, hospitals have not been allowed to refuse treatment even if patients cannot pay for the services. The understanding of emergency rooms as a destination was described by a man who was formerly homeless (ID 11):

It's like you have one thing and everything leads up to, uh, like a disaster, you know? In the end, well, you end up in the hospital.[14]

The issues are not restricted to emergency departments, and we heard similar sentiments from physicians and nurses who worked in the inpatient hospital setting, in pediatrics, and on adult medical care units. One internist (ID 25) told the story of a woman who was hospitalized because she reported she was vomiting twenty times a day and could not keep anything down. She was weak and suffering from abdominal pain. She had been fired from work the week prior and was living with her boyfriend. As the internist delved further into the social circumstances, the patient recounted how her boyfriend had just left for Washington, DC, that day, so she was now homeless. She had been evicted from her own apartment earlier because her niece had shot another girl there. The patient underwent a comprehensive battery of diagnostic tests. While she was in the hospital, the jury in her niece's case returned a verdict of manslaughter. The internist recalled:

> The woman was so happy to hear that it was manslaughter only, which meant her niece would not need to go to jail, that she ordered some fried chicken. She kept that down. . . . I don't think the woman was lying. She was symptomatic. We [at the hospital] are a safe place. It is warm; there is food. But the point is that the symptoms are contextual. She had more symptoms when she was newly homeless and scared and stressed; she had fewer symptoms when she was relieved and happy about her family situation. In both cases, the drivers of her symptoms are social, not medical.[15]

During the course of our research, we came to realize that seemingly remarkable stories like this were actually quite common in the experience of health care providers, suggesting that unaddressed social and emotional stressors are often at the root of patients' health struggles.

FRONT-LINE PERSONNEL ARE STRETCHED TO RESPOND TO PATIENT CONCERNS WITH LIMITED RESOURCES

Many front-line personnel described the challenge of providing care that meets the real needs of patients as all but impossible to overcome. Health care providers expressed frustration with the results of their efforts to meet increasingly complex patient needs in the midst of widespread cost containment efforts. Fighting a rising tide of paperwork and bureaucracy, providers of health care, whether physicians, nurses, or administrators, say that time has become a scarce resource of which they have far too little. Many of those working in health care facilities are weary of the repetitive pattern of admitting, treating, and discharging. They recall why they went into medicine—their desire to listen to patients and to have the skills necessary to help them feel better. Nevertheless, virtually everyone with whom we spoke expressed the feeling that their ability to treat patients was constrained by administrative, legal, and financial realities.

Because hospital clinics and emergency rooms serve as gateways for many hospital admissions, pressures on medical and social service staff in these settings are acute. As a program manager at a housing agency (ID 1) reflected:

> So [our people] go to those clinics where really, I hate to say it, [they are] just a number. I am sure there are some genuinely caring wonderful, compassionate medical providers within those systems, but they are overburdened and overwhelmed and, therefore, the follow-through is just not there.[16]

Emergency medicine physicians, who admit that they do not always have the opportunity to discuss a patient's lifestyle and environment in sufficient detail, expressed similar views. They experienced the same limitations not only in caring for patients who were poor or without support, but also in treating people of all socioeconomic backgrounds. As a chair of emergency medicine (ID 6) stated:

Honestly, it's hard to do; it's hard to invest a lot of energy in the backstory in the midst of the busy shift.[17]

A 1998 study by Jason Hollingsworth and his team from the Indianapolis University School of Medicine supports this view with data indicating that less than a third of clinicians' time in the emergency department is spent in direct patient care. The majority is spent on indirect patient care, including ordering tests, completing medical records, and arranging services; and more than 20 percent of their time is spent on non-patient-related activities, such as charting and making telephone calls.[18]

Even for primary care physicians, who are meant to be the main portal for patients seeking health care, making a full investment in collecting a patient's history and assessing current lifestyle can be difficult. The most recent evidence suggests that the average time a patient spends with the physician at a primary care visit is less than 15 minutes,[19] and nearly half of a primary care physician's time is spent on documentation and follow-up, outside the examination room without the patient present.[20] The stresses have created what author and consultant Dr. Ian Morrison, president emeritus of the Institute for the Future, termed "hamster medicine" in a 2000 paper in the *BMJ*—the experience of constant running and never catching up.[21] Gone are the days (for the most part) of house calls. Most doctor's offices are open an average of thirty to forty hours a week, and host practices of approximately 2,500 patients.[22] On the basis of recommendations from national clinical care guidelines for preventive services and chronic disease management, sufficiently addressing the needs of this size practice would require 21.7 working hours per day.[23] Although electronic means of communicating and retaining medical data were designed to save clinicians time, physicians do not view this as time saving, as this obstetrician (ID 31) said of her current-day practice:

The electronic medical record allows me to document more, and that information is helpful. But it definitely does not save any time;

it probably takes longer now. But we have more data, too. Still, there are too many alerts. It is so noisy. There is an alert for everything, and you get numb to it. If you stopped [to pay attention to] everything, it would really take forever, so sometimes you just click right by them.[24]

Nurses at the front line of acute care also experience inadequate time to address both the patients' medical needs, which they are trained to do, and their social needs, which they cannot avoid. A veteran pediatrics nurse (ID 21) in Boston described taxing interactions with drug-addicted mothers, who become her patients when their babies are born addicted to various drugs and in need of immediate weaning. Hospital policy allows these mothers to stay in the room with their newborns for the purposes of feeding them, either by breast or bottle depending on the particularities of their addiction. Nurses can become aggravated with the arrangement, as they spend time trying to manage relationships with the mothers, waking and prompting them to feed their babies according to schedule, holding their hands through social work consultations, and teaching them how to manage the stresses of a caring for a newborn, often with little lasting impact. Time spent on these activities carries with it enormous opportunity costs for nurses highly trained in medical and nursing care and less prepared for the in-depth social work and counseling care that falls to them on all shifts.

The mismatch between the desire to provide medical treatment and the practical demands of the job is incontrovertible. An internist (ID 25) put it this way:

I am sitting here writing a prescription [for] this person who has limited ability to afford the medication or have insight on the situation, who can't go outside because the neighborhood is unsafe . . . and I am totally unable to do my job. I need more support to do my job and to help these patients. Self-care skills need to be taught and we typically do not have the tools to do so at our disposal.[25]

The pediatric nurse (ID 21) who had become expert in caring for so-called drug babies echoed that sentiment:

> You get tired of it. I don't know what to do. You just learn to not take it personally. Some moms are in here every month. They come back and back and back. And then they take advantage of the situation. I mean, their lives stink, and they get food and sleep here. But after a while, seeing this day in and day out, it's pretty hard to take.[26]

The housing agency program manager (ID 1) summed up the similar effects of the stress felt by front-line workers in social services:

> This system is so saturated with people that are burnt out that I think, after a while, you tend to forget that you're helping humans.[27]

THE NEED FOR A MORE HOLISTIC APPROACH IS WIDELY ACKNOWLEDGED BUT REQUIRES PROFESSIONAL COLLABORATION BETWEEN HEALTH AND SOCIAL SERVICE SECTORS

The people at the front lines of both health care and social services widely acknowledged the full range of patients' needs and expressed dissatisfaction about the limited scope of services they are able to provide. In some cases explicitly and in others implicitly, many aspired to a type of care called "holistic" in nature. While the concept of holism has roots in the ancient Greek theory of the four humours, it applies to modern-day efforts to address individuals' physical, emotional, social, and even spiritual dimensions of health. Here we use the term in reference to the idea that the human body functions as an integrated system, rather than as a distinct physical or biological system. Adherents to holism often also endorse a view of medical care in which physicians and other caretakers should focus broadly on the provision of therapy for the whole patient, rather than focusing solely on the delivery of treatment for a given disease.

According to the World Health Organization (WHO) Constitution of 1948, health is "a state of complete physical, mental, and social well-being and not merely the absence of disease or infirmity."[28] But while the WHO was asserting this as the definition of health, the United States was building its medical complex. It did so particularly efficiently, first through the expansion of hospital-bed capacity with the Hill-Burton Act and later through the enactment of Medicare and Medicaid to pay for medical services. Hence, it is not surprising that reductionist and mechanistic approaches to medicine, which focus on eliminating disease rather than producing health in the WHO's definition of health, dominate. Paradoxically, the United States' overgrown investment in medicine combined with its inadequate attention to the many other inputs to well-being may itself be compromising people's health.

As far back as 1927, Dr. Francis Weld Peabody invoked a holistic perspective in his lecture to a graduating Harvard Medical School class on the importance of knowing one's patient. "The good physician knows his patients through and through, and his knowledge is bought dearly. Time, sympathy and understanding must be lavishly dispensed, but the reward is to be found in that personal bond which forms the greatest satisfaction of the practice of medicine. One of the essential qualities of the clinician is interest in humanity, for the secret of the care of the patient is in caring for the patient."[29]

That same year, the recognition that health required both social and medical services was highlighted in the *New England Journal of Medicine* in an exchange between Miss Ida Maude Cannon, the head of the first hospital-based social services department in the country and the administrator of Massachusetts General Hospital on the hospital's role in producing health, through an integration of medical and social perspectives:

MISS CANNON: An adequate modern hospital must be permeated with the social point of view . . . there has been a constant increase of the social obligations of the hospital, and, as I see it, the hospital social worker's position will become more and more important.

ADMINISTRATOR: From listening to Miss Cannon, I feel that she has touched on one point that is very important—that is, the relation of the social worker to the administration of the hospital . . . The work of the nurse and the doctor, and even the clerk, in relation to medical service, must be to a certain extent social in its approach, if there is to be a complete and thorough understanding of the patient's needs, and if the results in the care of the patient are going to be as good as they ought to be.[30]

As chronic disease came to replace communicable diseases atop the list of medicine's priorities, realms of an individual's life that had heretofore been considered private and therefore forbidden from physician inquiry, such as diet or marital relationships, came to be seen as important determinants of health. For treatments to be effective, consideration of these nonmedical determinants had to enter into medical treatment decisions.

In describing the lessons he had learned over twenty-five years of treating vulnerable populations, the executive director of a health and social service organization (ID 15) explained the necessity of building relationships with patients so as to understand them as whole people, not just a body with illness:

You can't take care of [people] unless you can, one, figure out how to go to them before they come to you because if you wait for them to come to you, it's the emergency room that you'll see them in. Two, it requires a relationship, and relationships take time, and nobody pays for that time. Three, you have to stick with it.[31]

Social service providers, including the clergy, agree. One community center director (ID 17) expressed a holistic view of the causes and potential solutions for illness among people in his community. In his view, one's life circumstances, self-perception, and social connections are fundamental to one's health. Addressing the troubling increase in obesity in his area, he reflected:

> But, you know, well, one of the things that I've experienced [is that] a lot of obesity . . . has to do with a lot of other kinds of situations going on. Some people are eating because they're frustrated; some are eating because they're stressed out. Some are eating simply because they're just disappointed with their life as it is. We can work through it, but they don't even want to discuss that because, you know, they don't want the public embarrassment.[32]

The increasing sophistication of medicine has led to increased specialization and, subsequently, a more reductionist, less holistic approach. Specialization can be crucial for addressing specific, often rare ailments, but such an approach has disadvantages as well. With such specialization, some needs, especially those that are outside traditional medical care and that seem extensive to address, can give way to a "silver bullet" mind-set where the right medicine is believed to be the best antidote for all woes. The housing agency program manager (ID 1) caring for a longtime client with HIV, who has only sporadic access to housing, explained it this way:

> We have a client who is HIV-positive. She was bleeding terribly from her nose. Blood was all over, and she was dehydrated. She had been to the emergency room and was hospitalized three times in seventy-two hours because they didn't take the time to really look at what the problem was . . . She was just dehydrated and needed some rest. But they patch them up and send them home without considering that she has no home where she can rest. They sent her home at midnight Thursday. Friday morning before seven, an ambulance went, came and got her again . . . Every time you admit someone, it's extra money, extra tests, and everything else.[33]

The myopic focus on using medicine as a quick and simple fix instead of addressing underlying social inputs to health is a challenge in treating people of means as well. One pediatrician (ID 81) who works in an affluent area described the tension he feels when parents request additional medical diagnostics and treatments for symptoms he knows can be better treated by more balanced diets, more routine exercise, and stronger community ties. For instance, he described parents' asking for costly genetic testing and hormonal screening to understand how their children are becoming overweight, without their attending to the root problems of lifestyle. He described a range of other troublesome situations for families—children doing poorly in school, talking back to parents, being cut from sport teams—in which parents seek solely medical solutions to what require nonmedical interventions to resolve.

Pursuing a holistic approach has been shown to be cost-saving, even if resource-intensive. The Preventive Medicine Research Institute conducted a demonstration project in collaboration with eight hospitals to determine whether comprehensive lifestyle changes could be a safe and effective alternative to bypass surgery or angioplasty.[34] After one year, almost 80 percent of participants were able to safely avoid heart surgery or angioplasty, and Mutual of Omaha calculated saving almost $30,000 per patient in the first year. In the words of the executive director of a health and social service organization (ID 15) emergency care may be the area where it is most possible to achieve the greatest savings:

> We spend a lot of money turning people in and out of the emergency room when you could probably spend a tiny bit of that getting to know them in the setting where they're comfortable and then work on it from there. We don't spend that money though, which is what is so funny.[35]

Collaborative programs involving health and social services have emerged from community centers, churches, senior centers, and health clinics. For instance, the director of a community center (ID 17), who was also a clergyman, described his Social Integration Program, in which the church community reached out to homeless shelters and started Sunday morning services. Attendees could receive a free breakfast and talk with people about ways to address their health and overall well-being.

> When they come in, they get a breakfast, they go through a variety of different programs that we do in collaboration with a number of the providers in the city. We do clinical work with them. We do job readiness. We have a computer lab that we allow them to use under supervision to go online. We show them how to fill out a job application online. We talk about anger management. We talk to them about bettering themselves.[36]

Like social service providers, health care providers also underscored the importance of the sectors' collaborating to be effective in delivering holistic care. A radiologist at a large hospital (ID 9) noted:

> [High-quality care] doesn't require high-level physician care, but it does require interaction with some type of either health care or social services . . . I think other chronic illnesses like asthma, chronic obstructive pulmonary disease, and so on are things that we could manage if there was a way of managing patients in between their hospital and doctor.[37]

In the absence of a partnership with social services, physicians described feeling impotent in the face of patient complaints, particularly after patients leave the hospital or doctor's office. Follow-up care to a medical episode can be sporadic due to a variety of factors, including challenging social conditions. Speaking in reference to one of his patients who was homeless, the chair of emergency medicine (ID 6) remarked:

> It is very tough to follow up on someone who's living on a park bench.[38]

The executive director of the health and social services organization (ID 15) illustrated the inadequacy of current approaches:

Our system has not got a place for [people living on the streets without steady housing] to go. These are people who get really sick, get really complicated, and we spent a lot of money on their [open heart surgery], but no money on their recovery . . . And ninety percent of them have an active substance abuse issue. When we tried to do substance abuse care, it was paid for by the Department of Public Health over here; it wasn't really in the system. The [hospital] psychiatry department, as wonderful as it is, was not interested in substance use. That is another system. And then for mental health, about sixty percent of the people in the street have a major psychiatric diagnosis. And yet, that care is by another department with another set of funding and another set of computers. We started to realize that we were taking care of people who have all three of these things, and none of these systems was talking to one another. So we started to realize that integration of care was the name of the game.[39]

Describing the "times when it works," the housing agency program manager (ID 1) emphasized cooperation among agencies as fundamental to helping clients with multiple challenges served by several agencies with different payment streams:

What we do is an "all treaters" call—everyone who is involved with the person, we will sit down at the table and discuss the person, what is the best care that we can give them. . . We can get three or four agencies working simultaneously side by side for one person; the key is communication and cooperation because if you don't cooperate, it doesn't get you anywhere.[40]

BARRIERS AND DIFFICULTIES IN ESTABLISHING RELATIONSHIPS BETWEEN SOCIAL SERVICES AND HEALTH CARE HAVE MANY ROOTS

The degree of coordination needed to provide more holistic care is rare, and the root causes of the lack of partnership are many. One considerable barrier is the lack of resources within the social services sector itself. Social service programs are often understaffed, with providers already stretched to cover too large a client base with too little time. The housing agency program manager (ID 1), who was balancing thirty-two high-need client cases simultaneously, regretted not having the time to secure people the help they needed before they landed in emergency departments or the court system. She mourned the loss of outreach staff that had been laid off due to state funding reductions:

> You talk to people [and] see that there's something wrong. [I think] we should just make that connection [to the relevant agency] like outreach staff used to do. [But those agencies] just don't have that kind of money anymore.[41]

The chair of emergency medicine (ID 6), when asked what resources would make his job easier, considered carefully and then responded:

> I would definitely have a social worker 24/7 who could actually take the time to try to do some of these interventions with some folks.[42]

This lack of resources results in unfulfilled tasks and backlogs in processing requests, leaving little time for social service agencies to establish new partnerships with health care providers, even if those partnerships might ultimately make it possible to provide holistic care efficiently.

A second barrier to coordination between health care services and social services is that different professional cultures, driven by distinct mission statements and models of care, prevail in each sector.[43] The ethos in social services is to meet the client where he or she is and to assess the client's motivation to change, as expressed by a veterans' community center director (ID 3):

> People come as often as they knew they need to, and for as long. I don't have any time limits on any of the programs here and it's all voluntary. And I think that's really important because you put

some motivation back on the individual . . . We normalize everything. It is important that we don't look at symptoms; we don't look at illness. We look at function and we look at what *you* [the client] want to work on, not what I want you to work on.[44]

Many health care entities, in contrast, have a more narrowly defined mission to provide medical treatment meant to address specific illnesses. Even as medical professionals may recognize social context as a contributing factor, their focus remains on medical treatment. A story from an internist (ID 25) illustrates the focus on medicine:

> I had a woman come in with abdominal pain, which we treated medically—all the work-up you normally do for hospitalized patients. She was hospitalized almost every month. And the day I saw her, when she came to the ED, she had a history that was tragic. She had recently been divorced and had been in a car accident. Her son had just dropped his premature baby girl, and the daughter had died. The woman had just lost her job, too. She had previously had an EGD, colonoscopy, blood tests, and it was not clear what was going on. But we stopped her metformin [a medication for diabetes], which may have been the reason for the abdominal pain. We'll see. I am sure it was contributing, but you know, with those events in my life, I would have belly pain, too![45]

Workers in each sector recognize the different approach in the other but often disagree over priorities. Some social service providers decry health service personnel for their narrow focus on a small piece of individuals' needs. The housing agency program manager (ID 1) reflected on her health care counterparts by saying:

> They will do an evaluation, and then they quickly start looking for a discharge date . . . [Some] clinicians . . . have been in the system so long that they feel they've heard everything, and they're not willing to believe that a person can change.[46]

Conversely, health care professionals may view the social service sector as essential but not reliably available due to underfunding and lack of coordination. In the words of the experienced pediatrics nurse (ID 21):

> The social workers are great; we get along well and they can really help us. But we don't always have enough around. They don't get paid enough for the tough jobs they have.[47]

These biases are overcome in select situations when parties recognize their dependence on the other, but generally, real differences in culture persist. Hospitals operate twenty-four hours a day, seven days a week; many social service agencies are open only standard hours on weekdays. Most health care personnel hold advanced degrees in their field of work; social service workers at many nonprofit agencies may work with only a bachelor's degree. Health care is primarily interested in curing diseases and mending injuries; social services are focused on rehabilitating people and reducing harm over the long term. Most health care interactions still feature doctors as experts whose advice a patient follows closely; social service providers generally prefer to see themselves as equal partners with clients in addressing client needs.

The differing models of care also give rise to different data monitoring systems, which are not linked so as to facilitate shared decision-making. Often, concerns over privacy and technical barriers to information sharing prohibit interdisciplinary collaboration between sectors. The hospital-based radiologist (ID 9) described the practical challenges:

> Even if you got past the privacy issues, it is very hard to tie in all of the information that was useful for all three parties—the hospital-based provider, outpatient-based provider, and social services—to be able to capture what an individual is thinking or feeling at a given point in time, to know whether intervention is necessary or, in fact, unnecessary.[48]

Health care providers indicated that, although they see the value in the social determinants of health, they do not have time to invest in and manage relationships with social service providers. As the emergency medicine chair (ID 6) put it:

> It's really tough and I'm underresourced. It would be great to throw a team at these people and have the team follow up on them and pursue them and get them into treatment and help them stay sober and all that, but [we do not have the resources].[49]

A third formidable barrier to coordination between the health care and social service sectors is the lack of financial incentives to do so. Health care providers are generally rewarded for increased numbers of patients treated and the complexity of medical care provided. If referrals to social services for nonmedical needs reduce the need for medical treatment, such coordination may not be in the provider's financial interest. In these situations, social services may be perceived as crowding out the business of the health care provider. The executive director of a health and social service organization (ID 15) reflected on the closing of a diabetes clinic that had addressed the nonmedical issues exacerbating patients' disease:

> Fundamentally, a health care industry that keeps everyone healthier is an industry that has reduced its customer base and needs to shrink. But every year, the medical school and the hospital explicitly set goals to increase revenue and volume. No one sets a goal to do fewer of anything. At [hospital name], we had a super-successful outpatient diabetes center: so successful that it reduced the number of hospitalizations, amputations, etc., dramatically. So the hospital shut it down because it lost them money. In a country like the United States in which there is limited central management and every industry (health care, social services) stands on its own, it is extremely difficult to get one organization to voluntarily collaborate with another that has the potential to put the first one out of business.[50]

The same executive director (ID 15) further described the challenges of coordinating between health care and social services. In his view, the provision of expensive medical interventions sometimes limited the resources available for essential social services. He highlighted how the lack of coordinated investment in both medical and social services resulted in ineffective care:

> We kept realizing we have access to all this very high-tech medical stuff for people who, when they come back to where they live, can't do any of the stuff that we spend a lot of money on. And then there's no money to help sort out their social situations, so that they can actually comply with their diabetes care.[51]

Hospital administrators also recognized that perverse incentives in the reimbursement system favored high-cost care over high-value care. One president of a midsize city hospital (ID 14) highlighted the effect that financial incentives had on her efforts to create a contextually appropriate and financially sound organizational strategy:

> In our institution, we have a pediatric service. We are a mile and a half from a children's hospital—you know, the top-ranked pediatric hospital, and when I got here, we were in very, very tough financial shape. I thought, "Okay, maybe we should do something," so I thought, "Maybe there's something creative we can do with pediatrics." So we have a pediatric intensive care unit (PICU), [which I was thinking we could merge with the one in the children's hospital]. But everyone said, "Oh, you know, you have to keep it, 'cause it's how we get pediatric trauma," but PS, we're not getting that much pediatric trauma, nor *should* we get that much pediatric trauma, and so I said, "Well, why don't I close the PICU? It's six beds. It's not that full." And then we looked at the contribution margin with the PICU and without, and we were better with the PICU in it [so we didn't close it].[52]

Paradoxically, insurers continue to reimburse for neonatal and pediatric intensive care services at very high rates nationwide, while less-pricey but essential services are poorly reimbursed. Approximately 630,000[53] American infants and children receive such care every year at a daily rate of $3,500, many of whom accrue expenses totalling more than $1,000,000 in the case of a prolonged stay.[54] Meanwhile, the programs to prescribe proper nutritional supplements or provide critical clothing and transitional items for children going to foster care after their hospital stay are supported only by an uncertain stream of charity. The hospital offers two programs for people with nutritional and shelter needs. This hospital president (ID 14) said:

> We have a food pantry, which is therapeutic, so your doctor gives you a prescription for food. It started in pediatrics, where one out of three kids was presenting with hunger as their chief complaint, particularly on weekends when school-based programs were closed . . . Our food pantry started because pediatricians had cans of peaches in what should have been medicine cabinets. And the great thing about it is the [prescription filling for food] is in our medical record. So when you go back to your oncologist, and he says, you know, "How're you doing?" "Well, I'm feeling a little weak." "Well, I saw that you didn't fill your food pantry prescription. Do you need some help with that?"
>
> One of my favorite programs is something called Pieces of Home, which is a program that gives age-appropriate backpacks to kids who have to go to foster care. So they have something. So if you're two, you get, like, a blanket and a snuggly and a book. We always give a book. If you're fifteen, you get a pair of pajamas that kind of fit you, and an iPod. You know, so you have something you can stick in your ears and zone out, because kids often go immediately into the shelter from here . . . [55]

The fate of these programs, and others like them, is uncertain in the long term, as the return on investment for such outlays is difficult to measure. Still, those who work on the front lines are adamant that, for many patients, these programs are the best value in the hospital. Even so, efforts at holism continue to be undermined by fears among health care organizations that successful collaboration with social services may diminish the potential for revenue.

Providers throughout the health care arena know that the impact of their work is being diluted by the chasm between health care and social services. The United States has the most sophisticated medical technology in the world, which, for insured people, is widely and almost immediately available. Still, many illnesses cannot be prevented or treated successfully with medical care alone. The role social services can play in preventing illnesses, mitigating repeat occurrences, or helping people manage chronic health conditions, is appreciated but underutilized, according to care providers, clients, and patients.

THE PEOPLE WE INTERVIEWED EXPRESSED themes that sum up the predicament: first, the health care sector is bearing the brunt of a missing or underresourced social services sector; second, front-line personnel with limited resources are stretched to respond to patient concerns; third, the need for a more holistic approach to caring for people's health and social needs is widely acknowledged but requires professional collaboration between health and social services; and, fourth, many barriers and difficulties exist in establishing relationships between health and social services, stemming from multiple causes.

Together, these themes shed light on the spend more, get less paradox of health care in the United States. The front lines reflect what the numbers and history evidence—that Americans treat health care and social services as two separate systems, and those systems do not often work in concert. Health care delivery, financing, and regulatory systems are largely independent from social services, and without more consistent strategy and planning, the distribution of health and social services in the care of people, particularly those with high needs, can be misaligned. The damaging impact of this misalignment is felt most keenly by people born in profound poverty, but the pain is experienced far beyond these neighborhoods as well.

Based on how inadequate the coordination is, it is easy to think that there are better ways. But what would that look like? Given the long history in the United States of a lack of coordination between and even separation of the health care and social service sectors, it may be helpful to look abroad for alternative models. Based on their spending and outcome patterns, which demonstrate substantial investment in both health and social services and excellent health outcomes, countries in Scandinavia may provide key lessons to this end.

CHAPTER 4

LEARNING FROM ABROAD

WHILE THE UNITED STATES' HISTORICAL experience and current approach to delivering health can be discouraging, a global survey of health system design and practices offers creative and potentially useful approaches. Over the past forty years, several emerging economies, including those of Singapore, Rwanda, Brazil, and Mexico, have gained academic and even some popular attention for the health reform efforts they have undertaken. In each case, the country dedicated itself to providing more equitable, high-quality care, with substantially fewer resources than those at hand in the United States. Their successes suggest to us that the United States is suffering from a gluttony of riches and should, in theory, be capable of more.

At times, the United States has sought to learn from other nations that have crafted successful models of health care, looking most often to culturally familiar countries, such as Canada or the United Kingdom. In so doing, Americans have overlooked the true health care stars of the global community—the social democracies of Scandinavia (see Table 4.1). While the health outcomes in the United Kingdom and Canada remain only moderately better than those of the United States, Scandinavian countries, such as Sweden, Denmark, and Norway, truly outperform the United States.

TABLE 4.1. COMPARISON OF HEALTH OUTCOMES BY COUNTRY, 2007 OECD DATA

	Infant mortality (Deaths per 1,000 live births)	Life expectancy (Years)	Low birth weight (% of total live births)	Maternal mortality (Deaths per 100,000 live births)
Sweden	2.5	81.0	4.1	1.9
Denmark	4.0	78.4	6.7	14.0
Norway	3.1	80.6	5.1	6.8
Canada	5.1	80.7	6.0	6.5
United Kingdom	4.8	79.7	7.1	7.1
United States	6.8	77.9	8.2	12.7

Scandinavia's success in achieving excellent health outcomes at reasonable cost has captured academic attention for several years now. Although Scandinavian countries differ in specific programs offered and degree of decentralization, academic and lay literature have come to conceptualize them as variations on a common theme, known as "the Scandinavian model."[1] Taken together, Sweden, Denmark, and Norway (the social democracies of Scandinavia) have more physicians and hospital beds per ten thousand people than are available in the United States,[2] and the publicly financed health insurance systems in these countries cover 100 percent of citizens.

In contrast, roughly 15 percent of people in the United States remained uninsured in 2012, prior to recent reforms. Yet Scandinavian countries still spend only slightly more than half of what the United States spends per capita on health care. The Scandinavian approach has consistently achieved the best health outcomes in the world at a reasonable cost for the last decade. For instance, as of 2007, Sweden's infant mortality rate was 2.5 per thousand live births compared with 6.8 infant deaths per thousand live births in the United States. Some, but not all, of this discrepancy may be due to more aggressive efforts to save preterm births in the United States; however, Sweden boasts better health outcomes in several other areas as well. Maternal mortality was 1.9 deaths per 100,000 live births, compared with 12.7 in the United States. Self-rated health also differs considerably; 38 percent of Scandinavians compared with only 28 percent of Americans consider themselves to be in very good health.[3]

Total health expenditures in Sweden, Denmark, and Norway were 11.8, 10.1, and 8.9 percent of the GDP, respectively, whereas health spending comprised 16.3 percent of the US GDP in 2007, climbed to nearly 17.4 percent of the GDP by 2009, and may reach 20 percent of GDP by the year 2021.[4] Scandinavia's comparatively modest rate of health care spending growth is evidence of savvy investing and political restraint, which have helped these countries maintain Standard and Poor's AAA credit rating while much of the rest of Europe has faced grave financial struggles. Many Americans dismiss these Scandinavian systems as being "socialist" and therefore irrelevant, but a nuanced comparison reveals timely lessons for the American experience.[5] Although their methods may appear quite different, the United States and Scandinavia share societal goals of economic, social, and technological advancement. Therefore, it is well worth exploring how Scandinavians conceptualize and deliver health care.

To aid in the analysis, we combined data from a number of sources, including about twenty in-depth interviews with Scandinavian policymakers and practitioners, and the World Values Survey.[6] The World Values Survey is an international source of empirical data measuring individuals' values regarding views on politics, economics, nationalism, trade, and health. The data come from an in-person survey, conducted in the relevant language, of more than one thousand randomly selected people in more than fifty-five countries, including Sweden, Norway, and the United States.

Before we undertook an in-depth examination of the Scandinavian system, we wanted to make sure there was good reason to think that its lessons would have relevance to the United States. We knew that influential media characterized the United Kingdom's experience with the National Health Service as a cautionary tale about the ill effects of long-term government dependence,[7] and we feared the same critique regarding Scandinavia's health care experience. Therefore, before detailing the important distinctions, we took care to ensure that there was substantive evidence of shared values among residents of the United States and Scandinavian countries as reported in the World Values Survey.[8] Quite a few areas of overlap were apparent, which helped us to understand the key differences that also emerged from our analysis.[9]

Perhaps the most fundamental value that people in Scandinavia and in the United States share is personal freedom. History would tell us that freedom is the raison d'être for the United States—the root of its founding ideology;[10] however, we found Americans' views of their own freedom, and of their ability to control their own lives, to be similar to those expressed in Scandinavia (represented by Sweden and Norway in this survey). The survey asked, "Some people feel they have completely free choice and control over their lives, while other people feel that what they do has no real effect on what happens to them. Please use this scale where 1 means 'no choice at all' and 10 means 'a great deal of choice' to indicate how much freedom and control you feel you have over the way your life turns out." On this item, people across countries indicated virtually identical views of their freedom, with scores of 7.7 in the United States and 7.8 in Scandinavia (Appendix B).

American and Scandinavian residents also reported similar levels of involvement in political action. In particular, the same percentages of people surveyed across the United States and across Scandinavian countries had signed a petition or participated in a boycott in the last five years. Self-ascribed political leanings were also similar.

In response to the item "In political matters, people talk of 'the left' and 'the right.' How would you place your views on the scale where 1 means 'left' and 10 means 'right'?," the average responses were 5.7 in the United States and 5.6 in Scandinavia. Given the tendency to depict the Scandinavian model as socialist, one might suspect that the robustness of social welfare in Scandinavia reflects a shared left-ist political leaning among its citizens; however, responses in Scandinavia were almost identical and statistically indistinguishable from responses in the United States. Undeniably, the same score may signal varying views in differing national political contexts. Specific programs and agendas endorsed by the "right" or "left" vary by country. Nevertheless, within their own contexts, the Scandinavian and American people both report themselves as being close to the middle of the political spectrum. Survey respondents in both regions viewed themselves as moderate.

The likeness extends to views about competition, where we had anticipated marked differences, given the pervasive endorsement of free-market competition and technological sophistication in the United States. Data from the World Values Survey told a different story. People were asked to place their views on the following scale.

Competition is good.   **Competition is harmful.**

It stimulates people to work   It brings out the worst
hard and develop new ideas.   in people.

1   2   3   4   5   6   7   8   9   1 0

The results surprised us. Ratings were identical in the United States and in Scandinavia, at 3.4 on the 10-point scale. This finding was particularly relevant to counter arguments that heretofore have deemed Scandinavian countries overly socialist, and thereby extraneous to the United States' experience. On the contrary, we found Scandinavians to be mostly open to the potential benefits of competition. A Norwegian health policy adviser (ID 65) indicated that competition from the private sector could provide a beneficial solution to their current challenge of long waiting times for treatment in the public sector:

> The main things [we should consider in thinking about reform] should be the quality of care, what the public actually spends, and results. If some of the simple procedures could be done in the private sector, and we could do cancer and all the complicated treatments in the public hospitals, that might be a good division of labor.[11]

Although the manifestation of competition in the United States and Scandinavia may differ, Americans and Scandinavians place equal faith in competition as a vehicle for progress in a modern society.

Views on the contributions of science and technology were also not substantively or statistically different between the United States and Scandinavia. This was unexpected because Americans' investment in medical science and technology dwarfs that of most other industrialized countries. For instance, in 2009, the United States had more magnetic resonance imagining, computed tomography scans, PET scans, and mammography scanners than many other industrialized countries, and utilization of imaging for medical care and complex procedures, such as knee replacements, is considerably higher in the United States than anywhere else in the world.[12] Nevertheless, based on the World Values Survey data, the United States and Scandinavia were very much alike in their endorsement of science and technology.

The World Values Survey asked, "All things considered, would you say the world is better off, or worse off, because of science and technology? Please tell me which comes closest to your view on this scale: 1 means 'the world is a lot worse off' and 10 means 'the world is a lot better off.'" Responses in the United States and Scandinavia were neither statistically nor materially different, weighing in at 7.2 and 7.1, respectively. This indication of similar values is substantiated by each country's national spending patterns, as domestic investment in research and development as percent of GDP is actually similar between the United States (2.7 percent of GDP) and key Scandinavian countries, including Sweden (3.6 percent of GDP) and Denmark (2.6 percent of GDP).[13] Rates of pharmaceutical research comprise 18 percent of all business research and development in the United States, 12 percent in Sweden, and 27 percent in Denmark.

In summary, people in the United States and Scandinavia share many important core values. This finding is notable and supports a previous statement from the American College of Physicians that the United States should be able to adopt some health care approaches from our Scandinavian peers.[14] According to the data from the World Values Survey, the people of these countries do not differ in their views of personal freedom and self-determination, their political participation in such activities as petitions and boycotts, their perceptions of their political leaning right or left, their beliefs that competition can be effective, and their endorsement of science and technology as means to make the world better.

RECOGNIZING THE SIMILARITIES BETWEEN PEOPLE in the United States and Scandinavia provides a solid foundation on which meaningful discussion of key differences may be built. Such differences, very much apparent from our analysis, helped us understand the cultural roots of decisions that have shaped distinct approaches to health care delivery. Key differences include views on the role of government and the social contract, tolerance of income inequality, level of trust in others, and overall conception of health and the determinants of health (see Table 4.2 and Appendix B).[15]

TABLE 4.2. SUMMARY OF HIGHLIGHTED SIMILARITIES
AND DIFFERENCES

Value Similarities Between Scandinavia and the United States	Value Differences Between Scandinavia and the United States
• Importance of personal freedom	• Scope of social contract
• Sense of political voice, action, and right/left leaning	• Views of income equality and social mobility
• Advantages of competition	• Degrees of trust in "the other"
• Benefits of science and technology	• Conception of health

Some may find such topics as the "social contract" too abstract for a practical discussion of health care, but collective views about the role of government have far-reaching implications when it comes to the question of who is responsible for promoting health. We anticipated that fundamental values and norms, rooted in demographic and historical features, would shape Scandinavians' perceptions of the social contract in ways that are different from Americans' perceptions, and therefore affect their approaches to health and health care. The data supported this premise.

The social contract, most famously described by Rousseau in his classic 1762 *Of the Social Contract, or Principles of Political Right*, is an implicit agreement among members of a community to submit a certain degree of their personal freedom to a government that will protect them from one another and from nature.[16] Rousseau's conception of this contract is far from stale political theory; it lies at the heart of any number of decisions that drive health policy.

Scandinavians view the social contract as a broad-based agreement involving substantial commitments on the part of both government and citizenry. Generally, government is viewed as a benevolent force whose role is to care for the good of society. In return, citizens participate (perhaps most famously through taxation of private income) in the creation of a common pool of resources that then is dispersed at the discretion of the government. This understanding of the symbiotic relationship between the governors and the governed provides solid foundations for the building of the Scandinavian welfare state and orients public discourse toward the collective, rather than individual, good.[17]

This conception of the social contract is also grounded in the Scandinavian value of universalism. In the context of welfare policy, the term *universalism* refers to the belief that services should be made available to all individuals. According to Robert Erikson, professor of sociology at the University of Stockholm and author of *The Scandinavian Model*, universalism is the "cornerstone" of the post–World War II Scandinavian approach to social welfare programs, including those targeting health care.[18] A Norwegian diplomat (ID 69) we spoke with echoed this sentiment, describing her nation's welfare state as one in which citizens know to "take only what they need and contribute what they can."[19]

Consistent with these social norms, the government provides public education, health care, child allowances for families with children, pension rights, public housing support, and other social programs leading to improved welfare.[20] As one Danish senior health policy analyst (ID 32) told us:

> That's the second paragraph in our health law . . . everybody is guaranteed equal access . . . In Denmark, if you live [here as a] citizen, you have these rights.[21]

This rights-based equality is central to the Norwegian welfare state as well. Not only is everyone covered by the public system, but no one can refuse the state-supported benefits due to them, even if they could afford to secure such services themselves. This is done to ensure parity among citizens. A Norwegian neurologist (ID 68) described the lengths to which the Norwegian system would go in order to preserve this value:

> A good example of [our view of equality in the welfare state] is if a billionaire said, "I don't need child benefits. I have enough money. I think it is nonsense that society should transfer this money to me because I have enough money." The argument would be [that] what you are really then arguing for is that we should start to provide these benefits based on [financial] need. [But we would not do that here.] They [the billionaires] would get [the services] because they had a child. These rights are for *all*, so you may not need them, but that's the way it works. By law.[22]

The Scandinavian enthusiasm for an expansive role for government in multiple domains of their public and private lives is likely to be disconcerting for many Americans, and merits some brief historical context. As described by Nanna Kildal, a researcher at Stein Rokkan Centre for Social Studies, and Stein Kuhnle, professor of comparative politics, at the University of Bergen, the legitimacy of this model has evolved through centuries of historical, social, and cultural influences.[23] The early integration of church and state bureaucracies during the Protestant Reformation in the 1500s established a tradition of citizens' depending on the government for the provision of key welfare necessities. The government performed this role without competition from churches (the main purveyors of such welfare services in the early American colonies) and left little role for market-based welfare services. In the words of the Danish senior health policy analyst (ID 32):

> We equate society and government much more than Americans do. I mean, for four hundred years, Denmark, had what we called

[a] dictator king, and he owned everything. So government and the society was one.[24]

In preindustrial times, the agrarian people of Scandinavia had rights and were protected by the government, enfranchised as full citizens even if they did not own capital. In more recent times, the devastation of World War II brought people in Scandinavia together in their fight against Nazism and German occupation. From the chief of the Norwegian health care workers' union's perspective (ID 66):

> I think there is not as much individualism now as [there was] before because, after the war, everybody had to join together to build everything up.[25]

This history paved the way for the modern-day social contract, wherein the government provided basic rights accepted by the citizenry, with an understanding that participants in the system would comply with efforts to make the nation prosperous and promote agreed-upon social norms.[26]

The American experience reflects a decidedly different view of government. The history and cultural mores of America, beginning with the experiences with King George III in the colonial period, have shaped a long-standing conception of a government at risk of becoming overly authoritarian, bureaucratic, meddling, and out of touch. This opinion has proven a remarkably durable component of the American worldview, reflected in President Ronald Reagan's famous 1986 declaration that the nine most terrifying words in the English language were, "I'm from the government and I'm here to help."[27] In contrast, Scandinavians we interviewed, who live in relationship with a government that is very much present in their lives, expressed appreciation for the role of government as well as dedication to its continued, and even expanded, role in the future. As American journalist Sharmi Albrechtsen, living in Denmark, described the culture:

> Big government is everywhere—even places you don't expect it. Since all health and education services are fully funded by the state, it is actually very often that one has government intervening . . . mostly in a good way. For example, after the birth of my daughter I was visited repeatedly by an at home nurse [employed by the government]. She gave me advice on breast-feeding and other helpful tips. In addition, she offered to put me in touch with the other women in my neighborhood who also had given birth recently.[28]

Consistent with differing conceptions of the social contract, values regarding the role of government in democracy differed significantly between the United States and Scandinavia. Although democracy was embraced strongly by the people of both regions in the World Values Survey, Scandinavians were significantly more likely to view the redistributive function of government (such as taxing those who are rich to subsidize those who are poor) as an essential feature of democracy. In particular, people in Scandinavia compared with those of the United States had more affinity with the viewpoints that government ownership of business and industry should be increased and that government should take more responsibility to provide for everyone as needed. It would surprise few historians that Americans expressed tepidity in this regard. As noted by *Newsweek* senior correspondent Howard Fineman, it took no less than a constitutional amendment to institutionalize an income tax in the United States, more than 125 years after the Constitution was written.[29]

People in the United States, however, were significantly more likely than those in Scandinavia to endorse as essential features of democracy that criminals are severely punished, that the army takes over if the government is incompetent, and that the economy is prospering. Taken together with the Scandinavian views, these data suggest two distinct views of the social contract—one (in Scandinavia) that emphasizes the role of government in providing social protection and the other (in the United States) that stresses government's role in providing protection from criminal, military, and economic threats.

Closely related to the varying notions of appropriate roles for government is the divide in values concerning individual independence. Scandinavians maintain that everyone should be working, not only to get ahead as an individual, but also to maximize the production in society and sustain a robust national economy. Speaking on behalf of her countrymen, the Norwegian union chief (ID 66) emphasized the extent to which the Norwegian government and public agreed upon the importance of work in society:

> We have to—everybody has to—have a good job. This is simple.
> So, high development and high employment is very important.
> This is the basic for everything [in Norway].[30]

Americans typically desire independence and value the hard work and success of the individual. The resentment many Americans feel over others' dependence on government is a layered sentiment. Although the English poet John Donne famously asserted, "No man is an island,"[31] Fineman reminds readers in *The Thirteen American Arguments* that in eighteenth-century America, "You very nearly could be [an island]" given the expansiveness and fertility of the land."[32] Self-sufficiency seemed attainable. The legacy of this sentiment is a suspicion of government actions that bail out troubled businesses or households, thereby repudiating the value of independence.[33]

Equally troubling for many Americans, however, is that government provision of financial assistance almost always requires a redistribution of income from one citizen to another. Even if Americans can accept that others need the support, substantial discomfort with sacrificing one's own hard-earned income to support others persists. Data from the World Values Survey indicated that Americans were significantly less likely than Scandinavians to view taxation of the rich to support the poor as an essential feature of democracy. For many Americans, increased social welfare programs have become a euphemism for "my hard-earned tax dollars" going to support strangers of unknown moral fiber. Consistent with Fineman's analysis,[34] there remains a distinction in the American mind between naturally ordered fairness, which is laudable, and socially engineered redistribution, which is not.

In addition to the resentment over remitting one's tax bill, Americans express concern about the moral consequences of government support on the recipient. Some feel that the availability of government unemployment payments weakens people's resolve to work and fosters overdependence on government programs. To this point, author Charles Sykes paraphrases Margaret Thatcher in his 2012 book *A Nation of Moochers*, writing, "The problem with moochers is that sooner or later they run out of Other People's Money."[35] The pervasiveness of such a view was substantiated in the World Values Survey, wherein people from the United States were significantly more likely than Scandinavians to agree that "it's humiliating to receive money without work" and that "people who do not work become lazy." This latter view was expressed by a pediatrics nurse (ID 21) in an inner-city hospital in the United States:

> You just have to wonder. If these services weren't free for them [Medicaid recipients], would they be here? I don't think so. If you offer something free, I am sorry—there are always going to be people who just take advantage. They don't have to find other ways, [because] they [can] just show up here. So maybe we should not offer so much.[36]

Widespread suspicion about insidious mooching and overdependence manifests itself in the restrictions Americans often place on government supports and welfare. In 2012, the national food stamp program, formally known as the Supplemental Nutritional

Assistance Program (SNAP), provided federal aid to 46 million Americans with low or no income. Beneficiaries received the cash equivalent of about $133 per month to be spent on food, using an Electronic Benefit Transfer card. Originally supported as a type of farm subsidy, the food stamp program has never provided income directly to recipients; rather, it has issued coupons or electronic transfers to purchase only food, ensuring the money could not be diverted elsewhere. In addition to supporting American agriculture, such programs increase Americans' comfort in the belief that their taxes will be put to good use; however, the constraints put upon the use of food stamps also limit recipients' independence and personal agency.

Americans accept constraints on food stamp recipients' independence so as to ensure that their tax dollars are not misused by recipients to purchase less worthy goods than food, as well as to bolster the farm economy. In contrast, many Scandinavians accept taxation as a necessary corollary to their own vulnerability, believing that the taxes they pay are going to fund programs for people who need them, which might one day include their own family, or even themselves. Recipients are not overly stigmatized, and the fears of others' becoming dependent or taking advantage of government programs are less ingrained. As an administrator of a large health system in Denmark (ID 37) said when asked whether people in Denmark feared some people would become dependent on social welfare programs and therefore stop working hard:

> [Our] social welfare system is based on what we call "right and duty." You have a right to a minimum income . . . but you also have a duty to work. If you cannot find work yourself, the municipality will provide you [with] a job. These jobs will often be picking weeds from public parks, working in supermarkets, cleaning, etc. Those who are not able to work due to sickness or old age have no duties. So basically, the average Dane accepts the high taxes and the relatively comprehensive welfare system based on a presumption that only those who can't work don't have to work. The level of welfare also has to be lower than the entry level wage.

> There is comprehensive control with those who claim to be too
> sick to work. They have to go through [a medical approval process]
> of sorts . . . Often the work [offered by the municipality] is unat-
> tractive. If you don't show up, you get no money.[37]

The health administrator with whom we spoke (ID 37) went on
to say:

> In the US, you're all about personal freedom. But it seems to
> me when it comes to poor people you control their choices. In
> a Danish setting, we haven't had food stamps and controlling
> government programs like that since 1933. We would consider
> it disrespectful. Those people who are unable to support them-
> selves have a legal right to a minimum income from the gov-
> ernment, and we anticipate they will make good decisions for
> themselves. We may be more comfortable with social control
> overall, but [we are] more freedom-giving than Americans for
> people who are poor.[38]

National investments in safety net programs reflect each nation's
conceptualization of the social contract. Whereas Sweden, Denmark,
and Norway each spend 16 to 21 percent of their GDP on social welfare services (e.g., old-age assistance, housing subsidies, family supports, and employment programs), the United States spends less than
10 percent of its GDP on these services.[39] Commensurate with this
spending, experts in European social service policy assert that publicly provided social services for children and older adults are more
widespread in Scandinavia than anywhere in the world.[40] Although
this may seem like a domestic policy choice rooted in the politics
of the day, these types of large-scale allocation decisions reflect the
Scandinavian belief that government has a fundamental responsibility to provide basic human services. A Norwegian neurologist (ID
68) described what might seem counterintuitive to Americans—that
receiving government support was *more* acceptable than receiving
support from a neighbor:

It is more dignified to go and receive services or support from the government as opposed to going to ask your neighbor. If you have a certain condition, [or] if you are in a certain position, there is a right, and you can say "I have these problems." You know your rights. You don't need to elaborate on your misery in order to be seen as something worthy of getting a benefit. It is the rights-based approach.[41]

As a corollary to the American preference for a more limited role of government in social protection, data from the World Values Survey also suggest a greater acceptance of income inequality in the United States than in Scandinavia. Specifically, the World Values Survey posed, "How would you place your views on this scale? 1 means you agree completely with the statement on the left; 10 means you agree completely with the statement on the right."

Incomes should be made more equal.	We need larger income differences as incentives for individual effort.

| 1 | 2 | 3 | 4 | 5 | 6 | 7 | 8 | 9 | 10 |

The United States rated significantly higher than Scandinavia (6.2 versus 5.6) in responses to this question, a result that is consistent with the steady increase in income inequality in the United States since the 1960s. The United States now tops most of our Western European and Scandinavian peers in income inequality, as measured by the Gini coefficient, a measure of income inequality.[42] According to estimates by the US Census Bureau, in 2010, people in the lowest income quintile made only 3.3 percent of the country's income, whereas people in the top quintile made 50.3 percent of the country's income.[43] The inequality is even starker if we examine overall wealth, which includes both assets and income. According to the Congressional Research Service, the top 1 percent of Americans holds nearly 35 percent of the wealth.[44] The top income quintile generated an average income more than fifteen times greater than that of the bottom quintile in 2010, and by 2011, this ratio was 16 to 1. The equivalent ratio in Sweden was 3.5 to 1.[45]

Income inequality such as that seen in the United States has been linked to increased violence and distrust, poorer health, elevated anxiety, and poorer economic growth.[46] In their book *The Spirit Level*, Professors Richard Wilkinson from the University of Nottingham and Kate Pickett at the University of York identify extreme income inequality as a driver across countries of any number of "social corrosions," including lack of community life, violence, drugs, obesity, mental illness, and ill health generally.[47] Wilkinson and Pickett review study after study quantifying the psychological distress and social anxiety experienced by people living in societies with more extreme income inequality. Despite what many might assume, the studies show that the anxiety Americans feel is not isolated to a certain class; those at the top of the socioeconomic gradient feel the stress in equal measure to those at the bottom. Robert Putnam outlined a number of similar societal dangers resulting from a disintegration of American community life, or what he called a decline in social capital, in his 2000 best seller, *Bowling Alone*.[48]

Some scholars have suggested that Americans accept increasing income inequality because they do not know the extent of the problem.[49] Professors Michael Norton and Dan Ariely, from Harvard and Duke Universities, respectively, found in a survey of more than five thousand people in the United States that Americans severely underestimated the income inequality in the country. When asked about what type of income distribution they would choose for their country, Americans described a more equal income distribution. Specifically, they described a distribution like Sweden's, where the top quintile control just over 32 percent of wealth, and the bottom quintile control approximately 10 percent of it. (As it stands now in the United States, the top quintile controls about 84 percent and bottom quintile controls approximately 1 percent.)[50] The study is useful, although the researchers did not ask people what they would be willing to pay (for instance, through higher taxes) to achieve the levels of equality they desired. Generally, Americans eschew the notion of paying nearly 50 to 60 percent of their income to taxes, as is required in Scandinavia, choosing instead to subscribe to a conception of an American Dream in which unfettered market competition and hard work can propel citizens up the socioeconomic ladder without government assistance. Many Americans view disparities between people who are wealthy and poor as a key motivator for people to work hard to improve their own financial circumstances. Furthermore, based on the widespread belief that people can improve their own lot in life and general resistance to the idea of structural barriers to success, the concept of redistributive justice may appear unnecessary and even detrimental to the country's economic well-being.[51]

Since the nineteenth century, the promise and perils of social mobility have been a recurring theme in American cultural discourse, as seen in books from Benjamin Franklin's *Autobiography* and Horatio Alger's *Ragged Dick* to F. Scott Fitzgerald's *The Great Gatsby*, and such films as *Citizen Kane*, *Avalon*, and more recently, *The Pursuit of Happyness*. As Jim Cullen describes in *The American Dream*, "American readers and writers have had tireless appetites for tales of poor boys (and later girls) who, with nothing but luck and ingenuity, created financial empires."[52]

The potential to move from rags to riches, particularly for immigrants, remains a powerful cultural meme. The result is widespread allegiance to a view of the United States as a nation of "self-made men," a term Cullen cites as being first used by Senator Henry Clay in an 1832 speech.[53] As long as people believe that equality of opportunity is assured to all, the American Dream can serve as a tonic in the face of concerns regarding social welfare programs or health benefits.

But the data do not support this elegant vision of social mobility. Empirical evidence from the past twenty years suggests that climbing the ladder of success is far less common than Americans would like to believe.[54] As summarized in Victoria Griffith's 2001 *Financial Times* article titled "The Myth of Social Mobility," which reviews research by David Zimmerman, professor of economics at Williams College, long-term average income in America was primarily predicted by parental earnings. Griffith states, "Of children [in the United States] born into the bottom quartile, 40 percent stayed there; an additional 29 percent moved up just one quartile in income. Because these numbers measured earnings alone, rather than inherited wealth, they probably understate the stability of socioeconomic class."[55]

More recently, in 2006, Markus Jäntti of the Department of Economics and Statistics at Åbo Akademi University in Finland compared social mobility in the United States and Scandinavia, revealing that the bottom quintile of income distribution is far "stickier" in the United States than in Scandinavian nations.[56] Using data from the National Longitudinal Survey of Youth and the Panel Study of Income Dynamics in the United States, Jäntti reported that 42 percent of the offspring born to fathers in the lowest quintile of income remain in the lowest quintile of income. The corresponding percentages are much smaller in Sweden, Denmark, and Norway (26, 25, and 28 percent, respectively). In the United Kingdom, the proportion is 30 percent. Additionally, the analysis showed that moving from the lowest to the highest quintile of incomes is less likely in the United States than it is in Scandinavia or the United Kingdom (occurring for only 8 percent of the population in the United States and for 11 to 14 percent in the other countries). Thus, even as Americans may believe that people can pull themselves up by their bootstraps in a democratic, free-market, capitalist society, the data reveal a "sticky" lower class that generally retains its constituents for generations. As Jäntti concludes, the exceptionality of the American state may be less about its famed liberty, democracy, and economic mobility and more about its marked economic immobility, particularly among the lowest-income group.[57]

Also prominent in the findings were disparate expressions of trust among US and Scandinavian residents—trust in family, trust in people in one's neighborhood, trust in people one meets for the first time, and trust in other nationalities. On all of these items of the World Values Survey, people from the United States were significantly less trusting than were people from Scandinavia. These country-level differences in values regarding trust have been documented for more than a decade,[58] although previous studies have not connected these views regarding trust to health system choices. Americans' responses to the two questions that follow highlighted fears of being taken advantage of and of losing in a zero-sum game of life: "Do you think people would try to take advantage of you if they got a chance, or would they try to be fair? 1 means 'they would try to take advantage of you,' and 10 means 'they would try to be fair.'"

People would try to   People would try to be fair.
take advantage of you.

1   2   3   4   5   6   7   8   9   1 0

How would you place your views on this scale? A 1 means you completely agree with the statement on the left; 10 means you completely agree with the statement on the right.

People can only get rich at   Wealth can grow so there's
the expense of others.   enough for everyone.

1   2   3   4   5   6   7   8   9   1 0

To the first question, the United States placed at 5.8 versus 7.2 in Scandinavia, indicating Americans agreed more that people will take advantage of others if they have the chance. To the second question, the United States ranked statistically lower than Scandinavia as well (6.2 versus 6.6), suggesting a greater affinity with the zero-sum mentality in the United States. The data suggest that Scandinavians are less likely to expect financial gain by certain individuals to come as a result of loss by others. A Swedish professor of economics (ID 41) outlined his contrasting view, citing a need for inclusivity and trust to make the model work for all:

> [Our approach] works if it's reasonably inclusive . . . You're supported in childhood and adolescence. Regardless of your family background, you participate in the same health care, the same schooling, the same way of life as most others . . . you kind of support the others who are being supported in this way. And it is great for unemployment, sickness, childbearing, and so on. The expectation is that you work—until you reach an age when you don't work. And then, you're again supported [through pension].[59]

This idea of trust and inclusivity extends to values about immigrants. People in the United States were more likely than their Scandinavian counterparts to agree with the statement that "when jobs are scarce, employers should give priority to citizens over immigrants." The survey also posed a more macro-level question: "Thinking of your own country's problems, should your country's leaders give top priority to reducing poverty in the world or should they give top priority to solving your own country's problems?"

Top priority to reducing poverty in the world.				Top priority to solving my own country's problems.					
1	2	3	4	5	6	7	8	9	1 0

Again, the scores differed significantly, with the United States at 8.0, reflecting a strong preference for focusing on national problems, whereas Scandinavians, at 6.0, identified more with the challenges of the global community. These values are reflected in Scandinavian governmental actions. Sweden, Denmark, and Norway spend nearly 1 percent of their gross national income on foreign development aid, respectively, whereas the United States devotes only about a fifth of 1 percent of gross national income to foreign aid, even when philanthropic giants, such as the Bill & Melinda Gates Foundation, are included in the global aid figures for the United States.[60] When asked about government aid, the Danish senior health policy analyst (ID 32) underscored the role of the government in taking care of the community, broadly conceived:

> We have a good conscience. I mean, you can compare it to some extent to a church community.[61]

The generosity of concern for global well-being was explained by one Norwegian diplomat (ID 69) as arising from both benevolence and enlightened self-interest. She explained that Norwegian empathy emerged after World War II:

> We have experienced what it is to be poor and [now] wealthy. I think the Marshall Plan, which helped to rebuild our country after the war, has been underappreciated; this was where our benevolence began. Because we know the value of international aid, we feel an obligation to be generous with development aid . . . Also, we know what it is to be dependent on the United Nations [UN]— so we are ready for a larger social compact.[62]

THE CONCEPTIONS OF HEALTH IN the United States and Scandinavia also differ in fundamental ways. Scandinavians view health as a means to an end, rather than simply an end in itself. This perspective was clear among people we interviewed and has been documented in official reports of the National Committee for Public Health in Sweden. For example, one such report reads: "All people are of equal worth and the individual should be free to act . . . all people should have an equal chance to realize their efforts. For this to be possible, it is necessary that the major differences between the health of different groups should be reduced. The Committee has chosen not to define what health means. Health is a subjective assessment where each individual has his own view. [Our] proposals aim to prevent ill health, which restricts the freedom of the individual."[63]

This viewpoint clarifies what people expect of their health and hence their health care providers. Scandinavians suggested that they pursued good health in so much as it would allow them to work, to take vacation on the Archipelago, eat the foods they wanted to eat, and be around to see successive generations of their family be born and grow. This perspective was further articulated by a high-ranking staffer at the Danish Health and Medicines Authority (ID 33):

> People . . . should know that health is not the goal of life. But health is definitely a means that you can use to choose exactly the life you want because if you don't have health, then your possibilities . . . cannot flow and grow . . . We have also tried to work . . . with the municipalities [to say] maybe you can use health, not because you want to make people healthy, but because actually health can then also help people learn better and it can help people in getting a job.[64]

In contrast, many Americans have become consumed with the notion of health as an end in itself. In his 1998 book *False Hopes*, medical ethicist Daniel Callahan of the Hastings Center described the culture of American medicine as unrealistically geared toward the attainment of "perfect health." This would be a recipe for failure and bankruptcy of the system, he warned, as perfect health is unattainable. Unfortunately, Americans have failed to correct their course since his admonition.[65] In 2012, one prominent East Coast hospital system debuted a new corporate slogan: "Because your health means everything."[66] Positioning health in such a way implies that health is both the result and the inherent goal of a prosperous life, rather than a precondition for achieving such prosperity. Scandinavians seem to be under no such illusion.

Another way in which Scandinavian and American conceptions of health differ markedly is in the view of what causes ill health and what is needed to produce good health for society. In adopting a holistic approach to creating health for their populations, Scandinavian countries have more fully embraced the importance of investing in nonmedical determinants of health than has the United States. Practically speaking, this outlook manifests in the substantial attention these countries pay to buttressing services pertaining to housing, the physical environment, conditions at work, supportive social environments, family allowances, income support, unemployment support, and other social services, rather than more medications, hospital days, and medical procedures. The Norwegian neurologist (ID 68) described this approach, which limits use of expensive medical care:

> What we fear in the Norwegian health care system is a development where you care for chronic problems by hospitalizing patients. The idea [in Norway] is to try to manage people in local communities, outside hospitals.[67]

Such an approach, consistent with the World Health Organization's definition of health and an overwhelming body of health literature, derives from the belief that socioeconomic circumstances are more powerful than medical care in fostering health at the population level. The contrasting approach, wherein personal suffering is understood primarily as a medical problem with predominantly medical solutions, is known as "medicalization" and has been used to label how Americans handle many natural rhythms of life[68] including birth,[69] childhood,[70] and death.[71] As documented by Sherwin Nuland, clinical professor of surgery at Yale University and National Book Award winner for *How We Die: Reflections on Life's Final Chapter*, many Americans have fallen prey to the idea, now avidly marketed by many big players in the health care industry, that medicine can offer a remedy to nature.[72] Recent analysis indicates that this penchant for medical approaches results in high health care expenses, in the range of several billion dollars per year.[73]

Nowhere is this truer than in care for people who have terminal illnesses. Evidence of the past three decades indicates that 25 to 30 percent of Medicare spending is for care of only 5 to 6 percent of Medicare beneficiaries, who die within one year.[74] One would expect the last year of life to be the most expensive as people suffer with more severe, complex, and prolonged illness. But it does not have to be as expensive as it is in the United States. Hospice, which takes a holistic view of health, seeks to address medical and nonmedical symptoms for people whose life expectancy is deemed to be less than six months. Accordingly, hospice uses an interdisciplinary team-based approach to care, addressing emotional, spiritual, and social needs with a host of social services that often include counseling, clergy visits, arts and music therapy, and physical or occupational therapy, to name a few. Notably, studies have repeatedly shown that hospice can positively influence patients' and families' experiences, as measured by improved patient and family satisfaction rates, reduced depression and better bereavement adjustment among survivors, and reductions in overall costs of care.[75]

In practice, every nation's approach to health care must balance funding for physicians, hospitals, pharmaceuticals, and other health care enterprises with funding directed at improvements in housing, child care, education, work climate, nutrition, and other support services. What Scandinavian governments do better than most is to balance "upstream" work to keep people healthy through adequate services in the social sphere, with "downstream" work of medical care for people after they have become ill. In accepting a broad view of the determinants of health, Scandinavian policies allow social and medical services to be planned and managed together, in many cases. Local governments—county councils or municipalities—are responsible for a pool of resources that has to finance both health and social services. For instance, Norwegians who face illness can count on a variety of municipality-funded social benefits designed to keep people functioning at home, with less need for expensive medical care in a hospital or nursing home. A director of health services for a municipality in Norway (ID 67) explained:

> Today you can get help for house cleaning, for shopping, and we also spend a lot of money to support or subsidize traveling in taxis to get anywhere [needed]. Not only to the doctor.[76]

Although the ability of these decentralized authorities to tax citizens differs across the countries, in all three contexts, local bodies run by locally elected officials are responsible for making choices between the financing of health and of social services to produce a tailor-made approach to health that best serves their community. This integration of power and control at the municipal level brings with it a critical sense of collective accountability for health, from which the United States may learn.

This perspective on health is consistent with Scandinavia's support for the welfare state and is reflected in the 2001 Swedish Ministry of Health and Social Affairs document *Towards Public Health on Equal Terms*: "The health of the population is affected by a range of what are known as determinants. These are factors that in part relate to the structure of society and in part to people's lifestyles and habits."[77]

This 2001 document formally recognizes the causal links between health and its social determinants, including employment, education, agriculture, culture, lifestyle, and housing. The report presents explicit objectives in each area, tying them with the expected health effects on the population. Furthermore, these lofty objectives are supported by detailed action plans that mandate local governments to set and achieve goals that are consistent with this framework.[78]

Similar documents and assertions can be found in Denmark and Norway.[79] For instance, in a 2003 report, the Norwegian Ministry of Health stated, "The health of the population results not least from developments and political choices outside a citizen's influence."[80]

When we asked Norwegian policymakers whether the assertions truly influenced policies and practices, they answered that they certainly did. To put the concept into practice, one high-ranking health official from Norway (ID 62) described a public measurement scheme and its effects:

> The main thing is the [national] public health indicators. That means that every municipality gets a chart . . . So that each municipality can really compare to another how they are doing on these indicators, and the citizens can go to elections and say that since . . . you're not doing a good enough job we [are going to] sack you. It has become very clear that health, including public health, is the responsibility of the municipality as a whole and should be worked with in each of the different sectors.[81]

Similarly, Scandinavian national policy documents programs that have characterized health of the public as a "social responsibility," thereby reinforcing that health is not solely a private issue determined by individuals in relationship to their physicians; rather, it is a collective good determined by and reflected in society at large.[82] This perspective was well articulated by the Danish senior health policy analyst (ID 32), referring to the value to society of supporting people who cannot support themselves:

> It's part of [our] mentality that the society, which in our part of the world is the government, has both a responsibility but also a self-interest because it's inefficient to have [people who cannot work] out there, [and not] to help them.[83]

The Norwegian union chief we spoke with (ID 66) reiterated the importance of high employment to the national agenda:

> We can't afford that people fall out of the system. Because then we
> don't get them back [to participate through employment] in the
> welfare state.[84]

Not surprisingly, American scientists have arrived at similar conclusions as to what percentage of health status is governed by which
medical and nonmedical factors. For instance, experts assert that the
vast majority of health gains in the last century have been due to
environmental, economic, and social circumstances, with only 10
percent of all gains attributed to medical care.[85] US government documents *Healthy People 2000, 2010,* and *2020,* highlight the roles of
socioeconomic and lifestyle choices on people's health and advocate
for services that address underlying inequalities in access and disparities in services. The influence of these and other similar reports in
the United States, however, remains limited. The crucial need for
attention to broader determinants of health is well documented, but
the funding shift required to implement such a vision remains elusive
in a political landscape characterized by diffuse power.

In the end, the United States, with a more limited view of the
social contract, leaves its people to rely on the purchase of medical care as the main lever for attaining or improving health. Poor
health and challenging socioeconomic circumstances that pose
challenges for health are, in some Americans' views, artifacts of
personal choices made in a private sphere; society therefore bears
limited responsibility to correct for them. The government can ed-
ucate the populace on ways we could do better (think of the Let's
Move campaign that has been supported by First Lady Michelle
Obama since 2010), but only under selected, and usually dire, circumstances does the government intervene to fundamentally alter
the conditions in which people live. Even when government agencies endeavor to do this, Americans' esteem for individual liberties
and suspicion of government has resulted in reticence to endorse
such efforts.

DECISIONS ABOUT HOW TO DELIVER social and health services in Scandinavia are governed largely by the concept of local accountability. The strength of local government is apparent in comparative data from Scandinavia, France, Italy, and Great Britain, which show local government budgets accounting for larger percentages of total government spending in Scandinavia than in the other countries.[86] Additionally, more than 80 percent of national politicians in Sweden and Norway have held locally elected offices at some time, and turnout for local elections in Scandinavia is more than 80 percent, far higher than in Europe or the United States.[87] Tailoring specific programs and services to county-level or municipality needs is a core aspect of Scandinavian program designs. Importantly, the local level of government is charged with the responsibility not only for primary health care but for social services as well, allowing them to make informed decisions between different services in their efforts to meet the specific needs of their populations. Although federal norms are set to ensure that procured services are evidence-based, the specific packages of services are determined at more local levels. As a top Swedish policymaker and health economist (ID 40) commented:

> I think [this is] the whole point of the system. It should be local, but it should be reasonably equal.[88]

In Sweden, for example, health services are procured by locally elected county councils that have flexibility within their mandate to provide evidence-based care at the county level. At the same time, the county councils are largely responsible for social services and general welfare as well, theoretically enabling greater coordination and more explicit trade-offs between health services and social services to maximize well-being. According to Richard Saltman, professor of health policy and management and political science at Emory University and expert on the Swedish health system, county-based policies and programs to promote health, although challenged from time to time by reforms, remain at the core of the Swedish welfare state.[89]

Similarly, the Ministry of Health and Social Care in Denmark is responsible for establishing broad legislative and financial frameworks for both health and social policy, while responsibility for service design and provision are decentralized to thirteen counties and more than one hundred municipalities. These municipalities administer, via the work of a health visitor and case manager for each client, comprehensive services including home nursing services, psychotherapy, occupational therapy, pensions, recreational activities, transportation, rehabilitation and other services.

The level of coordination between the federal and local level allows for flexibility in designing packages of health and social care that cater to local needs, without jeopardizing the principle of equality that underlies the system. In cases where a municipality chooses to focus more heavily in a certain area, they must curtail budgetary expenditure in another. As the senior health policy analyst in Denmark (ID 32) explained:

> It is a closed system where eighty percent of [the] decisions, even though they are decentralized, are made within [the] public integrated system. So . . . if one department in a hospital goes beyond its budget, somebody else will have to be below it.[90]

Specific examples of integrated social and health services at the county level are many. For instance, in 1984 the Danish municipality of Skaevinge began a 24-hour integrated health and social care service, using a multidisciplinary team to coordinate services needed by older people with the goals of promoting better self-care and independence as well as reducing unnecessary hospitalizations. Evaluation results over a ten-year period (1986–1996), reported by the Danish National Institute of Social Research in 2003, are impressive. During this time, operational expenditures decreased by

30 percent, despite the aging of the population. Use of bed days at hospitals was reduced significantly for all citizens in the county, and reported health status in the county improved.[91] Other local experiments funded by pooled resources for social services and health care include the 1992 establishment of "24-hour acute rooms" in the municipality of Rødding, Denmark. "Acute rooms" are staffed around the clock by nurses with access to a general practitioner for medical treatment and therefore provide an alternative to expensive, unnecessary hospitalization. As of 2003, hospitalization rates in Rødding were lower than in neighboring municipalities. Furthermore, citizens reported high rates of satisfaction, especially as they received care closer to home and avoided hospitalizations. In Norway between 1993 and 2000, the program known as TIPS reduced the median duration of untreated pschosis among young people from twenty-six to five weeks through the use of community education campaigns and low-threshold outreach detection teams. These teams work with mental health providers and GPs to identify and arrange treatment. The impact has been demonstrated in clinical trials and shown to be sustained after more than ten years.[92]

In Scandinavia, municipal governments maintain discretion over how they allocate the resources between social and health services (among other responsibilities). In Norway, more than four hundred municipalities, representing between 500 and 500,000 residents, are governed by locally elected officials who are responsible for creating a composite set of government services tailored to meet both the social welfare and health care needs of their communities. Primary care and social services are financed and coordinated by the municipality, and more expensive, specialty care is financed by the state and managed through regional health authorities. Financial incentives, such as municipality cofinancing of specialty care, have recently been introduced to improve coordination. General practitioners may be contracted by the municipalities to spend 20 percent of their time on public health services in the municipalities, and some report spending ample time on coordination of other social supports for their patients. The director of health services for a Norwegian municipality (ID 67) said:

> Most of the coordination for the patients is done by the doctor. The doctor, him or herself, gets in contact with the housing authorities to discuss the case and the economic support and so on. So doctors in Norway spend a lot of time on these tasks.[93]

In sum, our Scandinavian experience offers several takeaways that might inform American efforts to address the high spending and limited health outcomes in the United States. First, acceptance that health is determined by more than medical services is fundamental to shaping a different approach to health care. Second, a willingness to work closely at local levels to streamline the interaction between health and social service providers, so as to use each efficiently, can be effective. Last, the clear assignment of accountability for the health of a defined population to locally elected government, in the case of Scandinavia, enables coordinated budget allocation decisions with relevant feedback at the local level as to what works, allowing flexibility in investments over time. Translating these takeaways into an American context will take effort, but the concepts of a holistic view of health, acceptance of the social determinants of health, and clear accountability for health help forge a path worth pursuing.

DESPITE ITS STRENGTHS, THE APPROACH to health care in Scandinavia is not without problems.[94] Waiting times for government services can be long by American standards; and despite efforts to equilibrate access to health care through universal coverage, disparities based on education still persist. Furthermore, health care expenditures are increasing steadily requiring greater taxation, which is challenging the sustainability of the government-based model.

People in Scandinavia have long worried about waiting times for health care services, particularly specialty care. The data show that Swedish people tend to find long waiting times tolerable, while it seems unlikely that many Americans would accept such delays in care. Current Swedish national standards mandate that each patient be assured a visit with a primary care government-assigned physician within seven days and consultations with a specialist within ninety days after a referral is made.[95] Emergencies are to be treated immediately, but OECD data from 2010 document substantially longer waiting times for care in Sweden than in the United States.[96] For nonemergency, specialty care, more than half of people referred to a specialist waited four weeks or more in Sweden, whereas only 20 percent waited this long in the United States.[97] Stories of individuals who have had significantly longer wait times are common in the Swedish press.[98]

In addition to longer waiting times, overall health care expenditures per capita in Scandinavia are climbing. Between 2001 and 2007, health care expenditures increased about 30 percent across Scandinavia (compared with an overall 3 percent inflation rate).[99] Although the acceleration of health care spending pales in comparison to the 50 percent increase during the same time in the United States, the Scandinavian public is concerned. Scandinavian countries have experimented with various purchaser-provider financing schemes, increased patient choice and competition, and spending caps; nevertheless, sizable annual increases in costs remain a challenge, particularly with the national guarantee to provide universal access to services meeting a universal standard of quality. Continued control of the growth rate in health care expenditures is at the forefront of Scandinavian policymakers' minds.

Furthermore, Scandinavia has generally achieved strong health outcomes with reasonable health expenditures in what has been largely an ethnically and culturally homogeneous region with limited immigration, at least relative to the United States. The degree to which differences in homogeneity matter remains open to debate, and social challenges related to expanding minority populations are emerging in the Scandinavian nations. Although Scandinavians exhibit far more inclusive attitudes toward immigrants than do Americans, their acceptance of others does not always translate into easy answers for addressing the social and health care needs of expanding minority populations in Scandinavian nations. The current wave of immigration to Scandinavia, comprised mostly of people from Middle Eastern and African origins, has prompted considerable cultural dissonance.[100] Many Scandinavians support the development of programs designed to assist immigrants in integrating into key resources, such as schools, employment, and benefit programs. Others, in contrast, worry that such assimilation programs may dilute minority cultural life. Sweden's Act on National Minorities and National Minority Languages of 2010, for instance, forbids "policies and practices aimed at the assimilation of persons belonging to national minorities."[101] This legislation asserts that "every person belonging to a national minority has the right to use freely and without interference his or her minority language in private or public."[102] Even so, speaking the national language is strictly enforced in Scandinavian schools, and signs of disapproval of minorities, not unlike in the United States, can be found.

The Norwegian health policy adviser (ID 65) reminded us that this discord should be expected, given the fact that Norway's history with immigration, beginning with a first wave in the 1970s, is "very much shorter than in the United States."[103] As an example, in Denmark, a new term has been coined, "New Danes," which refers most commonly to Middle Eastern and African Muslims. As has been the case in Sweden, these immigrants have been blamed for increasing violence in prisons, rapes, and unemployment.[104] Multiple people in leadership roles whom we interviewed commented on the complexity of accepting a language, religion, and social norms that are not Scandinavian into their countries, noting that the foundation for national solidarity on which each country has long stood may be crumbling. The senior health policy analyst in Denmark (ID 32) reflected:

> Danes have been surprised at how poorly we have really socially integrated immigrants . . . About fifty percent of the Muslim immigrants have severe difficulties in becoming integrated, mostly because of cultural constraints.[105]

Similarly, in Norway, a diplomat (ID 69) confessed:

> Integrating immigrants is something the United States has done better than we have in this country. And it is complex . . . even though we have laws and norms that support solidarity. If you are here and a citizen of Norway, you have a right to a job, health care, and social support. But we are hearing that there is some hypocrisy because if you use your Pakistani name on a job application, you may not get an interview.[106]

These sentiments suggest an internal struggle to sustain the Scandinavian model in the midst of diversifying populations. The extent to which the comprehensive Scandinavian social contract, which is based on trust in fellow citizens, will survive the increasing ethnic, linguistic, and cultural heterogeneity of their population remains unknown.

Last, despite widespread popular support of the social welfare state, Scandinavians express concerns regarding the long-term sustainability of their government-based model. Waves of immigration are begging the question of how long the trust on which the system is built will hold. For instance, in Sweden, only 51 percent of non-European immigrants have a job, compared with more than 84 percent of native Swedes, and reports suggest that 75 percent of Somali immigrant children drop out of school.[107] Given these challenges, many are wondering whether the expansion of government programs has gone too far and if demands on the state will one day outstrip their ability to finance such benefits. As in the United States, the population in Scandinavia is aging, with fewer people of employment age supporting more people in retirement. The director of health services for a municipality in Norway (ID 67) put words to this fear:

> We have to realize that our helping system cannot take of *everything.*[108]

In reflecting on the current state of Denmark's system, the Danish senior health policy analyst (ID 32) commented:

> [The health system] was created in a sort of very simple way. And now, it becomes clearer that it's not as simple.[109]

In an effort to respond to these challenges, the Scandinavian system has recently been employing financing strategies more commonly found in the United States. While universalism and equality continue to influence social values underlying the health sector, institutional shifts are occurring. Particularly since the 1990s, public budgets needed to support programs consistent with espoused health values have tightened, and concerns about potentially reduced motivations to work have grown.[110] In particular, health reforms designed to foster experimentation with market-based incentives during this period became widespread, although the Scandinavian commitment to public financing of health care for all denizens has not waned. Market-oriented reform initiatives have included allowing patients to select between urban hospitals and family physicians, creating incentives for reduced waiting lists, allowing private provider organizations to emerge, and using performance-based purchasing schemes in which providers are financially rewarded for achieving benchmark indicators of quality. The Norwegian diplomat (ID 69) commented that Norway's system was actually "moving to a ground much closer to the United States in terms of individual choice."[111] Nonetheless, the reforms are considered "recalibrations" rather than paradigm shifts, and scholars suggest that wholesale deterioration of government commitments to health and welfare systems is unlikely.[112]

NEITHER SCANDINAVIA NOR THE UNITED STATES is immune from the reality of rationing in health care. Although many Americans experience health care resources as nearly infinite and cast European systems as dangerous and dogmatic limiters of care, every system rations in a way that is amenable to its populations' values. Scandinavians ration by regulating what procedures and medications will be available through the public system and in what time frame. *The Economist* has noted in particular their "pragmatism and tough-mindedness" in pushing through reforms, including those that limit availability of some health services.[113] Certain diagnostic procedures, surgeries, and medications make the cut and are available to all; others (such as expensive chemotherapy medications, multiple in vitro fertilization treatments, and other therapies) may not be available in the public system, although such rationing has faced political challenges.[114] If people want access to care that is not on the "approved list" or want care provided sooner than waiting times allow, they must seek such care through fringe-dwelling private systems. For Americans, the rationing scheme works not through wait times but through the mechanism of price. Consumers can choose to purchase whatever insurance plan they think best suits their needs and means, although specific insurance choices may be constrained by factors including employment, military status, age, and income. Once enrolled in an insurance plan, Americans become considerably more insulated from price as a rationing tool, although their choices of what physicians they can see and what services they can obtain can be circumscribed by provider network delineations. Still, Americans can go to the open market to seek top-of-the-line care from anyone they choose—if they are able to afford it.

Additionally, our analysis uncovers the complexity inherent in each population's efforts to live in accordance with the values it holds dear and to extend those values to groups who are marginalized. Scandinavians emphasize societal equality on the basis that all citizens—foreign born or native—have a right to benefits of the generous welfare state (including health care benefits). Yet, those viewed as outsiders (such as immigrants who do not learn the native language) may be denied access to benefits at the front lines. Similarly, Americans laud individual freedom but struggle to uphold this value in the treatment of those who depend on government. In many cases individuals are not provided cash benefits with which to exercise their individual freedom (as they are in most social democracies); rather, they are provided with a defined set of services deemed appropriate for government welfare recipients.

Scandinavia's approach to rationing has allowed for explicit negotiation in the political arena about national health care spending, which can be fairly accurately projected and, pending political support, controlled over time. Comparatively, the rationing in the United States is more implicit, wherein national health care spending decisions are made by tens of thousands of individuals and organizations navigating a semiregulated marketplace. Expenditures have been escalating for decades in the United States, and unchecked health spending is now being blamed by many as a main driver of the federal deficit, as well as a very real threat to international trade and long-term economic growth in the United States. Perhaps most disconcertingly, taming this unbridled growth in health expenditure will require a new vision of health and its determinants, as well as stronger collaborations between health care and social service sectors.

Can effective and efficient collaboration among the diverse actors who contribute to health (physicians, patients, housing and education experts, job training programs, and employers, to name a few) be achieved within a culture built on individualism and independence similar to that of the United States? Americans and Scandinavians share core values concerning freedom, competition, political moderation, and scientific advancement. Nevertheless, fully adopting Scandinavian models that rely on an expanded governmental welfare state and that necessitate cooperation among heterogeneous actors is politically unlikely in the United States and contrary to many Americans' values. Mirroring only selected pieces of the Scandinavian approach would likely also be problematic, given the interdependence and complexity of the health care system.

WHAT WE TAKE FROM THIS analysis is not concrete steps about what the United States should implement as far as reform, but rather, a new perspective on the scope and nature of the American health care challenge. Health policy debate in the United States has largely focused on curtailing spending, expanding access, and improving quality of health care services for several decades. Political parties disagree on the best strategy, as do the varied actors participating in the system. Little progress has been made, but stakeholders agree that reforms undertaken thus far are insufficient. The process of investigating the Scandinavian model calls attention to the deeper dilemmas inherent in the current American approach to health care. We learn from this kind of analysis that the cultural constructs related to trust, accountability, and conceptions of health are powerful influences that shape the health care sector. The ubiquitous impact of these values underlines the enormity of the challenges ahead for the United States in reforming its current approach.

Nevertheless, similar inspiration to that found in Scandinavia, albeit on a smaller scale, can be found on the front lines of America's health care system. There, uniquely American answers to the most challenging policy questions are being worked through and, in some cases, even answered, by clinicians and their allies. As many front-line health and social service organizations continue their efforts in the trenches, their work, described in the next chapter, offers hope that distinctively American remedies to our high health care spending and poor health outcomes may still exist.

CHAPTER 5

HOME-GROWN INNOVATIONS

AMERICANS PRIDE THEMSELVES ON THEIR well-earned reputation for developing new ideas to improve life. President Obama reinforced this sentiment in his 2011 State of the Union address: "The first step in winning the future is encouraging American innovation. . . What America does better than anyone else—is spark the creativity and imagination of our people."[1]

American ingenuity has been particularly pronounced in the area of health care technology. The United States invests close to 5 percent of its total health care expenditures in medical research and development and leads the world in the development of cutting edge medical treatments.[2] American laboratories have produced novel devices and therapies, including infusion pumps and nanotechnology, and now are blazing the path for immunotherapy and other treatments, believed to be the wave of the future for treatment of cancer and other diseases.

The United States has similarly created new and celebrated models of health care organization and financing. Efforts to align incentives more creatively have resulted in payment innovations such as capitation, which is a flat rate of reimbursement per person under a physician's care; diagnosis-related groups (DRGs), which are reimbursement rates based on diagnosis; and various pay-for-performance schemes. Experimentation with organizational designs has spurred the creation of multidisciplinary medical group practices, integrated delivery systems, and medical homes. Management innovations to improve quality and reduce costs of health care (sparked by the National Demonstration Project on Quality Improvement in Health Care in 1986 and adapted from Japanese concepts of continuous quality improvement) include total quality management (TQM), Six Sigma,[3] and a variety of other reengineering efforts. Many of these efforts have been emulated in European and other international contexts.[4]

Although hospitals and physicians may have worked to fine tune their operations and deliver high-quality, patient-centered care, the impact often starts and ends at the hospital door. By focusing only on health care, innovators overlook potential synergies between health care and social service sectors that, if leveraged, might result in cost-reducing ways to promote health. This narrow focus on health care alone can stymie or, in some cases, even damage the broader effort to improve the nation's health. Atul Gawande, an American surgeon and journalist, offers a metaphor for the shortfalls of such piecemeal approaches to change, "Anyone who understands systems will know immediately that optimizing parts is not a good route to system excellence."[5]

Discouragingly, many of these health care innovations in which Americans have placed so much stock have largely failed to deliver the desired outcomes or value. When we looked to the front lines of health care and of social service delivery, however, we found that those who interact most closely with patients are recognizing the intersections between the sectors as leverage points for improving health at reasonable cost, and pioneering a broader kind of innovation. Front-line staffs have come to this insight by listening to the perspectives of patients, many of whom, because of their ill health or limited resources or both, can benefit from the support of social services beyond the scope of traditional medical care. These may include transportation for an older person who can no longer drive to appointments, acupuncture for a person battling cancer, job placement for accident victims, or safe housing for survivors of domestic abuse. Many front-line staffs are working hard to devise innovative solutions to integrating care—even within an environment that structurally, financially, and culturally discourages such innovation.

In our investigation, we sought out and identified examples of American approaches that took this broader view of health into account and aimed to work across the traditional silos of care. We reviewed case studies representing a variety of geographic areas and business models and selected to profile in this book four organizations that each featured a spectrum of approaches. While these four are by no means the only organizations working to unite health and social care, we found them to be exemplary illustrations of effective integration. Their selection was based on a broad search of relevant research literature, Internet-based resources, popular press, and inquiries made through our research team's professional network. We visited each organization in 2012–2013 and conducted in-depth interviews with key clinical and administrative staff.[6] At each site visit, we collected and catalogued available data pertaining to costs and patient outcomes, and analyzed key themes pertaining to the site and its operation.

Inventive American models of care are evolving to serve segments of the population from well-off to cash-strapped. For people who can afford the highest-quality service, organizations that provide comprehensive, integrated services have evolved in response to clients' and providers' beliefs that medical care, alone, is not the solution. For those at the bottom of the income gradient, the same strategy of integrating medical and non-medical services has developed out of a need to attain the best health outcomes with limited resources. Here is what we saw.

LA PALESTRA, NEW YORK, NEW YORK

Just before the end of our meeting with Pat Manocchia, longtime owner and president of LA PALESTRA in New York City, he said: "The pain is never the problem." He was referring to physical pain, the kind that often brings prospective clients to his doorstep, complaining that they believe themselves to need surgery or rehabilitation on one body part or another. Although Manocchia has been expertly trained to rehabilitate star athletes from injury, LA PALESTRA is much more than a gym or physical therapy center. It is a hybrid organization that bridges the gap between fitness and medicine, providing programming to "integrate comprehensive medical treatments with individually tailored exercise programs."[7]

Since its inception in 1994, the flagship LA PALESTRA facility, called the Center for Preventative Medicine, has served nearly one thousand clients. The clientele come to LA PALESTRA with a range of health needs and goals: some are looking for a knowledgeable professional to oversee rehabilitation of a bad knee; others arrive interested in climbing Mount Kilimanjaro with LA PALESTRA's Expedition Series; some are seeking guidance in losing weight; and still others arrive with an interest in general health improvement. All pay out of pocket for the majority of their care.

Manocchia derived the inspiration for LA PALESTRA in 1993, after working as a personal trainer and reflecting on the wider fitness industry landscape:

> We have become a nation that is exercising more, and is obsessed with diet and physical appearance, but is simultaneously becoming obese, more medicated, and requiring more health care.[8]

He described being struck by the stark division between medical care and athletic training, two fields that preached improved health and better lives as goals. Several of Manocchia's earliest clients were physicians who agreed with his assessment of the similarities but noted that the professional cultures were at odds:

> Fitness guys thought medical guys fix things after they're a problem and don't know how to take care of themselves. Medical guys look at fitness guys like they are not educated, and only care about the way their "abs" look.[9]

Having been educated at an Ivy League college, Manocchia felt he could win the trust of the medical community so as to bridge this divide. He founded LA PALESTRA to provide health and fitness services of the highest quality, which would be delivered and enforced through an integrated team approach by professionals from multiple disciplines. While some passersby might still be tempted to call LA PALESTRA a gym, Manocchia's approach and staff are considerably more holistic. His is hardly a place where you can sneak in, get on a treadmill, and get out. Manocchia and his team want to know what brought you in the door and will conduct a full evaluation of your physical and mental health history before they begin monitoring weekly and monthly progress towards your goals.

> We don't address aesthetic requirements. Doing so is never successful in the long term. When you say "I want smaller love handles, I hear that you don't feel good. Why do you think you want that? Does it make you happy if you're that way? Everybody will love you then? The translation is, "I feel out of control. I want it back."[10]

According to LA PALESTRA's credo, this control, or sustainable functioning, can only be attained by addressing all aspects of clients' lives. Manocchia has assembled a staff representing an array of disciplines, who work in concert to tackle each complex challenge. A typical team includes representatives from internal medicine, orthopedics, nutrition, psychology, clinical social work, physical therapy, chiropractic care, cardiology, acupuncture, and massage therapy. The staff is affiliated with many of the most reputable acute-care health facilities in New York City, including Mount Sinai Hospital, New York Hospital/Weill Cornell Medical Center, the Hospital for Special Surgery, Beth Israel Hospital, as well as the New School.

Manocchia contrasts his initial vision with that of the original HMOs to explain his model of care. While HMOs ultimately manage only the costs of care, Manocchia was emphatic: "I want to literally manage people's *care*."[11] Many clients look to him for advice on how to decipher pain from injury, which procedure to pursue and which to avoid, which doctors to seek out, and which medicines to take. While we were with him, Manocchia fielded an e-mail from a client who asked how he should proceed in navigating the health care system on behalf of his elderly mother, who had just received disconcerting biopsy results from a suspected cancer lump. In light of such a broad-based mandate, Manocchia resists people's efforts to put him into the box of being a "trainer." When we asked what he would call his role, he did not miss a beat: "A caregiver." Then he recanted, "I don't know. I wouldn't put myself in a box."

The LA PALESTRA team takes an integrative approach to relieving clients' aches and pains. For them, intervening solely at the site of pain through traditional medical means may address immediate symptoms but in many cases is unlikely to resolve the actual cause. In fact, by not addressing the underlying issues, the traditional approach may predispose people to further injury, which can result in still more costly care. In Manocchia's view, pain is often the body's way of signaling that something foundational is not working:

> Pain is not the problem. The problem is the problem. Pain is the body's way of letting you know there is a problem.[12]

The intake process for new clients at LA PALESTRA reflects this holistic approach. Many clients are referred to LA PALESTRA by an orthopedist or primary care physician, whereas others are referred by friends and family or discover LA PALESTRA in the press. Regardless of how the client arrives, a checklist of preliminary measures of the client's functioning informs the care team about the way a body is working (or not). Ultimately, the client establishes a relationship with the novel one-stop health organization, where all diagnostic imaging and medical history can be stored, where an entire spectrum of physical and mental health care can be provided, and where they can go for advice on how to navigate the wider health care landscape. Each client is assigned a LA PALESTRA adviser who stays in communication with not only that client but the entire medical team, to ensure effective integration of exercise, rehabilitation, and other health needs.

A classics major in college, Manocchia named his business after ancient Greek gymnasiums (*palaestra*) that were central to the life of the community, and designed the physical space of LA PALESTRA to reflect this vision. The main facility was named "Best Health Care Project" by *Interiors* magazine, has been on the cover of *Interior Design* magazine, and has received design awards from *Modern Healthcare* and *Health Facilities Management* publications. Occupying 14,000 square feet on two levels, the main space contains a cardiovascular diagnostic and treatment area; physical therapy rooms; patient seminar and examination rooms; private changing rooms with nearly a dozen private bathrooms with spa-inspired showers and amenities; offices for doctors, technicians, and evaluators; a medical library; steam rooms; and a lounge with food and beverages available. There is a method to every detail. As we toured one of LA PALESTRA's gym spaces, we asked about a rough, exposed patch of stone wall that stood in contrast to the otherwise modern style of the space. Manocchia explained:

> We want to make sure people know that you don't have to be perfect to be beautiful. We integrate the flaws.[13]

In counseling and rehabilitating his clients, Manocchia advocates an integrative understanding of how to heal the body. Often, he finds that his clients have allowed key muscle systems to weaken—musculature patients may not even know they have—and have relied instead on isolated joints, bones, muscles, or tendons to accomplish necessary tasks. This overreliance is what causes the damage and ultimately the pain. Your knee hurts? Manocchia may suggest considering the way your feet strike the ground as you run. Back problems? Let's retool the way you transfer your weight while swinging a golf club. Sometimes it is even more basic. Manocchia mimicked a standard prescription, talking with a new client:

> You haven't eaten a vegetable in a month, and you sleep three hours a night. We're going to address that first.[14]

Evaluating and strengthening supporting systems in this way has allowed LA PALESTRA's clients to avoid any number of costly medical procedures. Clients that choose not to address these core issues remain vulnerable to recurrences of the same pain from which they previously suffered. Manocchia described this phenomenon with his signature wit:

> By making pain quiet, you lose the ability to figure out what the actual problem is. Aspirin is not a cure for a hangover. Not drinking forty beers is the cure for the hangover.[15]

Importantly, LA PALESTRA's approach acknowledges that the implications of injury and illness are never purely physical.

> As a professional athlete, if you sprain your ankle, you are not [going to get] out of shape. You will be doing therapy, lifting weights, and being active. The inherent psychological trauma of an injury is thereby mitigated by the fact that you are still doing stuff. Not for her. (He pointed to a woman lunching nearby.) If she falls down skiing, it will take a week to see her primary care physician, and then after that, she's going to go to a specialist and then go get X-rays and tests and then . . . meanwhile, she is in a brace, afraid to

cross the street, disrupting her life, disrupting her sleep, not eating the same way.[16]

Recognizing the connections between medical and nonmedical issues that challenge people's well-being has been a key motivator for Manocchia. In contrast to the health care sector on which most of his clients have historically relied, he has built a business to support people in the full range of their health needs.

Based on this kind of refusal to conform, LA PALESTRA has managed to clear several million dollars in profit over the past decade, and boasts a client roster that includes some of the highest-profile celebrities in arts, entertainment, and sports. In 1996, Manocchia and his team created a twelve-week weight management program for the purposes of reducing the risk of weight-related illness. Staff worked with participants to make lifestyle modifications through behavioral, medical, nutritional, and mandatory weekly exercise consultations, yielding impressive results: an average reduction of approximately 7 percent in body mass index (BMI), 10 percent in body fat, and 18 percent in cholesterol. LA PALESTRA's marathon training program, now in its eighteenth year, has achieved similarly impressive results. Through an integration of medicine, exercise, and nutrition, LA PALESTRA has achieved a nearly unheard-of 100 percent marathon completion over more than fifteen years of training.[17] These empirical successes, along with hundreds of personal transformation stories, have helped to grow the LA PALESTRA model. Six additional locations, including one in the Plaza Hotel, have opened in New York City since 2010, with two more under construction.

ERRERA COMMUNITY CARE CENTER, VETERANS ADMINISTRATION, WEST HAVEN, CONNECTICUT

Before Laurie Harkness, MSW, PhD, created the Errera Community Care Center (ECCC), she worked alongside all the other US

Department of Veterans Affairs (VA) providers "on the hill" at the VA Connecticut Healthcare System's West Haven campus. "On the hill" refers to the VA medical center campus, which looms large on an incline overlooking the street below. In her role as a social worker, Harkness had acted as the head of a hospital-based outpatient post-traumatic stress disorder (PTSD) clinic to provide therapy primarily to Vietnam War veterans. PTSD afflicts nearly 30 percent of these veterans over the course of their postcombat lives, and the clinic was a prestigious one, having been recognized as part of the VA's National Center for PTSD. Yet, Harkness felt increasingly dissatisfied. She was not getting the results she felt were possible.

> After about eighteen months, I became very frustrated. We were good, thoughtful clinicians, yet week after week, I was saying, "What's going on? Why are we not helping these people qualitatively change their lives in the community? What are we missing?"[18]

Harkness recognized that the clinic was catering to the wrong side of the patient interaction. Rather than being designed for the patient's convenience and betterment, it had been designed with the provider in mind.

> Our veterans were spending their days going from program to program . . . We were asking people struggling with mental illness to come into the comfort of our offices and talk about their feelings [in order to help them]. It was just backward. That was [for] my comfort, actually, my office hours. Why are we [only] open until four thirty P.M. if we are trying to get people back to work? Why aren't we open in the evenings and on weekends? So I went to the chief of psychiatry and I said, "I'm stepping down."[19]

After leaving the clinic in 1994, Harkness began to craft a vision for a veteran-centered model of care. She imagined a place that brought a full range of clinical and social services together under one roof, including the high-end PTSD treatment she had been offering "on the hill" as well as vocational rehabilitation, housing assistance, substance abuse treatment, and most importantly, a sense of community. In other words, she dreamed of providing the care that she knew her clients needed but that fell beyond the scope of her formerly limited, health care provider role. Harkness described her advocacy in the early days:

> [I argued that] you co-locate programs, and you get the veterans out of the institutional setting because, when they're in the institution, everybody feels they are a patient. What are the hallmarks of a patient? Let's see—passive, helpless, things are done sequentially, and well, that is not how people recover. That is not how people learn to live the lives they want or dream of.[20]

In light of her strong reputation as a creative social worker and a leading scholar within the VA, Harkness was able to secure institutional support for her vision, and ECCC became a reality that same year. The center, which is funded in full by Veterans Affairs, has evolved over the last two decades to become a leading innovator in the integration of the psychosocial and biomedical approaches to wellness. ECCC prides itself on being a "one-stop shop" for veterans, having removed several common structural barriers to care. The physical space bustles with mental health professionals, counselors, case managers, lawyers, housing experts, clinicians, job training experts, nutritionists, case managers, and exercise therapists. During years spent serving people with mental illness, substance abuse, homelessness, significant psychosocial issues, or all of the above, ECCC changed and grew based on what clients needed. In the early 1990s, ECCC created the Compensated Work Therapy Program in response to clients' desires to return to work after combat and trauma. ECCC saw the opportunity to use employment therapeutically, and now relies heavily on this program to staff its own facility. What ties the diverse professionals at ECCC together is a core belief in the potential for every individual to recover and an unflappable commitment to empowering clients to help them meet their goals.

To distance ECCC from the clinic on the hill, Harkness made several changes to the traditional health care delivery model. Perhaps most notably, she moved the main hub of service delivery from the hospital into the community. This entailed both a physical, half-mile move off the hill as well as more nuanced strategic shift. The operating hours of the center fit the schedules of working and nonworking clients alike. Patients can be seen at seven A.M., and many groups meet in the evening. In addition, ECCC's in-house services are augmented by a number of extension services available to veterans 24 hours a day in their residential communities. These services include case management, rent support, help with meals, and transportation. By moving veterans out of an institutional environment, their independent living skills can be fostered and social reintegration is more likely. Primary care services and referrals to more advanced medical care are made available close to clients' homes.

Harkness also recognized that having to send clients off the VA campus to access certain services was diminishing the effectiveness of their care. One ECCC client (ID 12) recalled feeling ready to enroll in a community-based detoxification program after being admitted to an emergency room the night before. Unfortunately, after taking an expensive cab across town to begin a new chapter of his life, he was turned away. He laughed when he remembered the reason. "They told me I couldn't enroll because I wasn't drunk or high."[21] As many addicts would, he took this as license to go on several more benders involving high-risk drug use and sexual behavior before finding a place in a detoxification program several months later. He reflected on the ordeal matter-of-factly: "I could have died."[22]

In response to narratives like this, Harkness chose to co-locate a broad range of health care and social services in ECCC's central hub building. The center's services, which are open to all eligible

veterans, include primary care, legal services, mental health counseling, exercise and weight control classes, a gym, a kitchen with
cooking and nutrition classes, substance rehabilitation services, job
training and interview preparation, and housing support services.
The ECCC utilizes the recovery model of care in which the veteran
is the most important member of the treatment team; the veteran's
dreams, wishes, and preferences determine how the recovery process
unfolds. Enhancing this is the interdisciplinary nature of the work,
which is apparent in the frequent staff meetings and team consultations, where staff from different fields weigh in about how to best
address a client's needs. Almost half of the staff are veterans themselves, and many have been served by ECCC programs before joining
the provider team. Harkness explained the interrelationship between
medical treatment and other services:

> We at the Veterans' Administration historically offered [medical]
> treatment but the veterans don't [typically] get housing, you don't
> get jobs, you don't get family support. We had the model totally
> backward. Without a safe, affordable place to live and without
> something meaningful to do with our day, the carousel is going to
> keep going round and round.[23]

In addition to broadening the scope of services provided, Harkness and her staff have worked at changing the tenor of care and
allowing veterans to be more active participants in their healing.
Concretely, ECCC creates opportunities for veteran voices to be in
constant dialogue with providers. Clients take on key tasks of running ECCC on a day-to-day basis, such as orienting new clients,
managing the community lunch program, and advocating for new
services (such as better computers, legal advice, more physician access, or more gym equipment) to support client-centered services.
Clients are represented in governance mechanisms as well, as they
write and co-sign all new policies of ECCC and serve on the Community Mental Health Advisory Board. Most revealing, veterans

recognize the benefits of the co-location and teamwork at ECCC to meet the needs of clients. As Harkness quoted one of the veterans served by ECCC:

> Teamwork permeates the entire ECCC. Veterans are part of the team. Veterans are involved in receiving care, improving care, and giving care . . . People enjoy their jobs and love to come to work. Veterans welcome new veterans, set up, clean up, prepare lunch, lead groups, do peer counseling, and do peer education. People care.[24]

The impact of this comprehensive approach has been documented extensively.[25] In 2012, ECCC served 4,828 unique veterans and placed 300 veterans in employment. Between 2009 and 2012, 100 homeless veterans moved into non-VA permanent supportive housing, and almost 600 homeless veterans moved into subsidized permanent apartments through the Department of Housing and Urban Development–VA Supported Housing Program. ECCC staff have created or are in the process of finding 200 new independent housing units for ECCC clients. The VA has repeatedly honored the ECCC as a Center of Excellence for the Care of Individuals with Serious Mental Illness and also designated ECCC a national model for psychosocial rehabilitation and recovery services. In 1999, Harkness received the Olin E. Teague Award, the highest award given to a clinical provider in the VA system. In 2005, she was the first nonmedical doctor and first VA-affiliated provider to receive the Excellence in Community Mental Health Services award from the National Alliance for Mental Illness.[26]

OCEAN PARK COMMUNITY CENTER, SANTA MONICA, CALIFORNIA

"Los Angeles still bears the dubious distinction of being the homeless capital of the world," John Maceri reminded us in the summer of

2012.[27] As the executive director of Ocean Park Community Center (OPCC), he knows well how challenging the task of rehabilitating people who are chronically homeless can be. OPCC's mission is to empower individuals who have suffered extensive physical and psychological trauma, developed substance dependencies, and lost connection with friends and family while living on the streets. In pursuit of this mission, OPCC administers almost a dozen programs that range in size and scope. Maceri reflected on the breadth of services offered:

> We have a very broad portfolio of people who we serve and provide everything from meeting people's very basic human needs—food, clothing, showers, access to the rest rooms . . . all the way to [providing] financial support and housing, and a lot in between.[28]

While the center's clientele has grown to include victims of domestic violence and other people who are already housed, OPCC's mainstay has always been caring for people who are indigent or homeless. OPCC focuses on the "Housing First"[29] model, wherein it prioritizes attaining stable, permanent housing linked to supportive services for clients as a first step in their rehabilitation. The idea is that housing is necessary for any larger health outcomes or behavioral changes, such as less substance abuse and violence, continued treatment for mental illness, or recovery from a medical condition.

In 2007, in partnership with a nearby health center, Venice Family Clinic (VFC), OPCC opened a satellite clinic to help empower clients. Physician and director of homeless services Dr. Theresa Brehove runs the show, after working more than twenty years in private practice. She and another physician see patients in two small examination rooms, dispense most basic medications, and refer patients to a larger full-time clinic nearby if needed. Her work gives her the satisfaction of knowing that she is able to assist patients who previously may have had no access to care at all. In one case, she recalled a client who had been discharged from the hospital with two broken arms. The patient, who had marginal housing either in a shelter or on the street, complained that he did not know what he would do because he could not even wipe himself in the bathroom. OPCC found a way to house him under Dr. Brehove's care until his casts were removed.

Homelessness remains a costly problem in Los Angeles and across the United States. Experts suggest that more than 51,000 people may be homeless[30] on any given night in Los Angeles, and more than 630,000 people suffer this fate nationwide.[31] Several studies have demonstrated the health toll of living on the streets; more than two-thirds of America's homeless population suffer from mental illness or substance dependency, while nearly half have at least one additional chronic condition such as diabetes or hypertension.[32] The high costs of health care provided to people who are homeless have been well documented. For instance, in one five-year period, 119 people who were chronically homeless and tracked by the Boston Health Care for the Homeless Program incurred a total of 18,834 emergency room visits estimated to cost $12.7 million. In the 2006 *New Yorker* article "Million-Dollar Murray," Malcolm Gladwell famously attributed more than $1 million dollars in medical care to one homeless former US Marine.[33] Meanwhile, studies on the impact of providing housing, especially for people with chronic mental illness, have shown significant health care cost offsets.[34]

People who seek even temporary housing can be on waiting lists for as long as eight months in Santa Monica. Although taxpayers may not always recognize the hidden costs of homelessness, front-line providers and first responders in and around Santa Monica were keenly aware. As Maceri explained:

> The homeless population causes the community to burn up a lot of money on first responders, police, paramedics, and hospital ER visits. It is somewhat invisible to the general public because

they don't realize that they are paying those bills in their taxes. They call the cops and say, "Hey, this [homeless] guy is doing such and such . . . Someone should arrest him. Get him out of here." And the community thinks, well, there is no cost involved in that. But actually, there is a tremendous cost [in terms of public funding].[35]

Local police, paramedics, emergency room staff, and social service providers agreed with Maceri that there were a small set of people (often homeless with medical conditions, mental health and substance abuse issues) who repeatedly utilized these public services. In accordance with its community service mission, OPCC offered to take responsibility for these most challenging cases.

Everyone [in the community] thought something different needed to be done, and we said, "Well, look, give them to us."[36]

In 2009, Maceri saw the potential for an alliance between OPCC and a local hospital to both improve the health of his clientele and save money for the system. He selected St. John's Health Center, a Catholic hospital, as a potential partner, based on its explicit focus on providing charitable care. His pitch was for a new kind of collaboration between the social and health services sectors. OPCC would set up what it called a "respite care program" near one of its shelters, where people who had no home would be discharged to recover in a safe environment, rather than on the streets. In return, the hospital would fund OPCC staff time and agree to communicate with OPCC staff about emergency room visits and hospitalizations of people who were homeless. Maceri remembered the reaction of administrators at St. John's Health Center:

They were open to the idea. After having to look at their own data, they came back and said, "Hey, we're burning up a lot of money here, so, sure, let's try something different."[37]

Today, the collaboration has grown into a novel program named Project HEARTH, an acronym for "Healthcare for Empowerment to Access, Respite, Treatment, and Housing." Another local hospital has joined in the partnership as well. Twelve beds in one of OPCC's shelters have been set aside for the project, where recovering clients may stay for up to three weeks. There, a registered nurse performs checkups, reviews medications, and provides clients with education on caring for themselves independently once they leave OPCC. When she changes wound dressings, for instance, she does so with an eye toward instruction, hoping that clients will be better equipped to care for themselves the next time around. She is most pleased when she sees that people in the respite program are self-sufficient, in which case she takes a more passive but still supportive role, observing and reminding them about infection control practices and linking them to local support in their community when they move.

While staying at OPCC, clients of Project HEARTH are connected to the full range of OPCC's social services, including substance abuse support groups, mental health counseling, job training, and case management services to facilitate transitional and permanent housing. A member of the OPCC staff (ID 28) reflected on the essential link between housing and health:

> People are being housed, which has a huge impact on their ability to have a higher quality of life and receive ongoing medical care.[38]

As with all OPCC programs, the coordination among different nearby agencies is paramount to their impact. Maceri reflected on prior experiences losing clients in the process of coordinating referrals:

> The reason [this] interdisciplinary approach works so well is because it makes it easy for them to get passed on without giving

them a piece of paper that says, "Here, go to a mental health center that is five miles away."[39]

The decision to integrate medical services into the broader agenda of social service provision was prompted by OPCC's recognition that social, mental, and physical challenges are interdependent. Addressing only part of clients' needs without tackling their other needs was not resulting in improved health.

> A lot of [the clients] have been on the street for a while. They've drifted between different areas, and we really try to engage them to get them to start taking medication, to get into treatment. And then we have a lot of clients who abuse controlled substances as a form of self-medication. So our population is really defined by this tri-morbidity, in terms of medical conditions, mental illness, and then substance abuse. So we've really tried to integrate our response.[40]

OPCC has seen tremendous impact from the collaboration. Clients have been vocal in describing the improvement in their health care experience, improvements in self-rated health, and increased ability to take more responsibility for their lives.

Top leadership at St. John's Health Center indicated that the collaboration with OPCC was a wise financial investment. In February 2011, the hospital conducted a financial analysis comparing costs over a year for a sample of the same ten patients before and after their Project HEARTH stay. The average emergency room visit cost dropped from $1,726 to $462. Total emergency room charges for these same ten patients dropped from $37,977 to $6,928. Inpatient charges dropped from $34,009 per patient to $3,189, and the number of days of hospitalization per patient decreased from six days a year to two.[41] The director of community benefits at St. John's Health Center, Mary Luthy, believes the partnership is allowing the hospital to accomplish the two goals that the US health care system is chasing—improving patient care and saving money:

> When patients come into the emergency room, instead of hospi-
> talizing them, hospital staff know that they can send them back
> to OPCC. For the first ten patients on whom we used Project
> HEARTH, we saved $300,000 over the next year.[42]

Based on these early results, staff at OPCC believe the provision of medical care will remain part of its social mission for years
to come. According to Maceri, medical care is another entry point
through which social service agencies can engage and empower
people to care holistically for themselves. In this sense, the medical programming provided on-site is simply a new application of the
same approach that OPCC has taken for more than fifty years.

> If you give someone medical care, their mental health gets better.
> If you give them mental health care, they physically get better. It
> doesn't matter where you enter . . . You just get them connected
> to a support system. And then, and if you can help to get them
> housing, both physical and mental health get better. It all goes
> together.[43]

C-TRAIN, OREGON HEALTH SCIENCES UNIVERSITY
PORTLAND, OREGON

"Interdependencies between medical care and social determinants of
health exist whether we want to acknowledge them or not,"[44] Hon-
ora Englander, MD, affirmed over coffee one morning in Portland,
Oregon. She is an assistant professor of Internal Medicine at Oregon Health Sciences University (OHSU), and knows from firsthand
experience how powerful these interdependencies are for patients.
She told a story of a middle-aged, long-haul trucker, who initially
presented at the hospital with pneumonia and hypothyroidism. Later
it would become apparent that he also suffered from sleep apnea (due
to obesity) and depression. Although he was discharged with a list
of local clinics for follow-up care, he lacked transportation and the

money to pay for necessary medications and therefore did not receive the follow-up care he needed.

After discharge, the trucker developed progressive edema and fatigue, eventually losing his job (and later his house) because he could not stay awake due to his untreated health problems. He was admitted to the intensive care unit (ICU) for severe respiratory failure and hypothyroidism—and stayed for nineteen days at a cost of more than $130,000,[45] sicker than ever and incurring enormous bills. It was then that Englander met him and committed herself to finding a better way to treat this patient and others like him. She set out to change the way discharge planning and follow-up would be done in her community.

In her interview that morning, Englander described the resulting shift in her mind-set:

> So [I just figured that] if we're not getting the outcomes we want by not acknowledging these interdependencies, maybe we should try something different.[46]

What she had in mind was a new way of managing discharges from the hospital, particularly for vulnerable patients, such as the long-haul trucker. Before settling upon just what that "something different" should be, Englander and her colleague, Dr. Devan Kansagara, systematically collected data on what patients and clinicians thought of the current processes, asking them to identify gaps and opportunities for improvement. They sought insight from doctors, patients, nurses, hospital administrators, social workers, case managers, and community safety-net providers.

During the course of their investigation, many of her medical peers described the current state of discharge planning as chaotic and inconsistent. Their colleagues identified lack of insurance (15 percent of the hospital's patients are uninsured), unstable housing, poor social and family support, and mental illness as the complexities of transitioning from hospital to home successfully. Once back in the community, many patients struggle to access local resources that will provide needed health care and social support. According to Englander:

> The safety net around Portland is at capacity. It exists, but it's not robust enough to meet demand. Many patients don't have access to needed outpatient services, and for those who do, care is often not well coordinated.[47]

For Englander, the crux of the issue was clear: organizational responsibilities during these transitions were not clearly defined. In the words of one OHSU hospital administrator:

> We don't have a community contract where everybody acknowledges their role . . . my role as the sender is to do these things . . . my role as the recipient is to do these things . . . the "who" and "how" of the handoff. We never get close to that sort of formality, which is really what any smart handoff or transition would require.[48]

Englander described the reality even more pointedly:

> We were asking patients to essentially "walk the plank" after hospital discharge. No one knew what would happen once they dropped out of sight.[49]

She recognized and seized the opportunity to transform the way the hospital linked with the wider community. Today, she and Kansagara are creating partnerships between the hospital and pharmacies, clinics, and social service agencies. They have named their effort C-TRAIN, short for "Care Transitions Innovation," but are wary of calling it a separate program or project. Rather, they want it simply to be the new standard way of practicing medicine.

Four key design features characterize C-TRAIN. First is the presence of a transitional nurse who helps patients and clinicians anticipate care needs, coaches patients to help them manage their complex illnesses, and serves as the contact point for patients transitioning from the hospital to home. Transitional nurses measure success by increases in the percentage of discharged patients who keep their follow-up appointments and adhere to their prescribed regimens. Second is the assistance with prescriptions, both through teaching and by facilitating access to affordable medications. For people without insurance, C-TRAIN pays for thirty days' worth of medications after hospital discharge, which through judicious procurement of generic pharmaceuticals has an average cost of only $108 per person. This allows most patients time to be connected to state-run insurance plans and primary care, without missing critical doses of medications. Third is the provision of sustained primary care in clinics that can facilitate access to a host of social services and supports. "If patients are on C-TRAIN, we tell them they can come here for life," said one community health clinic physician (ID 76).[50] Patients referred from OHSU never wait in intake lines at the clinic, which can require weeks or months for patients without C-TRAIN. They are taken in immediately and assigned a provider, thanks to the hospital's prepayment system with the clinic. (C-TRAIN, which is funded by the hospital, pays outpatient clinics $1,620 per uninsured patient to serve as a medical home, essentially reserving spots on the clinic physicians' docket each week.) Furthermore, the clinics' administrators and counselors facilitate housing, disability benefits, rehabilitation services, acupuncture, cooking and nutrition classes, and other social services that clients seek. One community health physician (ID 76) at the clinic described the rationale as follows:

> They get right in. And from a systems perspective that makes sense because you're, sort of, taking the highest need people and funneling them in to primary care services.[51]

Fourth, C-TRAIN serves as a platform for hospital-wide quality improvement. A team of providers that includes nurses, pharmacists, and physicians from the hospital and clinics meets monthly to review patient cases and to identify ways to create a better system of care across settings that previously worked in silos.[52]

C-TRAIN realizes its multi-pronged approach is not a simple fix. It requires intensive collaboration among multiple organizations and disciplines, which often cannot share information as easily as they would like and may have different perspectives on a patient. Describing the complexity of caring for her patients, Englander recalled her frustration at what she called "the air conditioner story." She was referring to a story made famous by local policymakers who argued that high medical costs could be addressed with simple fixes. They repeated the story of an older woman with chronic pulmonary disease, who lacked an air conditioner, and who therefore landed in the hospital on hot, humid days. Englander, who recognized the importance of air conditioners, buckled at the oversimplification:

> If I hear the story of the air conditioner one more time, I might scream. It's not about air conditioners. That's like saying buying people scales will solve heart failure. The air conditioner is only the beginning.[53]

One of the clinics to which C-TRAIN refers many patients is the Old Towne Clinic, a community health center in downtown Portland. Old Towne Clinic offers a wider scope of services beyond routine medical care, and patients who receive primary care there are eligible to partake in the full breadth of services offered on-site, including outpatient substance abuse treatment programs, acupuncture, and cooking classes, in addition to the primary care visits with their physician. Old Towne Clinic staff often provide assistance with identifying housing resources, enrolling in insurance programs, and obtaining financial or legal services. One Old Towne physician (ID 76) remarked:

> Our patients probably get better health care than we do; the system
> is just built in a much more rational way—it makes sense. Everyone
> should be so lucky.[54]

While C-TRAIN may be working now, Englander remembers many initial barriers to its implementation. To begin with, C-TRAIN required redefining providers' roles. For example, hospital pharmacists needed to develop new skills in educating patients and had to fit more communication with outpatient pharmacists into their work flow. Within the hospital, residents grumbled that C-TRAIN required them to finish their discharge summaries more quickly than usual. C-TRAIN also demanded that nurses, physicians, and pharmacists think about care differently—anticipating needs after hospitalization and working closely as part of a multidisciplinary team. Englander summarized the challenges inherent in such collaborations as follows: "There were very real cultural barriers."[55]

Initially the hospital management also had concerns about investing more resources in a population that was already hurting the hospital's financial bottom line. Englander anticipated the resistance and took pains to establish a business case for her proposal and to market it to top hospital executives. Executive vice president Peter Rapp recognized C-TRAIN as an opportunity to begin transforming his hospital for the future. As he explained to us:

> We are an acute-care oriented place, meaning the opportunity cost
> of each bed is really quite high. We need to reorient our thinking
> [to focus on delivering complex care to very ill people].[56]

Rapp and other executives see innovations like C-TRAIN as a tool by which to better steward scarce resources and potentially keep more beds available for patients who require the highly specialized care for which OHSU is known. In Englander's view, the hospital expects to save money over the long term by "paying for care upstream [before people become acutely ill] in an outpatient setting" where the less complex care can be delivered more cost-effectively. The front-line providers are in agreement that "the goal is to be able to utilize emergency departments as they were initially intended: [for emergencies]."[57] According to Rapp, developing C-TRAIN was an opportunity to learn about care models for patients with lower incomes and limited insurance, knowledge he viewed as critical to success in the era of health care reform.

The preliminary results of C-TRAIN suggest that Englander's willingness to recognize the interdependencies between medical care and social services has been positive for patients. Based on data from a randomized controlled trial, Englander and Kansagara have found that patients who participated in C-TRAIN experienced significantly lower mortality risk and improved quality of care. The hospital continues to support the program, recognizing the value of the program to individual patients, the hospital, and the local community. C-TRAIN is proving beneficial for providers, too. Participating physicians, in particular, are expressing appreciation for the team-based approach to care. Recalling the success of one patient in particular, one Old Towne physician (ID 76) described a sense of professional fulfillment:

> It [was] a really coordinated medical intervention, and that was satisfying. I think it was an experience where I really got to be a physician. I think a lot of the times here we're, sort of, playing social worker, playing psychiatrist when we're not necessarily trained to do that. We do medical care, you know? And so it was very refreshing. The patient needed an internist and she got an internist and it worked beautifully.[58]

Englander acknowledges that the program began with the short-term vision of helping the neediest cases, but she reminded us that its approach would have value for most patients, saying "developing clinical care for the most vulnerable is good for everyone."[59] In her view, although C-TRAIN was piloted for a specific population, the lessons learned are spreading to other parts of the hospital, and other patient populations have begun benefiting from similar practices. This broader use for C-TRAIN responds to what one case manager (ID 74) expressed in our visit, "We are all vulnerable people in the hospital,"[60] suggesting patients from any socioeconomic background would benefit from having a designated person to help them coordinate and manage their care in a chaotic hospital environment. She explained:

> You've got twelve different people coming in. Most of them are asking the same questions over and over again . . . That can cloud anybody's ability to self-manage.[61]

According to the hospital administration, the impact of C-TRAIN on the quality of patients' experiences has been remarkable. Because of its success, C-TRAIN is now being scaled up at OHSU and expanded to cover three other local area hospitals. Furthermore, the OHSU Foundation has tapped Englander to consult on how to improve care for other groups of patients, including wealthy donors. One Old Towne physician (ID 76) we spoke with reflected on the impact of C-TRAIN on broader hospital policies and standards:

> I think what's interesting is C-TRAIN started as a quality improvement project, you know. And I think what it really did, is even though it was targeting a low-income "underserved" population, it really stepped up the quality area around transitional care in general at the hospital.[62]

The hospital's long-term vision for C-TRAIN is that it becomes a vehicle by which to establish a community contract, which would specify the responsibilities not only of inpatient and outpatient health care providers, but also of social service providers and patients themselves. Another C-TRAIN physician at Old Towne (ID 76) described her lesson learned in the following terms:

> Allocating money for social services, help with housing, disability, rehabilitation, anything that you can to make the person well should really be under our full umbrella of health care.[63]

When asked what incentive there might be for Americans to support payments for these social services, in addition to the more traditional health care procedures, the physician (ID 76) recalled the high bills her patients used to run up in hospitals, and responded:

> I think you're paying for it anyway and you're going to pay more for it until we can figure out how to spend the money correctly.[64]

THE ORGANIZATIONS REVIEWED IN THIS chapter have all been successful in improving health care for their respective populations. Identifying their common features may prove useful in constructing larger efforts to improve health nationwide.

The organizations demonstrated balance in their provision of health care and social services. They accomplished this by co-locating services in a single building (ECCC, LA PALESTRA), establishing contractual partnerships with complementary organizations (OPCC, C-TRAIN), or assigning a case manager to facilitate navigation across a breadth of services (OPCC, C-TRAIN).

In addition, the organizations valued an interdisciplinary approach, which operated on the premise of mutual professional respect. Staff members included people with expertise in medicine, mental health counseling and psychiatry, housing, financial counseling, nutrition, legal services, job training, physical and occupational therapy, exercise physiology, and transportation services. Clinical and management staff described initial challenges to team-based approaches that require collaboration across different disciplines, but these were overcome in time, as staff experienced the benefits of such collaboration. Coordinating care in this way allowed physicians to focus on what they are trained to do—provide medical care—while other staff took care of applications for disability benefits, housing, legal issues, and many more needs. The academic literature identifies this approach as enabling professionals to work at the "top of their license" and has demonstrated its potential for maximizing organizational efficiency.[65] Success in strategically dividing tasks in this way can be achieved only through what Atul Gawande has deemed a combination of ambition and humility—ambition for the right process, and humility to recognize the limits of any one discipline.[66]

The commitment to an ethos of client empowerment was also central in the four organizations. Staff deliberately avoided providing services that the patient or client could reasonably attain on his or her own. In this way, staff focused on helping clients and patients realize their own independence and potential for self-care. Providers were willing to do things with clients, but not for them. To forge a relationship with clients, many providers described the need to meet people "where they are" and to be willing to accommodate the unconventional challenges of clients' lives while supporting them to become independent and healthy.

In sum, all of the programs created structures that allowed the staff to approach patients or clients holistically, rather than as a set of independent problems to be addressed by various specialists. In some ways, each organization approximated the concept of a patient-centered medical home, although with even greater reach and coordination of services beyond medical care. All succeeded in breaking down the silos that previously separated providers and organizations that share a mission of improving patients' health and well-being. Their comprehensive approach bolstered rather than diminishing the client's own capacities to attain greater health. These programs, which are supporting clients without inviting overdependence, are being recognized as effective means to achieve better health by integrating health care and social services for diverse client bases. The benefits are clear—not only for Americans who are poor or homeless but also for those who are in the upper echelons of the income distribution in the United States. If the public subscribed to a holistic view of health and if incentive structures rewarded this kind of cross-sector collaboration, these approaches might be endorsed more widely in the marketplace.

CHAPTER 6

AN
AMERICAN WAY
FORWARD

ALTHOUGH THE APPROACHES HIGHLIGHTED IN Chapter 5 stand out in the current health care landscape, Americans have been at this juncture before, experimenting with models that encourage the promotion of health at reasonable cost for a defined population. Twice in recent history, the United States has launched major efforts to redesign the provision of health care so that it might be more effective and less inflationary: through public sector efforts in the 1960s and through largely private sector efforts since the 1970s. The public sector effort in the 1960s fostered neighborhood health centers, which were designed to provide a range of services to keep communities healthy and employed. The private sector efforts of the 1970s–1990s aimed to leverage health maintenance organizations (HMOs) to promote the health of their members at reasonable cost. Despite substantial investment, over time both movements were narrowed in scope, from fostering a holistic view of health to delivering medical care. Nevertheless, the way forward need not be "déjà vu all over again." Lessons learned from these experiments gone awry may help avoid the pitfalls of previous strategies and prompt more effective future reforms.

ALTHOUGH THE HEALTH CENTER CONCEPT had its roots in serving immigrants in the early 1900s,[1] the modern neighborhood health center movement grew out of President Lyndon Johnson's War on Poverty. The term *War on Poverty* represented the administration's moniker for a set of policies that sought to reduce poverty through increased job training and improved access to education, nutrition, and health care, particularly for children and families with low income. The Economic Opportunity Act of 1964 constituted the centerpiece of the War on Poverty, seeking to reduce poverty through the development of employment opportunities.[2] The Office of Economic Opportunity (OEO), which administered the funds to support poverty reduction programs, such as the Job Corps and Head Start, learned early on that it was going to be difficult to raise people out of poverty without addressing their health issues. Many would-be Job Corps and Head Start participants failed to participate in the programs on account of their poor health. In response, the OEO issued grants to people or institutions proposing new models for promoting health and welfare of vulnerable populations served by OEO programs. Drs. H. Jack Geiger and Count Gibson, from Tufts University Medical School in Boston, were the first to be awarded such grants, in 1965.

The neighborhood health center model, envisioned by Geiger and Gibson and first implemented in Boston and rural Mississippi, sought to provide a comprehensive approach to health by integrating health care services with broader community development efforts.[3] Advocates of the model recognized the interdependence of economic development and health. People who were housed and fed would be more likely to be healthy; healthy people were more likely to be employed; and employed people would become self-reliant, productive citizens for the nation. The model was predicated on the creation of one-stop locations where people could receive health care services as well as links to housing agencies, job training, and other support services. A holistic approach toward health defined the work of the centers. Community members served on the governing boards of the neighborhood health centers, a design feature intended to give the community a voice in governance and to foster responsiveness to community priorities.

The early success of the OEO neighborhood health center movement was impressive, growing from two centers in 1964 to fifty centers by 1968 and one hundred by 1971. During this time, the funding and administration of the neighborhood health centers lay within the auspices of the OEO,[4] as opposed to the Department of Health, Education, and Welfare (HEW), which housed more traditional government health care programs.[5] The placement within the OEO signaled the recognition that health was a means to achieve economic development. Supported by the OEO, neighborhood health center staff saw the provision of medical care as an integral part of a wider community development effort. Progressive supporters, including those in the US Public Health Service (PHS), saw the potential for the neighborhood health centers to expand beyond their original mission and become a core institution for the wider American health care system, including the middle class;[6] however, this potential would never be fully realized.

As the number of neighborhood health centers grew, their newfound visibility drew criticism from mainstream medicine.[7] Some segments of the medical profession feared that integration of health services and social services might divert resources from medical efforts or tarnish physicians' prized reputation as scientists. The movement also clashed with physicians' professional norms, espoused by the American Medical Association (AMA). Historically, physicians, often working in solo practices, had enjoyed a high degree of professional autonomy. Neighborhood health centers, on the other hand, required the assembly of interdisciplinary teams of providers rather than independent providers working in the traditional medical hierarchy. Physicians comprised a critical part of the staff at neighborhood health centers, to be sure, but nurses, social workers, financial counselors, and others were also accorded substantial value in the team approach. Moreover, neighborhood health centers engaged the community in the centers' governance, favoring community participation over professional dominance, thereby further limiting the autonomy that physicians had traditionally enjoyed. Additionally, as neighborhood health centers began attracting the middle class, they encroached on private practitioners' paying patient base.

In addition to opposition from the medical profession, fiscally and politically conservative politicians and policymakers also expressed concerns.[8] These stakeholders believed that the neighborhood health centers would create an unnecessary and unwanted financial obligation for the federal government if they were not adequately circumscribed to care for relatively small, disenfranchised portions of the population. Such an expansion of the federal government into health care amounted to an act of socialism in the eyes of some critics.[9] The threat of runaway costs, large federal deficits, and radical government intrusion into Americans' private lives fueled considerable public and congressional debate on the appropriate role of government in 1967.

Under pressure from these and other critical lobbies, legislators made key concessions to accommodate conservative opposition and sustain necessary funding. As part of a 1967 amendment to the Economic Opportunity Act, Congress required each center to provide care only for people below the poverty line, rather than for the community at large. Thus, although the funding for neighborhood health centers was spared being eliminated entirely, their mission was markedly narrowed. Neighborhood health centers were left serving only people who were poor, thereby no longer posing a threat to mainstream medicine or expanding the government's traditional role of funding safety net programs.

As OEO funding came increasingly under attack in the late 1960s, a coalition of Johnson-appointed HEW bureaucrats developed their own version of neighborhood health centers that could be institutionalized (and therefore more protected) within HEW. Beginning in 1968, HEW began providing grants to what were called "community health centers" to care for people who were poor. These centers focused more squarely on medical care rather than the full complement of services coordinated by the OEO neighborhood health centers. By 1969, two dozen community health centers were funded under the Comprehensive Health Planning and Public Health Services Act of 1966.[10] Support from the medical profession came from physicians who chose to fulfill government service commitments by practicing in the community health centers rather than enlisting in the military and serving in Vietnam.[11] By 1972, the HEW-supported community health centers grew to serve 850,000 people,[12] but, like the OEO-supported neighborhood health centers, the model continued to be pushed to the margins, serving predominantly people who were poor and otherwise vulnerable.[13]

The changing political tide, made apparent by the election of President Nixon, brought even more opposition to the neighborhood health centers and other Great Society programs funded by the OEO. Uncomfortable with what he perceived to be government overspending, Nixon opposed continuing funding for many of these programs, including expansion of the neighborhood health center movement. In his 1970 Veto Message on the Labor-HEW-OEO Appropriations Bill, addressed to the House of Representatives, Nixon expressed concern that the requested funding would be directed toward programs of a "low priority."[14] Nevertheless, HEW bureaucrats and Democratic members of Congress continued to support the concept of the health centers as an important safety net program. Hence, even as funding dissolved for OEO neighborhood health centers, funding continued for community health centers under the auspices of HEW, where all responsibility for health center administration was centralized in 1973.

Even when health centers were placed within the jurisdiction of HEW, advocates found sustaining financial support to be difficult, as the Nixon administration began to dismantle Johnson's hallmark OEO programs. In 1973, Congressional staffers drafted a bill to retain community health center funding (Public Health Service Act, Section 330) in which they made another key concession by suggesting a division between "primary" and "supplemental" community health center services.[15] Primary services (which would be required) included traditional medical, radiology, and laboratory tests, as well as dental care and transportation to health care services, while supplementary services (which would be discretionary) included nutrition counseling and support, health education, and social services. The separation was a tactic to safeguard traditional medical care against future budget cuts by Nixon and other administrations, even if the social services, deemed supplemental, were sacrificed. Over time, the bill drafters' premonition came to pass, and funding was restricted to so-called primary services. As reductions in federal grant funding continued, the HEW community health centers increasingly relied on Medicare and Medicaid reimbursement dollars, which funded exclusively medical services. As their dependence on Medicare and Medicaid increased, the community health centers faced new financial incentives, which rewarded the provision of medical care but not the non-medical services that might promote the population's health.

In 2012, more than one thousand HEW community health center organizations continued to operate out of approximately 8,500 locations. Taken together, these facilities provided care to more than 20 million people, 72 percent of whom fell below the poverty line.[16] Despite this considerable impact, many of these operations stand in stark contrast to the neighborhood health centers first envisioned by the OEO in 1964. The discrepancy between original vision and today's reality can be traced to functional limitations that were placed on the model. These limitations restricted the population served to people living below the poverty line and focused services largely on primary medical care services. Although the dilution of the original neighborhood health center model was necessary to sustain political viability, the impact of the movement may have been substantially less than its originators had hoped. What began as a flexible, community-based center of comprehensive care provision became a dispensary of medical care primarily for indigent people.

To some, the failure to sustain neighborhood health centers according to their original formulation is surprising, given the conceptual strength of the model, but in retrospect, this evolution might have been predicted. Like the broader policies and programs that made up the War on Poverty, the idea of neighborhood health centers was initiated from within the executive branch, with only limited input from Congress, interest groups, or the general public.[17] This top-down approach, which required government expansion, proved ineffective for making a sustained, large-scale change, and illustrates the contrast between the United States and Scandinavia. (There, innovations to integrate health care and social services have been successfully scaled through local and federal government, and supported by general tax revenue.) The limitations placed on community health centers also highlights the political power of the American medical profession and a broader cultural preference for spending in the realm of medical care over social services.

WITH COMMUNITY HEALTH CENTERS FOCUSED on the medical care of people who were poor, Nixon soon faced the challenge of maintaining the health of the rest of the population at reasonable cost. With the Vietnam War ending, the country was in the midst of the worst economy-wide price inflation in decades. The challenges in the health care sector were particularly acute, as the establishment of Medicare and Medicaid in 1965 had committed government to paying more and more for Americans' growing demand for medical services. The president searched for health care delivery innovations that would restrain the mushrooming medical industry and the government's outlay for health care. In a Special Message to Congress in

February 1971, Nixon outlined the predicament: "Our record [of investment] then is not as good as it should be. Costs have skyrocketed but values have not kept pace. We are investing more of our nation's resources in the health of our people, but we are not getting a full return on our investment."[18] Influenced by health policy adviser Paul Ellwood, MD, professor of pediatrics, neurology, and physical medicine at the University of Minnesota, Nixon unveiled a new national health strategy that would center on scaling up HMOs.

The HMO model sought to manage the health of a population at reasonable cost by increasing health promotion efforts and creating financial incentives for physicians to reduce unnecessary use of medical care. HMOs represented a private sector approach to delivery and financing of health care that was attractive to the Republican administration. The HMO model brought the delivery and financing of health care under a single organizational umbrella, using capitated payments (flat rates paid to the HMO on a per-enrollee basis) to deliver and finance care.[19] HMO enthusiasts believed that these design features would motivate physicians to limit unnecessary utilization and instead focus efforts on disease prevention and health promotion activities. Furthermore, the HMO model could prosper and be sustained in the private market alongside traditional insurers. For Nixon, the model was an ideal alternative to either extending neighborhood health clinics' reach or implementing national health insurance. He signed the HMO Act into law in December 1973.

The HMO Act of 1973 was limited in federal financial commitments but bold in concept. The legislation authorized $375 million in start-up grants (for nonprofit or public organizations) and loans (for for-profit organizations) to develop HMOs nationwide.[20] From the outset, government financial support for HMOs was to be catalytic only, entailing no commitment for long-term financing. The HMO Act also ensured that the federal legislation would supersede state laws that might otherwise impede the growth of HMOs (such as restrictions on group practices), and required employers that of-

fered health insurance to at least twenty-five employees to also offer
a federally certified HMO alternative to traditional insurance if an
HMO were available in the area. With these efforts, the government
jump-started an innovative, private-sector model that sought to
promote population health and restrain inflationary pressures. The
model would grow to insure the majority of employed individuals in
the United States over the next quarter-century.[21]

The government effort to stimulate national expansion of HMOs
was inhibited along the way by political concessions made to well-
organized adversaries. Immediate opposition arose from the medical
profession, as physicians again balked at the idea of surrendering the
freedom of solo practice to participate in group practices. Moreover,
many physicians voiced concerns that the establishment of financial
relationships with HMOs (which provided disincentives to giving
more care) could endanger the sanctity of the doctor-patient relationship, giving patients reasons to mistrust physicians.[22] Factions
within the AMA considered HMOs, particularly those that salaried
physicians, an instrument of socialism.[23] (This and several other critiques levied against HMOs ran parallel to those made against neighborhood health centers a decade earlier.) To address these concerns,
the HMO model diversified from only employing salaried physicians
or physician groups to allowing physicians to practice independently
without being salaried. The vast majority of the growth in HMOs in
the 1980s took this latter form. Although salary-model HMOs were
believed to be most effective in restraining unnecessary health care
utilization, the loosening of controls over physician practice was
deemed necessary to attract providers and take the HMO model
to scale.

The staunchest opposition to the model arose from Americans
who felt their choice of providers and procedures was being cur-
tailed by their HMO's provider restrictions. When employers offered
HMOs as a choice, employees who selected the model were satisfied,
but when HMO characteristics and controls found their way into

almost every kind of insurance, the public balked. Americans began to view HMOs (and managed care more broadly) to be overly prohibitive, limiting the physicians who could be accessed and denying payment except for approved care. To address these complaints, the original HMO movement evolved by the mid-1980s into a more generalized managed care movement, in which insurers established financial relationships with providers (physicians and hospitals) and provided incentives for more judicious use of services. Other cost containment tactics, such as requiring patients to secure approval prior to using services, directing patients to certain (less expensive) physicians, and financially penalizing patients more if they sought services "out of plan," were implemented by managed care organizations to control costs but retain patient choice. As organizations continued to accede to a disgruntled marketplace, they loosened even these restrictions.

Although these concessions diluted the original HMO model, the managed care industry nonetheless flourished by successfully controlling costs, for a time. During 1994–1999, the period in which the managed care industry reached its peak coverage and used its most aggressive tactics to limit costs, health care expenditures as a percent of GDP leveled off for the first time since the enactment of Medicare.[24] Despite this success in terms of reducing health care cost inflation, outrage from the American public and the medical establishment ensued. Particular acrimony was levied at managed care companies, which required patients and physicians to attain prior approval for medical treatment, often from a phone bank of nurses with no connection to the case. The curtailment of both physician autonomy and patient free choice regarding medical care drove a powerful cultural backlash against managed care, as the public became suspicious that managed care companies (and sometimes physicians) were profiting from denying payment for needed care. By the end of the 1990s, legislation in some states limited the use of highly restrictive utilization rules,[25] and employers began dropping insurance products that were most aggressive in rationing care. Partly as a result of this tempering of the restrictive practices of managed care, by 2001, health care spending resumed its acceleration.[26]

After rapid growth in market share in the late 1990s, HMO and managed care models constituted 97 percent of employer-based insurance plans by 2005, and including high-deductible health plans, continue to dominate the employer-based insurance market.[27] Employer-based insurance plans, Medicare, and Medicaid all now have elements of managed care built into them, including negotiated payment rates, utilization review, and quality assurance mechanisms. The research literature largely suggests that HMOs succeeded in reducing health expenditures, primarily by reducing health care utilization. The impact on quality is less clear.[28] Anecdotes of inappropriate rationing by HMOs persist in popular culture,[29] although the research literature has not found marked reductions in quality of care. The HMO or managed care model of cost containment was generally effective from a cost and quality standpoint, but ultimately was unacceptable to the American public. Individuals were particularly appalled by the thought of HMO and managed care companies' allowing staff to deny payment for care while these companies benefited from reduced utilization. Furthermore, as HMO physicians faced similar financial incentives, they came under increased scrutiny by patients,[30] who were concerned that their clinical decision-making was being unduly influenced by financial motives. More fundamentally, the restrictions in choice dictated by the HMO model conflicted with deep-seated norms of professional autonomy for physicians and personal liberty for individuals.

As a result of the concessions made to remain politically and economically viable, modern managed care models are quite distinct from the original HMOs envisioned by Paul Ellwood and President Nixon. In the course of their growth, managed care organizations have become focused on reducing health service use (and attendant costs) rather than on managing health, and the "new spirit of discipline" that Nixon implored the nation to embrace in announcing the HMO model never materialized.[31] Rather, managed care companies have had to limit their aggressive cost containment tactics in response to patient and provider complaints. As in the case of the neighborhood health center movement, alterations in the original visions of these models were necessary for their expansion, but the altered model has also proven less able to deliver the intended results—health at reasonable cost.

These complex histories reveal an American tendency to funnel resources earmarked for health toward medical care. Whether orchestrated in the public or the private sector, the initiatives ultimately succumbed to an ever-increasing focus on the provision of health services and dwindling attention to addressing the population's overall health—including social, environmental, and behavioral determinants. The medical profession has powerfully shaped how resources for health are deployed, and the American public, diffuse in its political voice and economic influence, has allowed it to lead in the distribution of health resources. These historical realities make clear that Americans have been complicit in the creation of the current approach.

THE PREDILECTION FOR MEDICINE HAS firm roots in American culture as well as American politics. This widespread tendency to rely on medicine for health solutions has been termed "medicalization," which Professor Paula Lantz at the George Washington School of Public Health has succinctly defined as the mistaking of health care for health.[32] Medicalization has complex beginnings born of the behaviors of many actors. In the 1970s, medical sociologists viewed medicalization as a method of social control,[33] although the impact on high costs did not draw much attention at that time. Nevertheless, with increasing sophistication of medical technology, the American tendency to medicalize patient concerns is widely recognized as contributing to health care cost escalation. Health care providers, all

kinds of medical services organizations, and patients as well contribute to the medicalization of America on account of their (sometimes
misplaced) faith in specialty care, medical technology, and the new-
est medications.

Concrete cases from patients and physicians we interviewed,
which we share in the following pages, illustrate how various actors may exert power to increase the use of expensive medical care
without commensurate improvement in health. The first story shows
how the medical environment can influence patients to opt for more
medical care than they might have otherwise chosen. The second
story demonstrates how providers impart expensive medical care that
they may view as excessive.

THE FIRST STORY WAS TOLD by a middle-aged woman we interviewed, who described her recent experience with the health care
sector. Despite being referred to a top-rated specialist physician, she
wondered whether the prescription she received was really what
she needed.

> A year ago, my daughter became more serious about tennis. I had
> always played a bit, but then I began playing several times a week
> with her. As a result, I developed a sore shoulder that was painful
> enough to crimp my professional and recreational activities. Like a
> lot of other forty-year-old women, I use my gynecologist for primary
> care and had not seen an internist for years. Without much of a
> foothold inside the medical profession, I asked friends and family
> for a good orthopedist, and the best shoulder surgeon in the area
> agreed to see me.
>
> On the day of the appointment, I was punctual in arriving
> at the office and expected my care to be delivered in a similarly
> prompt manner. Unfortunately, it turned into a long and weari-
> some afternoon. I began by completing the registration forms in
> duplicate and having a wristband affixed with my name and date
> of birth. After producing my private insurance card, I was shuttled
> to radiology, where the technician asked which shoulder hurt and
> positioned me for three shoulder X-rays.

After X-rays, I was led to an examination room, where a nurse eventually showed up with a checklist of questions. I began to describe the history of the injury, but the nurse seemed to be in a rush, so I sped through my story. We fell into the scripted questions, and the nurse entered my answers efficiently into the computer, without eye contact. With one foot out the door, the nurse assured me the orthopedist would be coming in shortly.

I waited unattended for what felt like too long. Frustration and anxiety conspired, and I stuck my head into the hall to assert for whoever was listening that I was leaving in fifteen minutes whether I had seen a doctor or not. Only then did paper start to fly, and an orthopedic surgeon-in-training appeared and pushed my arm around, asking what hurt. He explained, "You may have torn the labrum, which is the cartilage around the socket, and that causes the pain. You may need surgery." He left. Then the surgeon entered the examination room, affirming, "The X-rays look perfect, no broken bones!" I had to wonder why he had been looking for broken bones. He wrenched the arm around for another minute, identically but less forcefully than his trainee had done, and concluded the same.

"The shoulder socket is not quite right; the labrum may be torn or shredded a little; hard to tell without MRI [magnetic resonance imaging], so we will order that and see about surgery. Meanwhile you will start physical therapy. Physical therapy works fifty percent of the time; surgery works ninety-five percent of the time."

I asked why an MRI was needed and how it would change the course of action, but the question went unanswered. The surgeon continued, "The MRI is easy. We have several facilities right in the vicinity. The wait won't be long." And he left the room.

Squeamish about surgery and frustrated by my interactions with the office, I ultimately took a different path. I started physical therapy and muscle strengthening, and made a concerted effort to change the biomechanics of my tennis stroke, which ultimately proved successful in restoring pain-free motion.

As our interviewee recounted the story, she noted the pressure she felt to abide by the surgeon's recommendation to undergo an MRI and surgery. He was, after all, the expert and she had come to see him for his professional opinion. Still, she felt that the prescription was overdone. She was tired of doctors and medicine after only the first visit. Her mistrust was intensified by the bill our interviewee received several weeks after the visit. Although she knew insurance would cover it, the numbers were shocking. The bill for the X-rays and less than five minutes with the surgeon was $650. The approach the surgeon suggested would have generated considerably more revenue for him, the radiology department, and the hospital. The MRI would have cost another $2,000, and if surgery were deemed appropriate, a preoperation visit, several blood tests, a chest X-ray, and follow-up care would ensue. All in, the bill ultimately could have totaled more than $30,000. In addition, surgery may well have required hospitalization, during which many patients are exposed to a set of potentially infectious pathogens and can suffer from inadequate sleep, nutrition, and physical movement, all of which have been demonstrated to be risks for other health problems.[34] The question remains as to whether all this would be in the best interest of the patient's health, or the nation's pocketbook, particularly given the fact that surgery could remain an option in the future if less medically intensive approaches were pursued and failed.

Our interviewee's experience exemplifies what some critics cite as the heart of the American health care problem—financial incentives that lead to overtreating patients, made vulnerable due to their limited scientific knowledge and their deference to the authority of medical professionals.[35] Some commentators have even suggested that the financial incentives are so perverse as to give health care providers and organizations reason to pursue strategies that may keep people from becoming healthy. Journalist Shannon Brownlee epitomized this view in a commentary she provided for the documentary film *Escape Fire*: "If [our system] really was honest with itself, it doesn't want you to die and it doesn't want you to get well. It just wants you to keep coming back for your care . . ."[36]

Putting the issue of financial incentives and health care provider profits aside, the sheer enormity of medical resources available in the United States may also influence people to adopt a decidedly medical approach. These effects recall the fabled phenomenon described by American philosopher Abraham Kaplan in his book *The Conduct of Inquiry: Methodology for Behavioral Science*, "Give a small boy a hammer, and he will find that everything he encounters needs pounding."[37] Health care organizations regularly pay for television, radio, billboard, and online advertisements, encouraging Americans to make sense of a complex world through a medical lens. The phenomenon has been noted in economics as Roemer's law of demand,[38] in which the supply of medical services generates demand for these medical services. Study after study has demonstrated that, for insured populations, "a hospital bed built is a hospital bed filled."[39]

OUR SECOND STORY ILLUSTRATES A complementary perspective about the source of overtreatment. This perspective suggests that patients' demand for ever-faster and more sophisticated medical care is a major driver of cost. One West Coast pediatrician in particular offered a candid description of just such an interaction, wherein the parents of a young boy, Tyler, sought inordinate levels of medical care, far beyond the usual standards of practice.

> I have been treating a teenager, Tyler, who has been quite healthy up until last year, when he developed some trouble with headaches. The headaches come and go intermittently, but his parents, who love him dearly, have become very concerned about what the pains may be signaling about his health. They have done extensive research on the Internet, leading them to request a number of specialist workups. Because they are covered by the father's employer-based insurance plan, the family sees these additional workups as essentially "free care."
>
> His parents come to my office not looking for my advice but rather with very clear requests as to what they want to have done. Who am I to deny them? Their insurance is paying for the case, and I want to be able to give this family as much confidence as I can. This is really weighing on them, and we have a long-standing

relationship. I have also seen and treated Tyler's older siblings, and my son and Tyler play soccer together in town. So I have done what I can to help these parents find an answer that will satisfy them.

To date, the resulting workup on Tyler has included a complete allergy workup; a complete ear, nose, and throat workup; an infectious disease workup; an immunology workup;, a toxicology workup; a dental workup; and consults with three additional neurologists and several psychologists. Besides the appointments with and testing conducted by these specialists, Tyler has undergone multiple procedures. The parents have asked for several rounds of analysis on blood work, a CT scan, and MRIs to check for brain tumors or bleeds. This child has also been hospitalized and has had a lumbar puncture (spinal tap) to check for bleeding or spinal infection. I have not seen the actual bill, but I would bet that, once everything is tallied, including hospitalization, this was a quarter-million-dollar workup. The majority of this bill will most likely be covered by their insurance, as we have secured approval for each step of the process. Because the etiology of the persistent headaches has remained unclear, I have been able to make a case for more testing on behalf of the parents.

Specialists have told me that Tyler's parents are equally directive in their dealings with them. The parents demand that specialists order specific tests because their neighbor has told them about [his] nephew who had a brain tumor that went undiagnosed and he later died. The parents have even gone so far as to openly say, "If you don't do the test and it turns out that my son has a tumor, I will sue you."

So, I have ordered this whole series of medical tests over the course of several months, with no abnormal clinical findings. In my mind, this is very good news, as it indicates that these headaches are not a sign of any serious medical condition. My colleagues, too, have reached a general consensus that Tyler's headaches are most likely caused by a nonclinical condition. Some of my most recent discussions with him indicate to me that his pain may be born of a fear of school or what some would call tension headaches.

The effects of this extensive medical investigation have been pronounced on Tyler. He has become increasingly frightened about what is wrong with him as he has been ferried from one hospital and doctor's office to another. Mirroring his parents affect, he has felt disappointment in the lack of findings, and I have been concerned about his slipping into something of a depression. He has also lost several weeks of schooling.

Reflecting on his experience, the pediatrician described feeling conflicted at times about whether the tests were all needed, but he also understood that the parents, and increasingly the son, were anxious and wanted an answer. He had considered the expense, but he knew that the family was well insured, and he knew this was their preference. Having been the family's pediatrician for more than a decade, he wanted to comfort them by being as thorough as possible. He rationalized his actions as providing patient-centered care, which is respectful and responsive to individual patient preferences, needs, and values. In this case, the pediatrician believed that being patient-centered meant following the family's lead in their quest for medical certainty, even while his medical intuition suggested such a quest to be unwarranted. He also aimed to retain the high patient ratings he had always enjoyed in a very competitive marketplace for pediatric care. Asked where he would draw the line, he told us he did not know. He hoped that his suggestion of tension headaches as a diagnosis, which several of the specialists had echoed, would suffice. Particularly in light of the agitation that the process had caused Tyler, the physician was hopeful that the family would relent for a time, which may give the headaches an opportunity to resolve on their own.

These complementary perspectives of patient and provider reveal complex roots to American's cultural reliance on medicine to create health. In both cases, providers and patients are working toward their own self-interest given the health care choices they face. Health care providers are trying to make the best living possible by structuring days to see a maximum number of patients, in light of the demands that administrative and paperwork place on their time. Patients and their families are trying to extract as much certainty as they can from the medical complex and, in the case of well-insured families, are insulated from the costs of this effort. None of the actors in the American health care landscape deserves full blame for medicalization. All are merely acting in accordance with what the system allows and rewards. The challenge is to think strategically about what a more mutually beneficial system design may look like.

ADOPTING A BROADER VISION OF what produces health can have critical implications for the United States as it seeks the best health outcomes given the national spending level. Such a holistic approach is consistent with the vision of OEO neighborhood health centers and early HMOs, wherein physicians were meant to treat medical problems, and a multidisciplinary staff supported them by providing clients with or linking clients to services that addressed nonmedical causes of their ill health—such as housing, job training, nutritional support, substance rehabilitation, and other social services. Each of the innovative programs we visited in Chapter 5 had implemented some version of this vision, and many other front-line providers with whom we spoke expressed a desire to work in a more holistic system. In particular, those we interviewed underscored the importance of accepting the prominent role that social, environmental, and behavioral factors have on health, which allows the nation to avoid repeating the mistakes of our past and to extract ourselves from the current dependence on medicine. Although medical care is crucial to the health of individual patients with specific illnesses, the larger context in which people live is far more predictive of a country's health.[40]

The beginnings of such a holistic view of health can be detected already among portions of American society. Although the trend is slow, many individuals are embracing a broader view of health and are therefore seeking out healthier lifestyles and environments for themselves and their families. Businesses with a reputation for offering products for health-conscious consumers (e.g., Whole Foods Market, General Nutrition Centers, and Lululemon Athletica) have seen sizable market expansion. A new wave of positive psychology research, packaged in the form of peer-reviewed papers and popular books, has similarly pointed to the power of nonmedical determinants of health. Titles such as *Good, Better, Best: Simple Ways to Improve Your Nutrition, Health, and Life*; *Perfect Health: The Complete Mind/Body Guide*; and *The Seven Pillars of Health* have underlined psychosocial determinants of health for interested readers. Alternative medicines have also seen a rise in popularity, in some cases even finding welcome receptions in traditional medical settings. The Veterans Administration, for instance, now offers acupuncture for indicated conditions, while major academically affiliated hospitals, such as Massachusetts General Hospital in Boston, offer free acupuncture, Reiki healing, and massage therapy to patients undergoing chemotherapy.

Adopting a holistic view about the determinants of health could have a far-reaching impact on national spending choices. Individuals can benefit from adopting such a view for themselves. Furthermore, such a stance embedded more firmly in the broader culture may well relieve financial strain on the health care sector and the national deficit. Perhaps the greatest challenge will be in recognizing that holistic approaches to health are not only good for those who can afford them, but are relevant to all Americans. If taxpayers understood that health was largely determined by nonmedical factors, more strategic national investments that more efficiently align medical and nonmedical efforts to attain health might be possible.

In addition to embracing a holistic view of health as the new goal, establishing accountability for health is essential. Currently, the question of who is accountable for health can have any number of answers. Depending on one's politics and place in the system, health may be viewed as the responsibility of individuals themselves, case managers, physicians, health care organizations, the government, or some combination thereof. The largely unplanned approach to building a health care sector has resulted in a plethora of actors, many of whom take responsibility for particular health services or products, but with no single entity designated to be accountable for health. All participate, acting in accordance with their place in the system, while paying hidden costs for the creation of subpar health outcomes.

On account of Americans' resistance to the centralization of authority, assigning full accountability to one actor or another is an unpopular idea. Giving greater responsibility to the government is cast as socialism in some circles, and more mildly critiqued for limiting competition, fostering complacency, and tolerating inefficiency in others. Allotting more accountability for health to health care corporations raises suspicions of profiteering, particularly as consumers are often unable to evaluate their health care needs or judge the quality of health care accurately. Assigning responsibility to patients to manage their own health and health care is often considered unrealistic and carries its own risks. For instance, individuals who may decide to forgo vaccination threaten the population's herd immunity, and individual lifestyle choices can lead to chronic disease epidemics, the costs of which are borne by the larger community. Additionally, many prevalent diseases, due to either their urgency or neurological effects (life-threatening heart attacks, major depression, and dementia, to name a few), render individuals unable to make informed and considered choices on their own. Hence, assigning accountability for health to any single actor remains unsatisfying.

An alternative would be to share accountability. Yet, given a culture of individualism and personal freedom, many Americans continue to resist this idea as well. When poor health outcomes take center stage in the public discourse, all actors point fingers at one another. Evidence of this can be found most recently in media frenzies around Mayor Michael Bloomberg's so-called soda-ban, and the ensuing "anti-Bloomberg" law passed in Mississippi in 2013.

Setting aside the concerns that the Bloomberg law was imperfectly conceived and written, the public rhetoric around the core idea of accountability illustrated America's challenges in this arena. While New York's mayor, an Independent, aimed to foster a public sphere that was conducive to healthy lifestyle choices, Mississippi's Republican governor, Phil Bryant, reacted by preemptively banning any such legislation in his state on the grounds of personal freedom. Bryant was quoted as saying, "The responsibility for one's personal health depends on individual choices about proper diet and appropriate exercise."[41] He further argued that government should have no role in promoting or deterring such personal health choices. Many other Americans joined with Bryant in his belief that individuals should be free to act in their own interest, even in instances when doing so can damage their health. As Cara Buckley wrote in the *New York Times*, "[People] resented what critics deemed a 'nanny state' mentality on the part of Mayor Michael R. Bloomberg, who heavily backed the ban. Even with obesity on the rise, and despite the accompanying toll on health care costs, access to bucket-size sodas was widely seen as a matter of personal choice. 'If you want to drink large drinks and become obese, that's your right,' said Christopher Rivera, 19, of Mott Haven, at the Regal Cinemas movie theater on West 42nd Street."[42]

As an aside, some readers will recall that similar arguments were made throughout the latter half of the twentieth century in the face of government regulation of smoking. The advent of warning labels, federal and state taxes, and, ultimately, outright bans on smoking in public places invited ideological critiques of an overly zealous government restrictive of free choice. Despite these concerns, by 2011 the majority of US states had enacted their own form of statewide smoking bans and nearly 60 percent of Americans supported a ban on smoking in all public places (increased from 39 percent in 2001).[43] This history illustrates one instance in which the American populace has accepted limiting some personal freedoms in the name of population health, particularly in the wake of (initially unpopular) public health legislation.

As a practical matter, taxpayers bear the burden of individuals' poor health behaviors, although this interdependence often goes unrecognized. For example, Bryant and others failed to recognize that the person who is exercising their free choice by purchasing the "Big Gulp" is already sharing substantial health care costs with others. The obesity epidemic in Mississippi has claimed 35 percent of the state's 3 million people as clinically obese.[44] The increased health care costs for people who are obese compared with those who are not is between $3,000 and $5,000 per year.[45] Extrapolated to the state, obesity is associated with an average of an additional $4.2 billion in health care costs per year that is attributable to Mississippi's obesity epidemic. These costs are paid by both public programs (more than 30 percent of Mississippi residents are enrolled in Medicaid or Medicare) but also by private insurance companies, and both public and private payers share this additional cost with the rest of the country, through higher taxes and increased premiums.

This analysis reveals that Americans are already sharing the costs of ill health widely. Placing accountability solely on individuals seems inconsistent with the fundamental premise inherent in all insurance schemes, in which risks are pooled, or shared, for the financial protection of all. Given this interrelatedness, it appears in the interest of Americans to collectively address determinants of ill health. Poor health—such as obesity—results from a confluence of factors, some related to individual choices but others related to, for instance, massive marketing campaigns for food of limited nutritional value, government subsidies of corn and sugar, and built environments that limit physical exercise. Thus, fully addressing these factors that contribute to ill health and high health care expenses may require collective action, including multiple government, corporate, and societal actors, which Americans struggle to orchestrate. Shared accountability for health is already a structural reality, as long as we have insurance of any kind. The challenge is acknowledging this shared accountability within the confines of an American culture so defined by individualism.

"Live free or die" has been a popular refrain for Americans who feel that all would be best served by staying out of one another's affairs. In health, however, this approach has produced shoddy results. In the words of one reporter, the approach is one that amounts to "Live free *and* die," highlighting the dangers of American dedication to individual liberties and an ethic of self-reliance.[46] In truth, neither the approach that depends fully on individual accountability nor the one that relies exclusively on collective accountability can be successful over time. Rather, the integration of the two seemingly contradictory approaches opens doors for newly innovative solutions. Such integration requires both personal and community motivation to recognize and address health threats at multiple levels. It also necessitates a reframing of public discourse concerning individual freedom versus collective responsibility as a "both-and" rather than "either-or" issue. The work of actively balancing these values in the implementation of programs, the advancement of public discourse, and the formulation of policy may be daunting. Nevertheless, the hallmark words of F. Scott Fitzgerald bestow high praise on such an approach: "The test of a first-rate intelligence is the ability to hold two opposing ideas in mind at the same time and still retain the ability to function."[47]

How might the United States retain the strengths of its medical establishment while also incorporating strategies that address the social, environmental, and behavioral determinants of health? The United States is unlikely to raise taxes to support the expansion of social services, particularly in light of the current economic climate and endemic concerns about the inefficiency of government-administered programs. Similarly, the United States is unlikely to explicitly transfer funding from health care to social service provision, given the demonstrated political and economic power of the health care industry. But, conceptually, accountable care organizations (ACOs) could provide an opportune leverage point. As part of the Affordable

Care Act (ACA) of 2012, the Centers for Medicare & Medicaid Services launched ninety ACOs to provide and coordinate the health care of 2.4 million people in seven states,[48] and private insurance companies are starting to follow suit. An ACO is an organization of health care providers (hospitals, clinics, physicians) that is reimbursed for providing and coordinating all of the health care used by a designated set of people who receive the plurality of their primary care from the ACO providers. ACOs are responsible for the health care expenditures incurred by these people and, for an extra fee, the coordination of their care. As of 2013, large insurance companies and self-insured employers have also begun to experiment with making contracts with ACOs for the care of their insured groups, hoping that the model of coordination may reduce health care expenses without sacrificing quality. In 2013, several hundred ACOs exist, the majority of which are operated by large hospital systems or medical group practices.[49]

Although the ACO model could be a potential leverage point, its daring vision is being narrowed already, and its long-term solvency and impact is not clear. Within the first year of its design, the American tendency to narrow its focus on medical care rather than to acknowledge broader determinants of health was already evident. The ACO model was originally envisioned to pursue what was called the "Triple Aim."[50] The Triple Aim is the tripartite goal of (1) reducing health care costs, (2) enhancing patient experience, and (3) improving population health, where population health meant health outcomes for the group of people receiving care from the ACO providers. In translating this goal into the regulatory sphere, the Centers for Medicare & Medicaid Services have named thirty-three performance indicators on which ACOs will be financially rewarded. Unfortunately, population health was largely lost in the translation, and the resulting performance indicators pertain primarily to cost of care, patient experience, and health care quality (see Appendix C).[51] Given their medical roots, it should not be surprising that ACOs are eager to focus on quality, cost, and patient experience in health care, leaving the population health agenda aside. Population health is something for which many providers and administrators feel they cannot reasonably be held accountable.

The limits placed on the practical scope of the ACOs' mandate echoes the narratives of neighborhood health centers and HMOs, both of which started with a broader view of health and devolved to focus on medical care over time. Furthermore, without a more systematic examination of the perverse financial incentives driving increased volume throughout the system, ACOs that attempt to limit cost increases will likely face the same challenges that HMOs did in the late 1990s. The early path of the ACOs suggests that once again, Americans are diluting a potentially powerful tool in health reform and repeating the mistakes of the past.

To prevent ACOs from becoming yet another ineffective health care acronym, it is essential to develop incentive systems that reward the pursuit of health and its root causes. Imagine a regulatory shift that rewarded health care providers for attention to social determinants of health, and consumers for maintaining their health. One approach might be to establish ACO payment based on performance indicators that measured health and progress on social determinants of health. Examples may include the percent of an ACO's population that is at a healthy body weight, is not depressed, is employed, is housed, or is on track to graduate from high school or college. Measures would need to be tailored to the population, adjusted for socioeconomic status, age, and other factors, and refined so that they could be reliably assessed. Conceptually, however, assessing performance relative to nonmedical issues known to influence health is likely to motivate health care providers to work more closely with other sectors that are central to promoting population health.

The impact of creating incentives to achieve the goal of holistic health could be far-reaching. The surgeon who has to operate might ask a patient, "Tell me about your work schedule; when can we perform this procedure without compromising your position at work?," to preserve employment in the community. Pediatricians might be rewarded for working more closely with school-based nurses on asthma control and mental health, to allow young patients to maintain their school attendance. The hospital might be more motivated to further establish coordination mechanisms with the job training programs, housing officials, and educational entities in their service area.[52] If health care providers were to become motivated to help accomplish social goals as a critical pathway to health, a virtuous cycle based on the alignment of health care and social service providers can evolve that is impossible given today's outmoded health care models. Given the breadth of inputs into health, no single agency or player can be solely accountable; rather, the achievement of health will require shared accountability.

Embedded in the concept of ACOs is an opportunity for all Americans to become more accountable for the impact of individuals' actions on the nation's health. Recognizing the harsh reality of limited budgets at all levels of government may inspire the motivation necessary to do so. Poor health in any segment of the population, even the most marginalized, costs all taxpayers money. Therefore, efforts to improve health may be motivated not just by altruism but by enlightened self-interest.

INCREASING THE ACCOUNTABILITY OF ALL actors in the American health care landscape is bound to produce pushback. In an environment replete with medical technology and know-how, the public will struggle to redirect their gaze to alternative methods of attaining health. Individual disincentives for poor health choices, or policies that restrict personal liberties in an effort to improve people's health, unsettle some Americans and inspire others. To achieve the better health outcomes the country wants, Americans will have to be innovative in sharing accountability in culturally acceptable ways.

Health care organizations and physicians are also likely to be initially unenthusiastic about becoming accountable for health, rather than for merely providing medical care. Many may argue that they cannot possibly influence housing, employment, lifestyle choices, and other social determinants of health. The health care providers we spoke with, however, expressed feeling frustrated and exhausted by the health-compromising social needs that medicine cannot address but that patients expect their doctors to fix. The proposed approach could mitigate these frustrations by opening paths to coordinate medical care and social services more seamlessly. Effective coordination of this kind could reduce overuse of hospitals and emergency rooms, open hospital beds for more complex (and often more profitable) medical care, and reduce burnout among their medical staffs.

Any increase in the responsibility and power accorded to government to jump-start organizations (such as ACOs) that accept accountability for health is destined to face criticism unless the role is catalytic rather than dominant. Previous attempts to create a holistic approach to health—whether in the public sector for people who were poor or in the private sector for people with more means—have been castigated by adversaries as mechanisms of socialized medicine. This criticism helped defeat both neighborhood health center and HMO models, proving to be what physician Alan Brett, professor of internal medicine at the University of South Carolina, called the ultimate "trump card" of American public discourse.[53]

The public has, however, accepted government investments to kick-start private sector innovation in a variety of instances, including the seeding of the solar energy industry, funding early innovations through the National Institutes of Health Small Business Innovation Research (SBIR) efforts, and expansion of the HMO industry. To avoid extensive opposition, the role of government may be to foster experiments that create incentives for health care and social service organizations to work in concert and that enable strategically coordinated investments in both. The trouble remains that many previous reform efforts have managed only to rearrange the proverbial deck chairs on the *Titanic* of our health care sector.[54] The relative neglect of strategic investments to address the nonmedical determinants of health has been a critical impediment to achieving health at reasonable cost in the United States. Fundamentally altering Americans' perspectives on health and its determinants would set the stage for sustainable health reform—one conducive to the creation of a system able to care for the whole person. Although this kind of paradigm shift will be difficult to set in motion, it could provide a pivot point for redirecting America's investment strategy for health, and the key to unraveling the spend more, get less paradox of American health care.

CHAPTER 7

CONTINUING THE DISCOURSE

WE STARTED THE BOOK BY identifying what many see as a paradox. How could the United States devote so much money to health care and yet rank so poorly relative to other industrialized countries in key indicators of the nation's health? Per capita, the United States spends nearly double what some of its peers spend, but Americans lag behind in terms of life expectancy, infant mortality, low birth weight, injuries and homicides, adolescent pregnancy and sexually transmitted diseases, HIV/AIDS, drug-related deaths, obesity, diabetes, heart disease, chronic lung disease, and disability rates.[1] Some have argued that Americans' comparatively poor health is due to the larger proportion of people living in poverty in the United States than in the more generous welfare states of Scandinavia and Western Europe, but this thinking fails to explain why this poorer health ranking holds for Americans who are white, educated, employed, and high-income.[2] We have suggested that previous calculations have omitted an aspect of spending that is critically important for national health outcomes. This is spending on social services, an area in which the United States spends far less relative to its GDP than its peer countries. The new math unraveled the paradox. If we add together what countries spend on health care and what they spend on social services, the United States' place in the ranking of industrialized countries shifts considerably. This sum of spending is what might be called the national investment in health. In looking at the sum, no longer does the United States appear to be a massively big spender. Americans' spending on social services is far less per capita than that of counterpart countries. Taking both health care and social service spending into account, the United States spends a fairly average sum compared with its peer countries and, we argue, has fairly average health outcomes as a result.

This finding is consistent with what experts in public health have argued for decades: health is determined by far more than good genes and medicine. The scientific literature estimates that at least 60 percent of premature deaths, for instance, are caused by nonmedical factors.[3] Researchers have estimated that the health returns on education increase the value of educational investments by between 15 and 55 percent.[4] In light of the mountains of other findings like these, it stands to reason that to design an effective system—one that actually delivers health and not merely health care—requires a strategy for addressing social, environmental, and behavioral factors. Such a strategy would necessitate a more balanced investment formula, allocating funding more equally between medical and nonmedical influences on health.

Examples of such models are alive and well around the world. Perhaps the most successful model is that of Scandinavia, where health is viewed more holistically and budget responsibility for both health care and social services is centralized in local government. Of course, Scandinavians still fervently debate health care and social services allocation decisions; however, the discourse regarding these decisions occurs openly in the public sphere. Once consensus is reached in Parliament, local governments can move investments fluidly between sectors to achieve the greatest health value.

A comparative analysis of Scandinavian and American values, however, reveals the depths of the United States' challenges in casting a health care model to improve its population's health. Although Scandinavians and Americans shared similar views about personal freedom, competition, political action, and investment in technology, conceptions of health differ markedly. Consistent with the ideology of individualism, the American notion of health emphasizes the illness of the individual, which is to be addressed by medical care delivered through one-to-one doctor-patient encounters. Similarly, health behaviors known to cause harm, such as smoking, drug use, and poor nutrition, are largely viewed in the United States as individual choices and failings, whereas the Scandinavian approach reflects a broader view of health that is predicated upon shared responsibility for the larger community. This conception also recognizes the nonmedical determinants of health, which are best addressed through collective action. Moreover, Americans lack the trust in each other and in government enjoyed in Scandinavia. This distrust may explain the American resistance to shared accountability for health needed to address the social, environmental, and behavioral determinants of ill health.

Recognizing that Americans' divergent values and history prevent the United States' outright adoption of the Scandinavian approach, we sought out domestic innovators who were building models of health care delivery based on a new conception of health. We found exemplars in organizations serving Americans spanning the socioeconomic gradient and in varying states of health. The success of these organizations in providing exceptional care gave us hope that committed providers and managers can find practical means by which to embrace a more holistic view of health, improving health within the populations they serve without adding to the cost—and in some cases, reducing costs. Nevertheless, their work is contained within small microcosms; their long-term viability and the geographic scale-up of the models they have pioneered will be difficult to achieve given existing incentive structures and cultural norms.

We have argued that a paradigm shift in how Americans view health is required for these and other small-scale innovations to grow and have larger impact. Such a shift would be characterized by Americans' willingness to think broadly about the root causes of ill health and to accept the limits of medicine. Only then could large-scale innovations involving coordination among health care and social service providers be developed, valued, and sustained.

New paradigms mean little if not accompanied by concrete action. The United States could benefit from building greater accountability into the financial incentives and rewards governing health care provider organizations. In this area, the United States' inventiveness and freedom to experiment locally will serve it well. Experimentation with and evaluation of models that reward individuals and providers for addressing deeper determinants of health and joining forces in the pursuit of health are essential to finding an American way to address the spend more, get less paradox.

IN THE YEARS WE HAVE spent conceiving of and writing this book, we have had ample time to consider the criticisms its ideas may face. We have wrestled with our own, similar doubts from time to time. We have wondered if the scope of the work is too large, the goals too lofty, or the implications too dire. At the same time, we have wondered whether we paid adequate attention to certain flashpoint issues, such as mental health and chronic illness, which represent obvious intersections of health and social services. Reconciling and, at times, adapting our views in light of these concerns has been a meaningful exercise that strengthened the logic of our thinking. No doubt, the challenges that lay ahead are considerable, but confronting the deep roots of the spend more, get less paradox is a productive step toward effective reform. At this stage, we thought it wise to include discussion of some of the most pressing and enduring issues, which could not be fully addressed here, to prompt among readers a more authentic analysis of and continued discourse about core challenges.

We have prioritized several potential sources of apprehension concerning the analysis and implications of our work. First, we suspect some readers may be unconvinced by the data presented to support our thesis. Second, we anticipate that American readers in particular may dismiss the arguments in this book as pertinent only to people who face financial hardship and rely on safety net services. Third, we imagine some readers may be paralyzed by the complexity inherent in the relationships among health, social services, and health outcomes, and thus may consider strategic action all but impossible. Fourth, we worry that some readers will become impatient with the lack of a quick fix, and hence withdraw from the national dialogue surrounding national health investment strategy. Last, we are concerned that readers will recognize the advantages of a more holistic approach to health but find the economic reordering that might ensue unpalatable, despite the promise of sustained benefits.

We present here what we believe are strong rebuttals to these apprehensions. We do so in the hopes of overcoming, at least partly, the tendency to disengage with material that elicits psychological discomfort. This discussion aims to hold readers' feet to the fire, so that each may recognize the roles of the individual and the collective in both creating and addressing the problems of high health care spending and poor health outcomes. Some readers will be loath to accept our arguments without more data. Although the scientific literature provides robust evidence regarding the influence of social, environmental, and behavioral factors on people's health,[5] comprehensive evaluations that quantify the precise costs and health impacts of broad-based, nonmedical health interventions are less available. Solid housing, a nutritious diet, stable home life, a reasonable amount of sleep, and a steady job have all been linked to improved health so many times[6] that the studies are becoming uninteresting for new researchers to pursue.

The evidence concerning the health impact of employment, education, and housing is particularly considerable.[7] Unemployed and underemployed segments of the population have been shown to die younger and be in worse health throughout their lives than are those more gainfully employed, and this finding is persistent across countries and times. Some of this effect is attributable to the poverty that accompanies unemployment; however, even among people who were employed but lose their jobs unexpectedly, the health effects are marked. In a series of studies, researchers have documented that involuntary job loss in middle age is linked with poorer health, including increased depressive symptoms and two to three times' increased risk of heart attack and stroke over ten years. Health effects of education are similarly impressive. Education has been shown to be associated with longevity, and some of this effect is due to its influence on employment and income. Recent evidence, however, is also revealing the independent effect of education on health and length of life; even after accounting for socioeconomic status, occupation, and race, the effect of education is robust. Many studies have shown that the number of years of completed schooling is strongly predictive of good health.

More relevant for our purposes, studies are beginning to show that increased education can lower health care spending. For instance, in a study of older adults with asthma or hypertension, those with more versus less education were significantly less likely to be high spenders in health care. A recent Robert Wood Johnson Foundation report highlighted research that demonstrated that lack of college education accounted for up to 35 percent of the variation in premature death rates in the United States, and each added year of postsecondary school education was associated with a 16 percent decline in years of life lost before the age of seventy-five.

Last, investment in housing has been consistently shown to offset increased expenditures in health care among people who are chronically homeless and in poor health. This has been shown in randomized controlled trials and observational studies of Housing First programs. Housing First is a social service program that provides supportive housing for people who have been chronically homeless and suffer substance abuse and mental health issues. In a study comparing ninety-five Housing First participants and thirty-nine people wait-listed for the program, the total of housing and health care costs were reduced by nearly $2,500 per month per person for enrollees. Similarly cost-effective housing investments as well as state-based supportive housing investments have been used for chronically homeless veterans. In one of the largest contemporary randomized social experiments in housing, Professor J. Ludwig, working with the Department of Housing and Urban Development (HUD), randomly assigned 4,498 women with children to one of three groups: (1) housing vouchers for low-poverty tracks (where fewer than 10 percent of residents were poor) and counseling on moving, (2) unrestricted vouchers with no counseling, and (3) neither voucher type and no counseling. The study reported ten- to fifteen-year follow-up health outcomes and found markers for obesity and diabetes were significantly lower in the low-poverty voucher group, suggesting that elevating people to be in less impoverished housing is particularly effective. In another set of studies, economists Daniel Sullivan and Till von Wachter estimate a 50 to 100 percent increase in mortality rates for older male workers who lose their jobs.[8] A study published in the *The Lanclet* found that a 1 percent rise in unemployment rate is associated with a 0.99 percent increase in the suicide rate.[9] Assuming a link of that scale, the increase in unemployment would lead to 128 more suicides per month in the United States.

Nevertheless, undertaking comprehensive randomized trials of specific interventions—with long-term follow-up to demonstrate the set of activities addressing social, environmental, and behavioral factors that improve health and temper health care spending—has not been done and is not currently feasible.

The desire for certainty is in part an artifact of the scientific approach to health care. The scientific method calls for researchers to establish controlled experiments that provide unbiased and generalizable conclusions. These standards are considered appropriate for biomedical research, but can be unduly constraining in a study of complex human behavior that is replete with any number of dynamic and unpredictable processes. Reducing such complexity to a controlled intervention to which people are assigned randomly, or to a reliable set of quantifiable values, is often an impossible challenge. For instance, a researcher might be interested in estimating the impact of employment and housing on health. Randomizing study participants to receive jobs or a place to live may be both logistically challenging and ethically questionable, but such an experiment also quickly becomes uncontrolled insomuch as the job or housing creates ripple effects elsewhere in the individual's life that may meaningfully influence health. For instance, the job might allow the person to qualify for health insurance, while housing may reduce exposures to street violence and other health risks. Over time, the person's optimism and vitality may improve, but reliably pinning down what portion of the improvement in health is due to the job, or the housing, or the myriad of other changing elements in the person's life would be all but impossible.

Thus, while the scientific approach has fueled unprecedented medical and technical progress in many arenas, it has been of less value in conferring data that identifies a prescription for optimally addressing the multifaceted causes of ill health. Scientific methods are touted for their ability to identify the effect of a specific treatment controlling for all the other social, environmental, genetic, and lifestyle factors that might influence the health outcome. In examining broad health interventions, however, recognizing the impact of these larger factors is critical. What might be dismissed as a factor to control in a biomedical experiment, such as the presence of a family support system, is often a fundamental facet of the intervention from a complex systems perspective. As Garrett Hardin, ecologist and author, wrote, "When we think in terms of systems, we see that a fundamental misconception is embedded in the popular term 'side effects.' Side effects no more deserve the adjective 'side' than does the 'principal' effect. It is hard to think in terms of systems, and we eagerly warp our language to protect ourselves from the necessity of doing so."[10]

To address the challenge of multiple moving parts at once, researchers often turn to statistical regression analysis, which seeks to distill effects of jointly occurring factors into their component parts. Yet, these methods are less powerful in the face of feedback loops and nonlinear effects inherent in complex systems. As James Gleick, author of *Chaos: Making a New Science*, writes, "Linear equations are solvable . . . [They] have an important modular virtue: you can take them apart and put them together again. The pieces add up. [But] nonlinear systems generally cannot be solved and cannot be added together. Nonlinearity means that the act of playing the game has a way of changing the rules."[11]

Frustrated by the limitations of quantitative approaches, qualitative researchers have sought more descriptive approaches to documenting the impacts of programs through case studies, ethnographies, and open-ended interviews.[12] These studies provide in-depth understanding of complex phenomena but have been criticized for their lack of generalizability, and their inability to produce numeric evidence from which one could estimate national cost savings attributable to various interventions.

All this is to say nothing of the ethical challenges researchers confront performing studies in which key social services are withheld from participants in need so as to study their impact on health. One clinical researcher and director of pediatrics whom we interviewed (ID 80) recounted his experience of being denied funding to evaluate the impact of improved housing and legal services on hospital costs for children with asthma. He said:

> I tried to get NIH [National Institutes of Health] funding for a study of the impact of improved social conditions on asthma outcomes and costs. Families below the poverty level with a child

with asthma were going to be randomized to being offered a civil rights attorney, for example, from Legal Aid, and access to housing along with usual medical treatment versus just receiving medical treatment. The reviews were good scientifically, but NIH would not fund the study because the reviewers said it was unethical to not give someone the social intervention. It was pretty frustrating—we are being asked to get data on the effectiveness of addressing the social factors rather than just the medical ones, and then—they call it unethical because everyone knows how important those factors are! Pretty ironic.[13]

As this experience demonstrates, the medical research community has prioritized certain types of questions and intervention timelines that challenge efforts to gather evidence on social, environmental, and behavioral interventions to improve health. Most grant-making bodies prefer to fund research focused on simpler, more precise interventions (such as medications and surgical procedures) rather than large, unwieldy programs addressing systemic and structural issues. Narrowly defined lines of inquiry are favored based on the time and resources required to complete such studies but are unlikely to produce evidence about levers for transformational change in health care. As an internist we interviewed (ID 72) summarized:

The *big* question, the one that [NIH] would never want you to study because it is too broad, would really have the most impact.[14]

We join with readers and the broader scientific community in recognizing that we do not have the precise type of data to summarily demonstrate the health and cost impacts of specific interventions to address social, environmental, and behavioral determinants of health. Nonetheless, given the unequivocal evidence concerning the social, environmental, and behavioral determinants of health, current actions that target these determinants should be considered well founded, even as additional data about the most effective interventions accrue.

Additionally, we worry that readers will misconstrue the implications of our analysis as little more than a call for more robust safety net services to complement the current health care sector. This would be a misinterpretation of our work. The data we have outlined and the reasoning we have presented are relevant for all Americans, regardless of income bracket. As already noted, the discrepancy in health between the United States and its peer countries is apparent even among wealthy, well-educated, and white subgroups of the American public.

The notion that this book is all about people who are poor overlooks a fundamental part of our argument. LA PALESTRA, the comprehensive center to promote health described in Chapter 5, exemplifies a holistic approach to health for which clients will pay a premium to receive coordinated nonmedical services: nutritional advice, physical exercise training, sports psychology, and help navigating treatment options. The results of the approach have been impressive, and LA PALESTRA is extraordinarily popular among the wealthy community in which it is known. Similarly, the early successes of C-TRAIN, which links patients with needed social and health services after hospitalization, have earned it the reputation of being one of the most patient-centered programs at the hospital, and the program is therefore being expanded to serve wealthier patients as well. Last, the stories of Dwane, Barry, and Martha in Chapter 3, which repeat themselves daily in the lives of any number of individuals across the country, highlight the interplay between health care and social service needs for people of different ages and socioeconomic standing.

Certainly, for people who are poor, social services, such as housing, nutrition, and safe neighborhoods, are essential. Often, these services must be financed by taxes or philanthropy and supported by governmental policy and action. Hence, our reference to social services may summon for some readers images of government handouts, the "dole," and bloated bureaucracies. To be clear, our call for greater attention to social services emerged in response to the empirical importance of these services for health, rather than in furtherance of an ideological or political agenda. Investments in social services are particularly relevant for our discussion as additions to social capital, described by Robert Putnam as "features of social organization such as networks, norms, and social trust that facilitate coordination and cooperation for mutual benefit."[15] Putnam uses membership in a group as a common proxy for social capital, noting that joining an organization cuts in half an individual's chance of dying within the next year.[16] A litany of health researchers have followed his path in associating the abstract social-capital concept to health through a variety of creative measurements. For example, a person who has cancer may receive information, money, or moral support that allows him or her to navigate the labyrinth of modern medicine more effectively. The social trust and group membership that reflect social capital can also be leveraged to reduce risky health behaviors, such as smoking and binge drinking.[17] Conversely, a lack of social capital in an individual's network has repeatedly been linked with ill health.[18] In sum, researchers who have documented the effects of social capital on health have underscored the important effects of social service investment, even among people who do not live in poverty.

We anticipate that some readers will become immobilized by the complexity of the issues and will settle for responding haphazardly to the matters at hand rather than seeking a strategic approach. These readers may argue that because of the potential for unintended consequences of interventions in complex systems, it is preferable to limit intervening action. This more laissez-faire view is apparent from a long history of disjointed investments that have proven for policymakers and the public to be both wasteful and distracting from strategic alternatives. In the last decades, the United States has marched through a panoply of priorities, responding episodically to the threat of the day (mad cow disease, anthrax, avian bird flu, SARS, or obesity) without ever formulating a national health strategy or systematically buttressing our social service or public health infrastructure.[19] Some would say this is the American way. Speaking to this point, one health and wellness center service user (ID 59) declared:

> The United States is the ultimate in ADHD [attention deficit/ hyperactivity disorder] investing.[20]

The American preference for focusing on the immediate or impending source of pain without attending to underlying causes reflects a type of national investment myopia. This term refers to conditions in which people focus so intently on one aspect of a problem that they neglect other critical data in the landscape. Steven Most and Brian Scholl, professors of psychology at Harvard and Yale University, respectively, have referred to this phenomenon as "inattentional blindness." In a famous 1999 experiment identifying this phenomenon, participants were asked to watch a video of people, wearing black and white shirts, tossing a basketball back and forth.[21] Participants were asked to count the ball tosses in various ways. Partway through the video, a person in a gorilla costume walked across the scene. More than half of the viewers did not see the gorilla, even though it walked directly through their line of sight. They were concentrating on counting the ball tosses. The analogue to inattentional blindness in health care is a narrow focus on the immediate problem—the part of our body or our community that threatens to disturb our immediate function the most—while neglecting the root causes of the threat. The result is an expensive, short-term fix of superficial symptoms while neglecting the social, environmental, and behavioral factors that are necessary to sustain health.

If Americans are serious about moving away from myopia and toward a more sophisticated approach to coping with the complexity of health, some principles may be helpful that have been put forth by Professor Donella Meadows, former Pew Scholar in Conservation and the Environment and professor at Dartmouth College, for guidance.

In her book *Thinking in Systems*,[22] Professor Meadows highlights the need to locate accountability in a complex adaptive system so as to optimize outcomes. In the United States' health care sector, putting Meadows's teaching into practice would mean identifying ways by which actors (for instance, hospitals) feel the impact of their actions on other elements of the system (for instance, homeless shelters) and therefore have an incentive to limit the negative effects on other elements in their shared system. In a similar but slightly different way, we expect some readers will be bothered by the lack of a simple prescription and therefore disengage from the matter altogether. Generally speaking, Americans are an impatient and skeptical lot, focused mostly on actions that will render immediate and impressive results. When Prilosec, a drug to alleviate the symptoms of heartburn, was at its commercial peak, Americans spent more than $5 billion per year on it,[23] rather than changing their eating habits to avoid the onset of heartburn in the first place. The medical course of action takes fifteen minutes; the alternate may take months or years. It is easy to see how, in a culture of anxiety regarding time, the Prilosec option is preferred. The trouble is that Prilosec addresses the symptoms but masks the underlying dangers of poor eating habits, which in fifteen years could land one in the hospital with a heart attack. Short-term success, in this case, breeds long-term failure. And the inconvenient truth of health care is that people change habits slowly.

Nevertheless, we purposefully have avoided offering straightforward solutions for which we recognize the public is thirsty. If our book disappoints in this way, it is because of our deep belief that simple prescriptions will not be effective. Rather, we believe that changing the dialogue around health to be holistic and inclusive of nonmedical contributions is paramount to resolving the spend more, get less phenomenon in American health care. Only in the wake of such a shift will scalable and sustainable solutions emerge.

In calling for a reconsideration of social services and social capital in the United States, we are grappling with a timeless tension between individualism and community orientation. The data we have presented suggest that health is not as individualistic a concept as people in the United States may assume it to be. Unfortunately, public debate in the United States continues to frame health as a product of individual action, individual commitment, and individual accountability. Americans have persisted in this view long after building cost-sharing schemes into much of our health care insurance landscape, with disastrous impact on the national deficit. Perhaps even more irrationally, Americans have persisted in this view long after the data have demonstrated this individualist vision of health to be incomplete.

Increased public dialogue about the consequences of overreliance on individualism and medical approaches, and underinvestment in social capital, may help the country to recognize that the difference of opinion among Americans, regarding whether health is better addressed through individual or collective action, represents a tension to manage, rather than a problem that can be solved. Going forward, Americans would be wise to accept responsibility for patiently managing this tension, rather than aggressively aiming to solve a fictitious problem.

A final concern is that some readers will find the economic consequences of slowing health care expenditure too great a price to pay for better health nationally. The US health care industry has evolved to serve a purpose. Occupying 17.9 percent of the GDP in 2012 and employing one in eight working Americans,[24] the health care industry returns significant profit for any number of professional guilds, health care organizations, and publicly traded corporations. If embracing a holistic vision of health and developing shared accountability results in a shift of funds from health care to social services or a repurposing of health care funds to achieve population health outcomes, a substantial number of Americans may stand to lose. As a result, a number of stakeholders and their political lobbies are likely to actively resist a restraining or redirecting of resources consumed by the health care industry.

The work of altering such a mammoth industry will be arduous, and the effects of even a strategic downsizing would be difficult to rationalize to those families whose income was lost.

AT THE END OF THE journey that resulted in this book, we are still at the beginning of a long conversation about what course the United States might best pursue to tame spiraling health care spending and demonstrate global leadership in the arena of health outcomes. The argument we have made in this book challenges the status quo, suggesting that health care reformers are relying on the wrong levers of change in their efforts to improve the value of America's health care investment. We do not disagree with the statement that Americans spend more on health care and have worse health outcomes than our peer countries. But we do disagree with the common belief that the solution to this problem lies in reforming the health care sector in isolation. In our view, it would be in the interest of both the American government and people to recognize the ill effects that American underinvestment in social services and inattention to social capital have had on health.

We have aimed through this book to inspire in readers a sense of ownership regarding the United States' health care challenges. Not only have all actors contributed to creating the problems, but all are now suffering at the hands of them. Whether or not Americans are comfortable accepting their interrelatedness, people are interdependent on those with whom they share a common pool of resources. The ill effects that American underinvestment in social services and inattention to social capital exert on health are profound. Strategies that aim to resolve the spend more, get less paradox must therefore acknowledge and address these vulnerabilities, brokering new conceptual and programmatic linkages between the goal of health and its diverse determinants. These strategies require the consent, at least implicitly, of all actors in order to be successful.

No health care system in the world is perfect. All have advantages and disadvantages, and all manage the tensions inherent in rationing schemes built into the fabric of their designs. For the most part, the approach to promoting health that countries employ reflects the value base of their citizens. For decades, the United States has relied on reforming various methods of paying for health care or organizing its delivery, when in fact the problem has run deeper. Larger change, extending well beyond the scope of traditional health policy, will be required.

Our hope for this book is that it may come to constitute a small part of a new discourse, prompting Americans to reconsider the prices they pay and the benefits they receive from their health care sector in light of its many shortfalls. Shifting the paradigm of health will be difficult. Recognizing its social, environmental, and behavioral dimensions and embracing the need for both personal and shared accountability to address these elements of health runs counter to the American affinity for individualism and threatens a large, profitable medical industry.

It remains an American choice to forego taking bold action and to continue instead on the current path; however, the monumental costs associated with preserving the status quo continue to grow, and relief from the national health burden is unlikely without a new approach. To devise this new approach on the basis of evidence rather than ideology would represent a courageous step in the history of American health policy. To that end, an ever-growing body of literature suggests that broadening Americans' historically narrow focus on medicine in pursuit of improved national health may ultimately hold the key to unraveling the spend more, get less paradox.

APPENDIX A

ID 1	Program manager, supportive housing agency
ID 2	Director, adult day care center
ID 3	Director, community center for veterans
ID 4	Service user, community center for veterans
ID 5	Director of emergency services, medium-size hospital (200–600 beds)
ID 6	Emergency medicine chair, medium-size hospital
ID 7	Chief financial officer, health system
ID 8	Executive director, patient advocacy organization
ID 9	Radiologist, large hospital (more than 600 beds)
ID 10	Service user, community center for veterans
ID 11	Service user, community center for veterans
ID 12	Service user, community center for veterans
ID 13	Chief bariatric surgery nurse, medium-size hospital
ID 14	President, medium-size hospital
ID 15	Executive director, health and social service organization
ID 16	President, social service agency
ID 17	Director, community center and clergyman
ID 18	Police officer, police department
ID 19	Director, care coordination organization
ID 20	Program manager, care coordination organization
ID 21	Pediatrics nurse, medium-size hospital
ID 22	Chief executive officer, care coordination organization

continues

ID 23	Service user, health and wellness center
ID 24	Service user, large hospital
ID 25	Internist, large hospital
ID 26	Executive director, community center
ID 27	Director of community benefits, medium-size hospital
ID 28	Chief medical officer, community health clinic
ID 29	Service user, community health clinic
ID 30	Mental health counselor, housing coordinator, and case manager at community center
ID 31	Obstetrician, large hospital
ID 32	Executive director, Danish Institute for Health Services
ID 33	Chief executive officer, Danish Health and Medicines Authority
ID 34	American blogger in Denmark
ID 35	Deputy director, Danish health and social care agency
ID 36	Staff, Copenhagen Institute for Future Studies
ID 37	Vice president, Danish hospital
ID 38	Senior medical officer, National Board of Health in Denmark
ID 39	Mental health researcher, Danish Institute for Health Services
ID 40	Director, Swedish Board of Health and Welfare
ID 41	Professor of economics, Swedish Institute for Social Research
ID 42	Obstetrician, large hospital
ID 43	Service user, large hospital
ID 44	Service user, community health clinic
ID 45	Service user, community health clinic
ID 46	Service user, community health clinic
ID 47	Service user, community health clinic
ID 48	Service user, community health clinic
ID 49	Director, health care advocacy organization
ID 50	Professor of health economics, Norway
ID 51	Medical education coordinator, drug and alcohol rehabilitation center
ID 52	Director of health and community services, local government

continues

ID 53	Vice president of patient-centered medical-home development, health system
ID 54	Medical director, drug and alcohol rehabilitation center
ID 55	ID not used
ID 56	President, health and wellness center
ID 57	Behavioral health director, health and wellness center
ID 58	Service user, health and wellness center
ID 59	Service user, health and wellness center
ID 60	Professor of health economics, Norway
ID 61	Professor of health economics, Norway
ID 62	Former director general, Norwegian Health Directorate
ID 63	Acting director general, Norwegian Health Directorate
ID 64	Professor of health administration, Norway
ID 65	Health policy adviser, conservative party, Norwegian parliament
ID 66	Chief, Norwegian health care workers' union
ID 67	Director of health services, Norwegian municipality
ID 68	Neurologist, large hospital, Norway
ID 69	Ambassador, Norwegian Ministry of Foreign Affairs
ID 70	Medical director of health care business, armed forces medical center
ID 71	Internist, medium-size hospital
ID 72	Internist, medium-size hospital
ID 73	Executive vice president, medium-size hospital
ID 74	Transitional nurse and case manager, medium-size hospital
ID 75	Inpatient pharmacist, medium-size hospital
ID 76	Primary care physicians (2), community health clinic
ID 77	Director of care management, health system
ID 78	Project manager, medium-size hospital
ID 79	Executive director, hospital-based research institute
ID 80	Director of pediatrics, medium-size hospital
ID 81	Pediatrician, private medical practice

APPENDIX B

SOCIAL VALUES IN SCANDINAVIA AND THE
UNITED STATES: SIMILARITIES AND DIFFERENCES

Domain	Survey question	Response range	US score	Scandinavian* score	P-value**
Personal freedom	How much freedom and control do you feel you have over the way your life turns out?	1 = No choice at all 10 = A great deal of choice	7.7	7.8	0.191
Political voice and action	Signing petitions	1 = Have done 2 = Might do 3 = Would never do	1.3	1.3	0.279
	Joining in boycotts	1 = Have done 2 = Might do 3 = Would never do	2.1	2.0	0.272
	In political matters, people talk of "the left" and "the right." How would you place your views on the scale?	1 = Left 10 = Right	5.7	5.6	0.096

* Comprising responses from Sweden and Norway; Denmark was not surveyed.
** P-value calculated from t-tests.

Domain	Survey question	Response range	US score	Scandinavian* score	P-value**
Competition	How would you place your views on this scale? Competition is good. It stimulates people to work hard and develop new ideas (1). Competition is harmful. It brings out the worst in people (10).	1 = Competition is good 10 = Competition is harmful	3.4	3.4	0.916
Science and technology	All things considered, would you say the world is better off or worse off because of science and technology?	1 = A lot worse off 10 = A lot better off	7.2	7.1	0.142
Scope of social contract	How would you place your views on this scale? Private ownership of business and industry should be increased (1). Government ownership of business and industry should be increased (10).	1 = Private ownership should be increased 10 = Government ownership should be increased	3.6	5.0	<0.001

Domain	Survey question	Response range	US score	Scandinavian* score	P-value**
Scope of social contract (*continued*)	Please tell me how essential you think the following is as a characteristic of democracy. Governments tax the rich and subsidize the poor.	1 = Not an essential characteristic of democracy 10 = An essential characteristic of democracy	5.0	6.5	<0.001
	Please tell me how essential you think the following is as a characteristic of democracy. People receive state aid for unemployment.	1 = Not an essential characteristic of democracy 10 = An essential characteristic of democracy	5.8	7.1	<0.001
	Please tell me how essential you think the following is as a characteristic of democracy. Civil rights protect people's liberty against oppression.	1 = Not an essential characteristic of democracy 10 = An essential characteristic of democracy	8.0	8.6	<0.001
	Please tell me how essential you think the following is as a characteristic of democracy. Criminals are severely punished.	1 = Not an essential characteristic of democracy 10 = An essential characteristic of democracy	6.8	5.4	<0.001

Domain	Survey question	Response range	US score	Scandinavian* score	P-value**
Scope of social contract (*continued*)	Please tell me how essential you think the following is as a characteristic of democracy. The army takes over when government is incompetent.	1 = Not an essential characteristic of democracy 10 = An essential characteristic of democracy	3.7	2.5	<0.001
	Please tell me how essential you think the following is as a characteristic of democracy. The economy is prospering.	1 = Not an essential characteristic of democracy 10 = An essential characteristic of democracy	6.9	5.7	<0.001
Views of income equality and social mobility	How would you place your views on this scale? Incomes should be made more equal (1). We need larger differences as incentives for individual effort (10).	1 = More equal incomes 10 = Larger income differences	6.2	5.6	<0.001
Trust in one another	Trust in your family	1 = Trust completely 4 = Do not trust at all	1.3	1.1	<0.001

Domain	Survey question	Response range	US score	Scandinavian* score	P-value**
Trust in one another *(continued)*	Trust in your neighbor-hood	1 = Trust completely 4 = Do not trust at all	2.1	1.7	<0.001
	Trust in people you meet for the first time	1 = Trust completely 4 = Do not trust at all	2.7	2.3	<0.001
	Trust in people of other nation-alities	1 = Trust completely 4 = Do not trust at all	2.2	2.0	<0.001
	Do you think people would try to take advantage of you if they got a chance, or would they try to be fair?	1 = They would try to take advantage of you 10 = They would try to be fair	5.8	7.2	<0.001
	How would you place your views on this scale? People can only get rich at the expense of others (1). Wealth can grow so there's enough for everyone (10).	1 = Rich at expense of others 10 = Enough wealth for everyone	6.2	6.6	<0.001

Domain	Survey question	Response range	US score	Scandinavian* score	P-value**
Trust in one another (*continued*)	When jobs are scarce, is the priority citizens or immigrants?	1 = Citizens 2 = Neither 3 = Immigrants	1.6	2.5	<0.001
	Thinking of your own country's problems, should your country's leaders give top priority to help reducing poverty in the world (1) or should they give top priority to solving your own country's problems? (10)	1 = Reduce poverty in the world 10 = Solve own country's problems	8.0	6.0	<0.001

APPENDIX C

ACO #	Domain	Measure Title
1.	Patient/Caregiver Experience	CAHPS: Getting Timely Care, Appointments, and Information
2.	Patient/Caregiver Experience	CAHPS: How Well Your Doctors Communicate
3.	Patient/Caregiver Experience	CAHPS: Patients' Rating of Doctor
4.	Patient/Caregiver Experience	CAHPS: Access to Specialists
5.	Patient/Caregiver Experience	CAHPS: Health Promotion and Education
6.	Patient/Caregiver Experience	CAHPS: Shared Decision-Making
7.	Patient/Caregiver Experience	CAHPS: Health Status/ Functional Status
8.	Care Coordination/ Patient Safety	Risk-Standardized, All Conditions Readmissions
9.	Care Coordination/ Patient Safety	Ambulatory Sensitive Conditions Admissions: Chronic Obstructive Pulmonary Disease or Asthma in Older Adults (AHRQ Prevention Quality Indicator [PQI] #5)
10.	Care Coordination/ Patient Safety	Ambulatory Sensitive Conditions Admissions: Congestive Heart Failure (AHRQ Prevention Quality Indicator [PQI] #8)

ACO #	Domain	Measure Title
11.	Care Coordination/ Patient Safety	Percent of Primary Care Physicians Who Successfully Qualify for EHR Program Incentive Payment
12.	Care Coordination/ Patient Safety	Medication Reconciliation: Reconciliation After Discharge from an Inpatient Facility
13.	Care Coordination/ Patient Safety	Falls: Screening for Fall Risk
14.	Preventive Health	Influenza Immunization
15.	Preventive Health	Pneumococcal Vaccination
16.	Preventive Health	Adult Weight Screening and Follow-up
17.	Preventive Health	Tobacco Use Assessment and Tobacco Cessation Intervention
18.	Preventive Health	Depression Screening
19.	Preventive Health	Colorectal Cancer Screening
20.	Preventive Health	Mammography Screening
21.	Preventive Health	Screening for High Blood Pressure
22.	At Risk Population— Diabetes	Diabetes Composite (All or Nothing Scoring): Hemoglobin A1c Control (<8 percent)
23.	At Risk Population— Diabetes	Diabetes Composite (All or Nothing Scoring): Low Density Lipoprotein (<100)
24.	At Risk Population— Diabetes	Diabetes Composite (All or Nothing Scoring): Blood Pressure <140/90
25.	At Risk Population— Diabetes	Diabetes Composite (All or Nothing Scoring): Tobacco Non Use
26.	At Risk Population— Diabetes	Diabetes Composite (All or Nothing Scoring): Aspirin Use
27.	At Risk Population— Diabetes	Diabetes Mellitus: Hemoglobin A1c Poor Control (>9 percent)
28.	At Risk Population— Hypertension	Hypertension (HTN): Controlling High Blood Pressure

ACO #	Domain	Measure Title
29.	At Risk Population—Ischemic Vascular Disease	Ischemic Vascular Disease (IVD): Complete Lipid Panel and LDL Control (<100 mg/dL)
30.	At Risk Population—Ischemic Vascular Disease	Ischemic Vascular Disease (IVD): Use of Aspirin or Another Antithrombotic
31.	At Risk Population—Heart Failure	Heart Failure: Beta-Blocker Therapy for Left Ventricular Systolic Dysfunction (LVSD)
32.	At Risk Population—Coronary Artery Disease	Coronary Artery Disease (CAD) Composite (All or Nothing Scoring) Drug Therapy for Lowering LDL-Cholesterol
33.	At Risk Population—Coronary Artery Disease	Coronary Artery Disease (CAD) Composite (All or Nothing Scoring) Angiotensin-Converting Enzyme (ACE) Inhibitor or Angiotensin Receptor Blocker (ARB) Therapy for Patients with CAD and Diabetes and/or Left Ventricular Systolic Dysfunction (LVSD)

Source: CMS, *Accountable Care Organization 2012 Program Analysis: Quality Performance Standards Narrative Measure Specifications* (Baltimore: Centers for Medicare & Medicaid, Quality Measurement & Health Assessment Group, 2011).

NOTES

FOREWORD

1. US Burden of Disease Collaborators, "The State of US Health, 1990–2010: Burden of Diseases, Injuries, and Risk Factors." *JAMA* 310, no. 6 (2013): 591–608.

2. S. H. Woolf, and L. Aron (eds.), *US Health in International Perspective: Shorter Lives, Poorer Health*. National Research Council and Institute of Medicine (Washington, DC: National Academies Press, 2013).

3. See, for example, M. Marmot and R. Williams (eds.), *Social Determinants of Health, 2nd edition* (Oxford: Oxford University Press, 2006); and L. F. Berkman and I. Kawachi (eds.), *Social Epidemiology* (New York: Oxford University Press, 2000).

CHAPTER 1: THE PARADOX

1. S. H. Woolf and L. Aron, eds., *U.S. Health in International Perspective: Shorter Lives, Poorer Health* (Washington, DC: National Academies Press, 2013); M. Avendano, M. M. Glymour, J. Banks, and J. Mackenbach, "Health Disadvantage in US Adults Aged 50 to 74 Years: A Comparison of the Health of Rich and Poor Americans with That of Europeans," *American Journal of Public Health* 99, no. 3 (2009): 540–48.

2. S. Tavernise, "For Americans Under 50, Stark Findings on Health," *New York Times*, January 10, 2013, A3; A. Lewis, "Al's Emporium: Dead by 50? Thank You!," *Wall Street Journal*, January 14, 2013, http://online.wsj.com/article/BT-CO-20130114-703737.html.

3. N. Glazer, "Paradoxes of Health Care," *Public Interest* 22 (1971): 62–77.

4. J. S. Skinner, D. O. Stalger, and E. S. Fisher, "Is Technological Change in Medicine Always Worth It? The Case of Acute Myocardial Infarction," *Health Affairs* 25, no. 2 (2006): W34–47.

5. C. J. Truffer et al. "Health Spending Projections Through 2019: The Recession's Impact Continues," *Health Affairs* (Millwood) 29, no. 3 (2010): 522–29.

6. CMS, *Personal Health Care Expenditures; Levels, Annual Percent Change and Percent Distribution by Source of Funds: Selected Calendar Years 1970–2011* (Atlanta, GA: Centers for Medicare & Medicaid Services, Office of the Actuary, National Health Statistics Group, 2012).

7. OECD, *Health Data 2011* (Paris, France: OECD Publishing, 2011).

8. M. Kim, R. J. Blendon, and J. M. Benson, "How Interested Are Americans in New Medical Technologies? A Multicountry Comparison," *Health Affairs* 20, no. 5 (2001): 194–201.

9. OECD, *Health Data 2011*.

10. Woolf and Aron, *U.S. Health in International Perspective*; E. H. Bradley et al., "Health and Social Services Expenditures: Associations with Health Outcomes," *BMJ Quality and Safety* 20 (2011): 826–31.

11. *Fast Facts: International Comparisons of Achievement* (Washington, DC: National Center for Education Statistics, 2011), accessed May 1, 2012, http://nces.ed.gov/fastfacts/display.asp?id=1.

12. UNESCO, *Adult and Youth Literacy* (New York: United Nations Educational, Scientific and Cultural Organization, 2012), accessed May 24, 2013, http://www.uis.unesco.org/literacy/Documents/fs20-literacy-day-2012-en-v3.pdf. Some have argued that comparing test scores and literacy rates across countries is not relevant because in non-US countries, people in school being tested may be a selected population; however, this is less true in comparisons with OECD countries. Furthermore, even at the fourth-grade level, the United States has only a middle ranking in testing scores, and this ranking becomes worse in older ages.

13. As reported by CNN on November 3, 2011, larger percentages of the populations of Australia, Belgium, Canada, Denmark, France, Ireland, Israel, Japan, Luxembourg, New Zealand, Norway, South Korea, Sweden, and the United Kingdom than of the United States had graduated from college (see http://globalpublicsquare.blogs.cnn.com/2011/11/03/how-u-s-graduation-rates-compare-with-the-rest-of-the-world/); T. Julian and R. Kominski, *Education and Synthetic Work-Life Earnings Estimates*, American Community Survey Reports (Washington, DC: United States Census Bureau, 2011); OECD, *Education at a Glance 2011: OECD Indicators* (Paris, France: OECD Publishing, 2011); T. Nachazel et al., *The Condition of Education 2011* (Washington, DC: US Department of Education, National Center for Education Statistics, 2011).

14. Although record-keeping practices may vary by country, many of the European countries and the United States follow the World Health Organization guidelines for their definitions of *live birth*. (According to the WHO, *live birth* means the complete expulsion or extraction from its mother of a product of human conception, irrespective of the duration of pregnancy, which, after such expulsion or extraction, breathes, or shows any other evidence of life such as beating of the heart, pulsation of the umbilical cord, or definite movement of voluntary muscles, whether or not the umbilical cord has been cut or the placenta is attached. Heartbeats are to be distinguished from transient cardiac contractions; respirations are to be distinguished from fleeting respiratory efforts or gasps.) Eurostat, "Population and Social Conditions: Demographic Statistics: Definitions and Methods of Collection in 31 European Countries" (Luxembourg: Eurostat, 2003), May 24, 2013, http://ec.europa.eu/eurostat/ramon/statmanuals/files/KS-CC-03-005-EN.pdf; OECD, *Infant Mortality* (Paris, France; OECD Family Database, 2012); J. Kowaleski, *State Definitions and Reporting Requirements for Live Births, Fetal Deaths, and Induced Terminations of Pregnancy*, 1997 revision (Washington, DC: National Center for Health Statistics, 1997).

15. A. de Tocqueville et al., *Democracy in America* (New York: A. A. Knopf, 1945).

16. D. D. Eisenhower, "Farewell Address," January 17, 1961, accessed May 24, 2013, http://www.pbs.org/wgbh/americanexperience/features/primary-resources/eisenhower-farewell/.

17. B. Obama, "State of the Union Address," accessed May 25, 2013, http://www.whitehouse.gov/the-press-office/2012/01/24/remarks-president-state-union-address.

18. B. Obama, "Remarks by the President on the Economy in Osawatomie, Kansas," Osawatomie, Kansas, December 6, 2011, accessed May 25, 2013, http://www.whitehouse.gov/the-press-office/2011/12/06/remarks-president-economy-osawatomie-kansas.

19. L. Charles. "The Candidates and Foreign Policy," *World Affairs*, January/February 2012, accessed May 27, 2013, http://www.worldaffairsjournal.org/article/candidates-and-foreign-policy.

20. C. Schoen et al., "How Many Are Underinsured? Trends Among US Adults, 2003 and 2007," *Health Affairs* 27, no. 4 (2008): w298–309.

21. OECD, "Health at a Glance 2009" (Paris, France: OECD Publishing, 2009).

22. B. Starfield, L. Shi, and J. Macinko, "Contribution of Primary Care to Health Systems and Health," *Milbank Quarterly* 83, no. 3 (2005): 457–502.

23. M. M. Mello et al., "National Costs of the Medical Liability System," *Health Affairs* 29, no. 9 (2010): 1569–77.

24. S. Smith, J. P. Newhouse, and M. S. Freeland, "Income, Insurance, and Technology: Why Does Health Spending Outpace Economic Growth?," *Health Affairs* 28, no. 5 (2009): 1276–84.

25. D. Card, C. Dobkin, and N. Maestas, "The Impact of Nearly Universal Insurance Coverage on Health Care Utilization and Health: Evidence from Medicare" (New York:

National Bureau of Economic Research, 2004); some studies, particularly those regarding providing insurance for children, have found cost increases but of more modest magnitude. See J. Zwanziger et al., "Evaluating Child Health Plus in Upstate New York: How Much Does Providing Health Insurance to Uninsured Children Increase Health Care Costs?" *Pediatrics* 105, no. 3, suppl. E (2000): 728–32; J. L. Holl et al., "Covering the Uninsured: How Much Would It Cost?," *Health Affairs* 22, no. 3, suppl. (2003): 3–250.

26. Woolf and Aron, *U.S. Health in International Perspective.*

27. J. Bernstein et al., *Medical Homes: Will They Improve Primary Care?* (Princeton, NJ: Mathematica Policy Research, Inc., 2010); G. R. Martsolf et al., "The Patient-Centered Medical Home and Patient Experience," *Health Services Research* 47, no. 6 (2012): 2273–95; R. S. Brown et al., "Six Features of Medicare Coordinated Care Demonstration Programs That Cut Hospital Admissions of High-Risk Patients," *Health Affairs* 31, no. 6 (2012): 1156–66.

28. N. Kaye, J. Buxbaum, and M. Takach, *Building Medical Homes: Lessons from Eight States with Emerging Programs* (New York and Washington, DC: The Commonwealth Fund, 2011).

29. R. A. Paulus, K. Davis, and G. D. Steele, "Continuous Innovation in Health Care: Implications of the Geisinger Experience," *Health Affairs* (Millwood) 27, no. 5 (2008): 1235–45.

30. The Lewin Group, *Medicaid Managed Care Cost Savings—A Synthesis of 24 Studies* (Falls Church, VA: The Lewin Group, March 2009), accessed May 24, 2013, http://www .lewin.com/publications/publication/395/.

31. D. Peikes et al., "Effects of Care Coordination on Hospitalization, Quality of Care, and Health Care Expenditures Among Medicare Beneficiaries: 15 Randomized Trials," *JAMA* 301, no. 6 (2009): 603–18.

32. R. S. Brown et al., "Six Features of Medicare Coordinated Care Demonstration Programs That Cut Hospital Admissions of High-Risk Patients," *Health Affairs* 31, no. 6 (2012): 1156–66.

33. T. Lincoln, *A Failed Experiment: Health Care in Texas Has Worsened in Key Respects Since State Instituted Liability Caps in 2003* (Washington, DC: Public Citizen, 2011).

34. Census Bureau, *Health Insurance Coverage Status and Type of Coverage by State—All Persons: 1999 to 2010* (Washington, DC: US Census Bureau, 2011).

35. M. A. Hlatky et al., "Utilization and Outcomes of the Implantable Cardioverter Defibrillator, 1987 to 1995," *American Heart Journal* 144, no. 3 (2002): 397–403.

36. B. L. Jacobs et al., "Growth of High-Cost Intensity-Modulated Radiotherapy for Prostate Cancer Raises Concerns About Overuse," *Health Affairs* (Millwood) 31, no. 4 (2012): 750–59.

37. J. Carreyrou and M. Tamman, "A Device to Kill Cancer, Lift Revenue," *Wall Street Journal*, December 7, 2010, accessed May 24, 2013, http://online.wsj.com/article/SB100014 24052748703904804575631222900534954.html. Evidence suggests that IMRT results less damage to surrounding tissue; however, the experienced improvement in health and the cost-effectiveness of this approach is not yet fully known. For more literature on IMRT, see J. C. Hodges et al., "Cost-Effectiveness Analysis of SBRT Versus IMRT: An Emerging Initial Radiation Treatment Option for Organ-Confined Prostate Cancer," *American Journal of Managed Care* 18, no. 5 (2012): e186–93; P. L. Nguyen et al., "Cost Implications of the Rapid Adoption of Newer Technologies for Treating Prostate Cancer," *Journal of Clinical Oncology* 29, no. 12 (2011): 1517–24; D. J. Sher et al., "Cost-Effectiveness Analysis of SBRT Versus IMRT for Low-Risk Prostate Cancer," *American Journal of Clinical Oncology* (2012); S. Hummel et al., "Intensity-Modulated Radiotherapy for the Treatment of Prostate Cancer: A Systematic Review And Economic Evaluation," *Health Technology Assessment* 14, no. 47 (October 2010):1–108.

38. D. Callahan, "Health Technology Assessment Implementation: The Politics of Ethics," *Medical Decision Making* 32, no. 1 (2012): E13–19.

39. M. Marmot, "Social Determinants of Health Inequalities," *Lancet* 365, no. 9464 (2005): 1099–1104; M. G. Marmot and R. G. Wilkinson, *Social Determinants of Health*, 2nd ed. (Oxford and New York: Oxford University Press, 2006), x, 366; E. McGibbon, "Health

and Health Care: A Human Rights Perspective," in *Social Determinants of Health: Canadian Perspectives*, ed. D. Raphael (Toronto: Canadian Scholars' Press Inc., 2008), 318–35; R. G. Wilkinson and M. Marmot, eds. *The Solid Facts: Social Determinants of Health*, 2nd ed. (Copenhagen, Denmark: World Health Organization, 2003), 33; R. F. Schoeni et al., *Making Americans Healthier: Social and Economic Policy As Health Policy* (New York: Russell Sage Foundation, 2010).

40. Marmot and Wilkinson, *Social Determinants of Health*.

41. Ibid.

42. Schoeni et al., *Making Americans Healthier*; M. Wen, C. R. Browning, and K. A. Cagney, "Poverty, Affluence, and Income Inequality: Neighborhood Economic Structure and Its Implications for Health," *Social Science & Medicine* 57, no. 5 (2003): 843–60; D. L. Crooks, "American Children at Risk: Poverty and Its Consequences for Children's Health, Growth, and School Achievement," *American Journal of Physical Anthropology* 38, suppl. 21 (1995): 57–86; E. Brunner, "Socioeconomic Determinants of Health-Stress and the Biology of Inequality," *BMJ* 314, no. 7092 (1997): 1472–76; N. Kaye, C. H. Sharman, and J. Rosenthal, *Chronic Homelessness and High Users of Health Services: Report from a Meeting to Explore a Strategy for Reducing Medicaid Spending While Improving Care* (Washington, DC: National Academy for State Health Policy, 2008); B. D. Smedley and S. L. Syme, *Promoting Health: Intervention Strategies from Social and Behavioral Research* (Washington, DC: National Academies Press, 2000).

43. M. R. Cullen, C. Cummins, and V. R. Fuchs, "Geographic and Racial Variation in Premature Mortality in the U.S.: Analyzing the Disparities," *PLoS One* 7, no. 4 (2012): e32930.

44. E. A. Platz et al., "Proportion of Colon Cancer Risk That Might Be Preventable in a Cohort of Middle-Aged US Men," *Cancer Causes and Control* 11, no. 7 (2000): 579–88.

45. M. J. Stampfer et al., "Primary Prevention of Coronary Heart Disease in Women Through Diet and Lifestyle," *New England Journal of Medicine* 343, no. 1 (2000): 16–22.

46. Ibid.

47. F. B. Hu et al., "Diet, Lifestyle, and the Risk of Type 2 Diabetes Mellitus in Women," *New England Journal of Medicine* 345, no. 11 (2001): 790–97.

48. R. M. Whyatt et al., "Prenatal Insecticide Exposures and Birth Weight and Length Among an Urban Minority Cohort," *Environmental Health Perspectives* 112, no. 10 (2004): 1125–32.

49. C. A. Pope III et al., "Lung Cancer, Cardiopulmonary Mortality, and Long-Term Exposure to Fine Particulate Air Pollution," *JAMA* 287, no. 9 (2002): 1132–41.

50. E. Sabath and M. L. Robles-Osorio, "Renal Health and the Environment: Heavy Metal Nephrotoxicity," *Nefrologia* 3, no. 3 (2012): 279–86.

51. R. Zeig-Owens et al., "Early Assessment of Cancer Outcomes in New York City Firefighters After the 9/11 Attacks: An Observational Cohort Study," *Lancet* 378, no. 9794 (2011): 898–905.

52. M. Marmot, "Social Determinants of Health Inequalities."

53. For further discussion of this point, see J. M. McGinnis, P. Williams-Russo, and J. R. Knickman, "The Case for More Active Policy Attention to Health Promotion," *Health Affairs* 21, no. 2 (2002): 78–93; D. R. Williams, M. B. McClellan, and A. M. Rivlin, "Beyond the Affordable Care Act: Achieving Real Improvements in Americans' Health," *Health Affairs* 29, no. 8 (2010): 1481–88.

54. H. Hall, "Donations Barely Grew at All Last Year, 'Giving USA' Finds," *The Chronicle of Philanthropy* (2012); Independent Sector, "The Sector's Economic Impact" (Washington, DC: Independent Sector, 2012), accessed May 24, 2013, http://www.independentsector.org /economic_role.

55. HUD, *The 2009 Annual Homeless Assessment Report to Congress* (US Department of Housing and Urban Development, 2010).

56. A. Coleman-Jensen et al., *Household Food Security in the United States in 2010* (Washington, DC: US Department of Agriculture, Economic Research Service, 2011), 37.

57. V. Oliveira, *Food & Nutrition Assistance* (Washington, DC: Economic Research Service, US Department of Agriculture, 2012), accessed May 24, 2013, http://www.ers.usda.gov/topics/food-nutrition-assistance#.UV48vatoRTM.

58. C. Duhigg, "Millions in U.S. Drink Dirty Water, Records Show," *New York Times*, December 8, 2009, A1.

59. Bradley et al., "Health and Social Services Expenditures."

60. Some readers may be interested to consider the size of private philanthropy for social services and for health services. In 2007, according to the *Chronicle of Philanthropy* (March 30, 2011), philanthropic giving in the United States totaled about $310 billion. About $100 billion of this was directed to social services, and $25 billion was directed at health services. By way of contrast, the total of public and private spending for social services and for health spending was $1.2 trillion and $2.3 trillion, respectively, in 2007, demonstrating that the philanthropic portion of these social investments is modest. The Sector's Economic Impact, 2012, accessed May 28, 2013, http://www.independentsector.org/economic_role; H. Hall, "Donations Barely Grew at All Last Year, 'Giving USA' Finds, *The Chronicle of Philanthropy*, March 30, 2011; OECD, StatExtracts (Paris, France: OECD Publishing, 2012), accessed May 28, 2013, http://stats.oecd.org/.

61. We used 2007 data because it was the most recent year with comprehensive data on all expenditures and health outcomes.

62. Bradley et al., "Health and Social Services Expenditures."

63. Ibid.

64. The OECD data itemizes long-term care (such as nursing home care and home care), and we consistently classified it within health care spending.

CHAPTER 2: HISTORICAL PERSPECTIVES

1. J. H. Warner, *The Therapeutic Perspective: Medical Practice, Knowledge, and Identity in America, 1820–1885* (Princeton, NJ: Princeton University Press, 1997), xiv, 365.

2. J. M. Barry, *The Great Influenza: The Epic Story of the Deadliest Plague in History*, (New York: Penguin Books, 2005), 546.

3. R. Porter, *The Greatest Benefit to Mankind: A Medical History of Humanity*, 1st American ed. (New York: W. W. Norton, 1998), 681.

4. Warner, *The Therapeutic Perspective*.

5. C. E. Rosenberg, *The Care of Strangers: The Rise of America's Hospital System* (Baltimore, MD: Johns Hopkins University Press, 1995), x, 437.

6. Ibid.

7. P. Starr, *The Social Transformation of American Medicine* (New York: Basic Books, 1982), 55.

8. Ibid., xiv, 514.

9. For more information on this history, see Porter, *The Greatest Benefit to Mankind*.

10. K. M. Ludmerer, *Time to Heal: American Medical Education from the Turn of the Century to the Era of Managed Care* (Oxford and New York: Oxford University Press, 1999), xxvi, 514.

11. M. J. Zinner and K. R. Loughlin, "The Evolution of Health Care in America," *Urologic Clinics of North America* 36, no. 1 (2009): v, 1–10.

12. For more on the reform of medical education, see Barry, *The Great Influenza*, ch. 1 and 2, or Starr, *The Social Transformation of American Medicine*, ch. 2.

13. R. Stevens, *In Sickness and in Wealth: American Hospitals in the Twentieth Century* (Baltimore, MD: Johns Hopkins University Press, 1999), xxxviii, 432.

14. Ibid.

15. R. A. Kessel, "The A.M.A. and the Supply of Physicians," *Law and Contemporary Problems* 35 (1970): 267–83.

16. Rosenberg, *The Care of Strangers*.

17. Stevens, *In Sickness and in Wealth*.

18. Ibid.

19. Ibid.

20. In 1929, health care spending was 3.6 percent of GDP; by the 1990s, it was more than 16 percent of GDP. N. L. Worthington, "National Health Expenditures, 1929–74," *Social Security Bulletin* 38 (1975): 3; Centers for Medicare & Medicaid Services, Office of the Actuary, "National Health Expenditure (NHE) Amounts by Type of Service and Source of Funds: Calendar Years 1960–2008," last updated January 20, 2010, accessed January 15, 2013, http://www.cms.hhs.gov/NationalHealthExpendData/downloads/nhe2008.zip.

21. Porter, *The Greatest Benefit to Mankind*, 629.

22. J. Schiller et al., "Summary Health Statistics for US Adults: National Health Interview Survey, 2010," *Vital Health Statistics* 10, no. 252 (2012): 1.

23. C. J. Truffer et al., "Health Spending Projections Through 2019: The Recession's Impact Continues," *Health Affairs* 29, no. 3 (2010): 522–29.

24. R. Cunningham and R. M. Cunningham, *The Blues: A History of the Blue Cross and Blue Shield System* (DeKalb, IL: Northern Illinois University Press, 1997).

25. Ibid.

26. Ibid.

27. P. Flora and A. J. Heidenheimer, *The Development of Welfare States in Europe and America* (New Brunswick, NJ: Transaction Books, 1981), 417.

28. Starr, *The Social Transformation of American Medicine*.

29. Ibid.

30. Porter, *The Greatest Benefit to Mankind*.

31. *New York Evening Post*, quoted in *JAMA*, 99, no. 24 (1932): 2035.

32. M. R. Grey, *New Deal Medicine: The Rural Health Programs of the Farm Security Administration* (Baltimore, MD: Johns Hopkins University Press, 1999), xvii, 238.

33. "The Nation on Civil War in AMA," *California and Western Medicine* 47, no. 6 (1937): 432–33.

34. Grey, *New Deal Medicine*.

35. Ibid.; Starr, *The Social Transformation of American Medicine*.

36. K. Doherty and J. A. Jenkins, "Examining a Failed Moment: National Health Care, the AMA, and the U.S. Congress, 1948–50," paper prepared for the Annual Meeting of the Southern Political Science Association, New Orleans, LA, 2009.

37. Starr, *The Social Transformation of American Medicine*.

38. Ibid.

39. Porter, *The Greatest Benefit to Mankind*.

40. L. Shi and D. A. Singh, *Delivering Health Care in America* (Burlington. MA: Jones & Bartlett Learning, 2011); *Statistical Abstract of the United States: Vital Statistics 2012* (Washington, DC, US Census Bureau, 2012).

41. CMS, "National Health Expenditures, Selected Calendar Years 1960–2011" (Baltimore, MD: Centers for Medicare & Medicaid Services, n.d.), accessed May 28, 2013, http://cms.gov/Research-Statistics-Data-and-Systems/Statistics-Trends-and-Reports/NationalHealthExpendData/Downloads/tables.pdf.

42. People with end-stage renal disease (ESRD) were added as beneficiaries to Medicare in 1972 after successful lobbying of Congress by the National Kidney Foundation. For a more detailed history, see G. E. Schreiner, "How End-Stage Renal Disease (ESRD)-Medicare Developed," *American Journal of Kidney Diseases* 35, no. 4, suppl. (2000): S37–44.

43. P. M. Ellwood, *Assuring the Quality of Health Care* (Minneapolis, MN: InterStudy Center, 1973).

44. P. R. Kongstvedt, *Essentials of Managed Health Care*, 5th ed. (Sudbury, MA: Jones & Bartlett Publishers, 2007), xxi, 841.

45. M. S. Foster, *Henry J. Kaiser: Builder in the Modern American West*, American Studies (Austin: University of Texas Press, 1989).

46. M. Allen, "Declining HMO Market Has Blue Cross Mulling Options," *St. Louis Business Journal*, July 27, 2008, http://www.bizjournals.com/stlouis/stories/2008/07/28/story8.html.

47. D. Austin, *Human Services Management: Organizational Leadership in Social Work Practice* (New York: Columbia University Press, 2012).

48. Flora and Heidenheimer, *The Development of Welfare States*; C. Howard, "Is The American Welfare State Unusually Small?," *PS: Political Science & Politics* 36, no. 3 (2003): 411–16; OECD, *Society at a Glance 2011*, OECD Social Indicators (Paris, France: OECD Publishing, 2011); D. Rice and B. Sard, *Decade of Neglect Has Weakened Federal Low-Income Housing Programs—New Resources Required to Meet Growing Needs* (Washington, DC: Center on Budget and Policy Priorities, 2009); US Department of Labor, *Fair Labor Standard Act Advisor* (Washington, DC: US Department of Labor, 2010); K. Battle, *Restoring Minimum Wages in Canada* (Ottawa, ON: Caledon Institute of Social Policy, 2011).

Professor Christopher Howard, professor of government at the College of William and Mary, has argued that conventional measures of American government program spending underestimate the actual size of the American welfare state, suggesting that policies related to housing tax breaks, minimum wage legislation, and tort law confer additional "hidden welfare benefits." Nevertheless, even with these benefits added in, the United States' investment in social welfare is more limited than that of most other OECD countries, and much of its benefits accrue largely to people in the middle of the socioeconomic gradient rather than to people with lower income, who are most in need.

For instance, in 2008, the three largest housing-related tax breaks cost the US Treasury about $144 billion, according to the Center on Budget and Policy Priorities, but 70 percent of these tax break benefits accrued to households with income exceeding $100,000, suggesting that these benefits are largely absorbed by people with higher incomes who may not be in need of social assistance. C. Howard, "Is The American Welfare State Unusually Small?," *PS: Political Science & Politics* 36, no. 3 (2003): 411–16; OECD, "Society at a Glance 2011" (Paris, France, OECD Social Indicators, 2011); D. Rice and B. Sard, "Decade of Neglect Has Weakened Federal Low-Income Housing Programs—New Resources Required to Meet Growing Needs" (Washington, DC: Center on Budget and Policy Priorities, 2009); United States Department of Labor, *Fair Labor Standard Act Advisor* (Washington, DC: US Department of Labor, 2010); K. Battle, "Restoring Minimum Wages in Canada" (Ottawa, ON: Caledon Institute of Social Policy, 2011).

49. Flora and Heidenheimer, *The Development of Welfare States*; M. J. Graetz and J. L. Mashaw, *True Security: Rethinking American Social Insurance*, Yale ISPS Series 1999 (New Haven, CT: Yale University Press, 1999), x, 369.

50. W. I. Trattner, *From Poor Law to Welfare State: A History of Social Welfare in America* (New York: Free Press, 1974), xii, 276.

51. Ibid.; J. Axinn and H. Levin, *Social Welfare: A History of the American Response to Need* (New York: Harper & Row, 1975).

52. Trattner, *From Poor Law to Welfare State*.

53. Ibid.

54. J. V. Yates, "Report of the Secretary of State in 1824 on the Relief and Settlement of the Poor," *The Almshouse Experience: Collected Reports* (New York: Arno Press, 1971), 942, 951–52, 958.

55. Trattner, *From Poor Law to Welfare State*, xxxix, 424.

56. P. F. Pierce, "Veto Message, an Act Making a Grant of Public Lands to the Several States for the Benefit of Indigent Insane Persons," May 3, 1854, Washington, DC, http://www.lonang.com/exlibris/misc/1854-pvm.htm.

57. Yates, "Report of the Secretary of State."

58. L. M. Salamon and H. K. Anheier, *Defining the Nonprofit Sector: The United States* (Baltimore, MD: Institute for Policy Studies, Johns Hopkins University, 1996).

59. W. A. Nielsen, *The Endangered Sector* (New York: Columbia University Press, 1979).

60. A. Lincoln, Second Inaugural Address, March 4, 1865, http://avalon.law.yale.edu/19th_century/lincoln2.asp.

61. For more detail on this increasing economic disparity, see Axinn and Levin, *Social Welfare*.

62. Ibid., 89–99.

63. M. B. Katz, *In the Shadow of the Poorhouse: A Social History of Welfare in America*, 10th ann. ed. (New York: Basic Books, 1996), xvii, 391.

64. Ibid.

65. H. Sitkoff and University of New Hampshire Dept. of History, *Fifty Years Later: The New Deal Evaluated*, 1st ed. (Philadelphia: Temple University Press, 1985).

66. M. B. Katz, *The Price of Citizenship: Redefining the American Welfare State*, updated ed. (Philadelphia: University of Pennsylvania Press, 2008), 518.

CHAPTER 3: FRONT-LINE INSIGHTS

1. P. Q. Patton, *Qualitative Research & Evaluation Methods* (Thousand Oaks, CA: SAGE Publications, 2002).

2. AHA, *Fast Facts on US Hospitals* (Chicago, IL: American Hospital Association, 2012), accessed January 3, 2012, http://www.aha.org/research/rc/stat-studies/fast-facts.shtml.

3. R. Porter, *The Greatest Benefit to Mankind: A Medical History of Humanity*, 1st American ed. (New York: W. W. Norton, 1998), 671.

4. A. Gottschalk and S. A. Flocke, "Time Spent in Face-to-Face Patient Care and Work Outside the Examination Room," *Annals of Family Medicine* 3, no. 6 (2005): 488–93.

5. *Health Care's Blind Side: The Overlooked Connection Between Social Needs and Good Health* (summary of findings from a survey of America's physicians) (Princeton, NJ: Robert Wood Johnson Foundation, 2011).

6. Ibid.

7. Interview #6.

8. Interview #17.

9. Interview #5.

10. Interview #11.

11. Interview #5.

12. Ibid.

13. Ibid.

14. Interview #11.

15. Interview #25.

16. Interview #1.

17. Interview #6.

18. J. C. C. Hollingsworth et al., "How Do Physicians and Nurses Spend Their Time in the Emergency Department?," *Annals of Emergency Medicine* 31, no. 1 (1998): 87–91.

19. L. Kane, *Medscape Physician Compensation Report: 2012 Results*, MedScape 2012, accessed February 15, 2013, http://www.medscape.com/features/slideshow/compensation/2012/public.

20. Gottschalk and Flocke, "Time Spent in Face-to-Face Patient Care."

21. I. Morrison and R. Smith, "Hamster Health Care," *BMJ* 321, no. 7276, (2000): 1541–42.

22. Kane, *Medscape Physician Compensation Report*.

23. K. S. H. Yarnall et al., "Family Physicians as Team Leaders: 'Time' to Share the Care," *Prevention of Chronic Disease* 6, no. 2 (2009).

24. Interview #31.

25. Interview #25.

26. Interview #21.

27. Interview #1.

28. Preamble to the Constitution of the World Health Organization as adopted by the International Health Conference, New York, June, 19–22, 1946; signed on July 22, 1946, by the representatives of sixty-one states and entered into force on April 7, 1948 (New York: World Health Organization), Official Records, no. 2, 100.

29. F. W. Peabody, *The Care of the Patient* (Cambridge, MA: Harvard University Press, 1927).

30. "New England Hospital Association: Sixth Annual Meeting, May 5 and 6, 1927," *Boston Medical and Surgical Journal* 197, no. 19 (1927): 836–58.

31. Interview #15.

32. Interview #17.

33. Interview #1.

34. E. H. Guarneri, B. J. Horrigan, and C. M. Pechura, *The Efficacy and Cost Effectiveness of Integrative Medicine: A Review of the Medical and Corporate Literature* (Minneapolis, MN: The Bravewell Collaborative, June 2010), 8.

35. Interview #15.

36. Interview #17.

37. Interview #9.

38. Interview #6.

39. Interview #15.

40. Interview #1.

41. Ibid.

42. Interview #6.

43. For a full review of the distinctions and their history, see D. Austin, *Human Services Management: Organizational Leadership in Social Work Practices* (New York: Columbia University Press, 2002), 229–320.

44. Interview #3.

45. Interview #25.

46. Interview #1.

47. Interview #21.

48. Interview #9.

49. Interview #6.

50. Interview #25.

51. Ibid.

52. Interview #14.

53. R. S. Watson and M. E. Hartman, "Epidemiology of Children Receiving Critical Care Services," in *Pediatric Critical Care Medicine: Basic Science and Clinical Evidence*, ed. D. S. Wheeler, H. R. Wong, and T. P. Shanley (New York: Springer, 2007), 32; L. G. Cooper et al., "Impact of a Family-Centered Care Initiative on NICU Care, Staff and Families," *Journal of Perinatology* 27 (2008): 532–37.

54. J. Muraskas and K. Parsi, "The Cost of Saving the Tiniest Lives: NICUs Versus Prevention," *American Medical Association Journal of Ethics* 10, no. 10 (2008): 655–58.

55. Interview #14.

CHAPTER 4: LEARNING FROM ABROAD

1. For a full exploration of the Scandinavian model including its application to broad concerns of social welfare, see R. Erikson, *The Scandinavian Model: Welfare States and Welfare Research*, Comparative Public Policy Analysis (Armonk, NY: M. E. Sharpe, 1987), xi, 251. For a detailed analysis of its practical influence on Nordic health systems, as well as a discussion of variations in approaches across the Nordic countries, see J. Magnussen, K. Vrangbaek, and R. Saltman, *Nordic Health Care Systems: Recent Reforms and Current Policy Challenges*, European Observatory on Health Care Systems (Maidenhead, Berkshire, UK: Open University Press, 2009); G. Esping-Anderson and W. Korpi, "From Poor Relief to Institutional Welfare States: The Development of the Scandinavian Social Policy," in R. Erikson, *The Scandinavian Model*; B. Guldvog, "Strengthening Quality of Care in Four Nordic Countries," *Scandinavian Journal of Public Health* 37, no. 2 (2009): 111–16.

2. Despite the high availability of physicians and hospitals, in Scandinavia, medical salaries are far lower than those in the United States, and overall costs of care are managed at local and county governments to contain costs. WHO, *World Health Statistics 2012* (Copenhagen, Denmark: World Health Organization Global Health Observatory, 2012), 120–31. This number was calculated by using the number of doctors per one thousand of population and the total population to determine the total number of doctors in each Scandinavian country.

3. Cohen, R., and Martinez, M. *Health Insurance Coverage: Early Release of Estimates from the National Health Interview Survey, 2012.* Centers for Disease Control & Prevention, June 2013. www.cdc.gov.nchs/data/nhis/earlyrelease/insur201306.pdf

4. S. P. Keehan et al., "National Health Expenditure Projections: Modest Annual Growth Until Coverage Expands and Economic Growth Accelerates," *Health Affairs* 31, no. 7 (2012): 1600–1612.

5. M. Tanner, *The Grass is Not Always Greener: A Look at National Health Care Systems Around the World,* Policy Analysis (Washington, DC: Cato Institute, 2008), 613.

6. *World Values Survey,* 2005–2008 (Stockholm, Sweden: World Values Survey Association, 2012), accessed May 31, 2013, http://www.worldvaluessurvey.org/.

7. T. Dalrymple, "Britain's Cherished, Lousy National Health Service," *Los Angeles Times,* August 10, 2012; P. Wehner and P. Ryan, "Beware of the Big-Government Tipping Point: Socialized Health Care Fundamentally Changes the Relationship Between Citizens and State," *Wall Street Journal,* January 16, 2009, Opinion section.

8. For a summary of all survey items and responses for the US and Scandinavia, see Appendix B.

9. The World Values Survey is the best available international comparative data on values. Nevertheless, different cultures may interpret such terms as "personal freedom" or "the right" differently, and hence the comparisons should be interpreted in light of such limitations; regardless, broad patterns emerge and are informative.

10. This root is apparent in the writing of Thomas Jefferson at the early dawn of the country in 1774; Jefferson wrote, "The God who gave us life gave us liberty at the same time." See *A Summary View of the Rights of British America,* the Avalon Project: Documents in Law, History and Diplomacy 1774 (New Haven, CT: Yale University, 2009).

11. Interview #65.

12. D. A. Squires, *Explaining High Health Care Spending in the United States: An International Comparison of Supply, Utilization, Prices, and Quality* (New York and Washington, DC: The Commonwealth Fund, 2012); D. P. Ly and D. M. Cutler, "The (Paper)Work of Medicine: Understanding International Medical Costs," *Journal of Economic Perspectives* 25, no. 2 (2011): 3–25.

13. NSF, "Research and Development: National Trends and International Linkages," in *Science and Engineering Indicators: 2010* (Arlington, VA: National Science Foundation, 2010), Table 4–11.

14. NSF, "Research and Development: National Trends and International Linkages," in *Science and Engineering Indicators: 2010* (Arlington, VA: National Science Foundation, 2010), Table 4–18. Also, J. A. Ginsburg et al. "Achieving a High-Performance Health Care System with Universal Access: What Can the US Learn from Other Countries?" *Annals of Internal Medicare,* 148, no. 1 (2008), 55–75.

15. In many of these values, the United Kingdom and Canada fell somewhere between the United States and the Scandinavian countries.

16. J. J. Rousseau, *Of the Social Contract, or Principles of Political Right & Discourse on Political Economy,* trans. C. M. Sherover, 1st ed. (New York: Harper & Row, 1984), xl, 226.

17. For more on the social contract, see Erikson, *The Scandinavian Model.*

18. Erikson, *The Scandinavian Model.*

19. Interview #69.

20. Erikson, *The Scandinavian Model.*

21. Interview #32.

22. Interview #68.

23. Early-twentieth-century welfare efforts, particularly in health, were viewed within the doctrine of mercantilism. Healthy people brought wealth to the nation, and because many infectious diseases affected wealthy and poor, investment in public health efforts to limit such diseases were in the national interest. Much of this draws upon N. Kildal and S. Kuhnle, *The Principle of Universalism: Tracing a Key Idea in the Scandinavian Welfare Model,* 9th International Congress, Geneva, Switzerland, September 12–14, 2002. This approach was first documented for Americans in 1936 by reporter Marquis Childs, in his book *Sweden: The Middle Way* (New Haven, CT: Yale University Press, 1936), and revisited by the Swedish Institute for Social Research in Stockholm; see Erikson, *The Scandinavian Model.*

24. Interview #32.

25. Interview #66.

26. For more in-depth discussion of the historical and cultural underpinnings of the social welfare state in Scandinavia, see Erikson, *The Scandinavian Model*, xi, 251; and Kildal and Kuhnle, *The Principle of Universalism*.

27. R. Reagan, "The President's News Conference," August 12, 1986, Chicago, IL, *The American Presidency Project*, http://www.presidency.ucsb.edu/ws/?pid=37733.

28. Interview #34.

29. H. Fineman, *The Thirteen American Arguments: Enduring Debates That Define and Inspire Our Country* (New York: Random House, 2009), 98–99.

30. Interview #66.

31. J. Donne, *Devotions upon Emergent Occasions* (Ann Arbor: University of Michigan Press, 1959), li, 188.

32. Fineman, *The Thirteen American Arguments*.

33. THF, *The Auto Bailout: It's Not Something to Celebrate* (Washington, DC: The Heritage Foundation, 2012).

34. Fineman, *The Thirteen American Arguments*.

35. C. J. Sykes, *A Nation of Moochers: America's Addiction to Getting Something for Nothing*, 1st ed. (New York: St. Martin's Press, 2012), x, 307.

36. Interview #21.

37. Interview #37.

38. Ibid.

39. F. G. Castles, "Social Expenditure in the 1990s: Data and Determinants," *Policy and Politics* 33, no. 3 (2005): 411–30.

40. J. Sipilä and A. Anttonen, "European Social Care Services: Is It Possible to Identify Models?," *Journal of European Social Policy* 6, no. 87 (1996): 87–100.

41. Interview #68.

42. The Gini coefficient in this context is a measure of income inequality. A Gini coefficient of zero expresses perfect equality, where all values are the same. A Gini coefficient of one (100 on the percentile scale) expresses maximal inequality among values; R. V. Burkhauser et al., "Estimating Trends in US Income Inequality Using the Current Population Survey: The Importance of Controlling for Censoring," *Journal of Economic Inequality* 9 (2011): 393–415; Census Bureau, *Historical Income Tables: Income Inequality Table H-4* (Washington, DC: US Census Bureau, 2011); OECD, *OECD Factbook 2011–2012* (Paris, France: OECD Publishing, 2011).

43. C. DeNavas-Walt, B. D. Proctor, and J. C. Smith, *Income, Poverty, and Health Insurance Coverage in the United States: 2011* (Washington, DC: US Census Bureau, 2012), 60–243.

44. L. Levine, *An Analysis of the Distribution of Wealth Across Households, 1989–2010* (Washington, DC: Congressional Research Service, 2012).

45. DeNavas-Walt, Proctor, and Smith, *Income, Poverty, and Health Insurance Coverage*.

46. R. Sturm and C. R. Gresenz, "Relations of Income Inequality and Family Income to Chronic Medical Conditions and Mental Health Disorders: National Survey," *BMJ* 324, no. 7328 (2002): 20–23; I. Kawachi et al., "Social Capital, Income Inequality, and Mortality," *American Journal of Public Health* 87, no. 9 (1997): 1491–98; E. Weede, "Income Inequality, Average Income, and Domestic Violence," *Journal of Conflict Resolution* 25, no. 4 (1981): 639–54; K. Deininger and L. Squire, "Economic Growth and Income Inequality: Reexamining the Links," *Finance & Development* (1997): 38–41; P. Aghion, E. Caroli, and C. García-Peñalosa, "Inequality and Economic Growth: The Perspective of the New Growth Theories," *Journal of Economic Literature* 37, no. 4 (1999): 1615–60.

47. R. G. Wilkinson and K. Pickett, *The Spirit Level: Why Greater Equality Makes Societies Stronger* (New York: Bloomsbury Press, 2010), xv, 330.

48. R. D. Putnam, *Bowling Alone: The Collapse and Revival of American Community* (New York: Simon & Schuster, 2001).

49. M. I. Norton and D. Ariely, "Building a Better America—One Wealth Quintile at a Time," *Perspectives on Psychological Science* 6, no. 1 (2011): 9–12.

50. Ibid.

51. J. Heskett, "Income Inequality: What's the Right Amount?," *Working Knowledge* (Cambridge, MA: Harvard Business School, 2012), accessed May 31, 2013, http://hbswk.hbs .edu/item/6903.html.

52. J. Cullen, *The American Dream: A Short History of an Idea That Shaped a Nation* (Oxford and New York: Oxford University Press, 2003), x, 47, 60, 214.

53. Ibid.

54. G. Solon, "Cross-Country Differences in Intergenerational Earnings Mobility," *Journal of Economic Perspectives* 16, no. 2 (2002): 59–66; M. Jäntti et al., *American Exceptionalism in a New Light: A Comparison of Intergenerational Earnings Mobility in the Nordic Countries, the United Kingdom and the United States*, IZA Discussion Paper No. 1938 (Bonn, Germany: IZA [Institute for the Study of Labor], 2006).

55. V. Griffith, "The Myth of Upward Mobility," *The Financial Times*, January 21, 2001, Weekend section.

56. Solon, "Cross-Country Differences."

57. In his New Year's Address on January 1, 2013, by the prime minister of Norway, Jens Stoltenberg, agreed with the notion that the American Dream may be easier to achieve in Norway, saying, "The Americans have their American Dream. We have the Norwegian model. Our model may not sound as exciting, but it makes up for this by providing security. In a society where freedom goes hand in hand with security, more people are able to realize their dreams. What I am saying is this: It is easier to realize the American Dream in Norway than it is in America. We should be proud of this." (Oslo, Norway: Office of the Prime Minister, 2013), accessed February 27, 2013, http://www.regjeringen.no/en/dep/smk/Whats-new /Speeches-and-articles/statsministeren/statsminister_jens_stoltenberg/2013/prime-minister -jens-stoltenbergs-new-yea.html?id=710868.

58. P. Smith and M. Polanyi, "Social Norms, Social Behaviours and Health: An Empirical Examination of a Model of Social Capital," *Australian and New Zealand Journal of Public Health* 27, no. 4 (2003): 456–63; C. Mansyur et al., "Social Capital, Income Inequality, and Self-Rated Health in 45 Countries," *Social Science & Medicine* 66, no. 1 (2008): 43–56; M. H. Jen et al., "Trustful Societies, Trustful Individuals, and Health: An Analysis of Self-Rated Health and Social Trust Using the World Value Survey," *Health & Place* 16, no. 5 (2010): 1022–29.

59. Interview #41.

60. Gates Foundation, *Building Better Lives Together: 2011 Annual Report*, 2012 (Seattle, WA: Bill & Melinda Gates Foundation, 2012). *Who We Are: Annual Letter 2010* (Seattle, WA: Bill & Melinda Gates Foundation, 2010), accessed May 30, 2013, http://www.gates foundation.org/who-we-are/resources-and-media/annual-letters-list/annual-letter-2010.

61. Interview #32.

62. Interview #69.

63. "Towards Public Health on Equal Terms—National Goals for Public Health," *Scandinavian Journal of Public Health* 57, suppl. (2001): 1–68.

64. Interview #33.

65. D. Callahan, *False Hopes: Why America's Quest for Perfect Health Is a Recipe for Failure* (New York: Simon & Schuster, 1998), 330.

66. Winthrop-University Hospital, *About Us: Mission* (Mineola, NY: Winthrop-University Hospital, 2012), accessed May 30, 2013, http://www.winthrop.org/aboutus/mission/.

67. Interview #68.

68. H. G. Welch, "The Medicalization of Life," *Los Angeles Times*, March 15, 2010, Opinion section.

69. R. Kukla and K. Wayne, "Pregnancy, Birth, and Medicine," *The Stanford Encyclopedia of Philosophy* (2011), E. N. Zalta, editor.

70. P. Conrad, *Identifying Hyperactive Children: The Medicalization of Deviant Behavior* (Farnham, Surrey, UK: Ashgate, 2006).

71. J. D. McCue, "The Naturalness of Dying," *JAMA* 273, no. 13 (1995): 1039–43.

72. S. B. Nuland, *How We Die: Reflections on Life's Final* Chapter (New York: Vintage, 1995).

73. P. Conrad, T. Mackie, and A. Mehrotra, "Estimating the Costs of Medicalization," *Social Science & Medicine* 70, no. 12 (2010): 1943–47.

74. A. A. Scitovsky, "'The High Cost of Dying' Revisited," *Milbank Quarterly* (1994): 561–91; A. A. Scitovsky, "'The High Cost of Dying': What Do the Data Show?," *Milbank Quarterly* 83, no. 4 (2005): 825–41; J. Lubitz and R. Prihoda, "The Use and Costs of Medicare Services in the Last 2 Years of Life," *Health Care Financing Review* 5, no. 3 (1984): 117; J. D. Lubitz and G. F. Riley, "Trends in Medicare Payments in the Last Year of Life," *New England Journal of Medicine* 328, no. 15 (1993): 1092–96.

75. D. H. Taylor Jr. et al., "What Length of Hospice Use Maximizes Reduction in Medical Expenditures Near Death in the US Medicare Program?," *Social Science & Medicine* 65 (2007): 1466–78; E. H. Bradley et al., "Depression Among Surviving Caregivers: Does Length of Hospice Enrollment Matter?," *American Journal of Psychiatry* 161, no. 22 (2004): 2257–62; S. C. Miller et al., "Does Receipt of Hospice Care in Nursing Homes Improve the Management of Pain at the End of Life?," *Journal of the American Geriatrics Society* 50, no. 3 (2002): 507–15; R. L. Kane et al., "Hospice Role in Alleviating the Emotional Stress of Terminal Patients and Their Families," *Medical Care* (1985): 189–97; D. E. Meier, "Increased Access to Palliative Care and Hospice Services: Opportunities to Improve Value in Health Care," *Milbank Quarterly* 89, no. 3 (2013): 343–80; M. D. Carlson et al., "Hospice Characteristics and the Disenrollment of Patients with Cancer," *Health Services Research* 44, no. 6 (2009): 2004–21; A. S. Kelley et al., "Hospice Enrollment Saves Money for Medicare and Improves Care Quality Across a Number of Different Lengths-of-Stay," *Health Affairs* 32, no. 3 (2013): 552–61.

76. Interview #67.

77. "Towards Public Health on Equal Terms."

78. D. Raphael and T. Bryant, "The State's Role in Promoting Population Health: Public Health Concerns in Canada, USA, UK, and Sweden," *Health Policy* 78, no. 1 (2006): 39–55.

79. "National Health Plan for Norway (2007–2010)," in *Proposition to the Storting No. 1 (2006–2007)* (Oslo, Norway; Ministry of Health and Care Services, 2006); "Preventive Health Care and Health Promotion" (Copenhagen, Denmark: Ministry of Health, 2010), http://www.sum.dk/Aktuelt/Publikationer/Publikationer/UK_Healthcare_in_DK/Chapter 05.aspx.

80. J. Magnussen, JK. Vrangbaek, and R. Saltman, *Nordic Health Care Systems*.

81. Interview #62.

82. "Chapter 2: The Public Health Objective Bill (Govt. Bill 2002/03:35)—Extended Summary," *Scandinavian Journal of Public Health* 32, no. 6, suppl. 64 (2004): 18.

83. Interview #32.

84. Interview #66.

85. P. Lee and D. Paxman, "Reinventing Public Health," *Annual Review Public Health* 18 (1997): 1–35; R. G. Wilkinson and M. Marmot, *The Solid Facts: Social Determinants of Health* (Copenhagen, Denmark: World Health Organization, 2003); D. R. Williams and P. B. Jackson, "Social Sources of Racial Disparities in Health," *Health Affairs* 24, no. 2 (2005): 325–34; J. M. McGinnis, P. Williams-Russo, and J. R. Knickman, "The Case for More Active Policy Attention to Health Promotion," *Health Affairs* 21, no. 2 (2002): 78–93; M. Marmot, "Social Determinants of Health Inequalities," *Lancet* 365, no. 9464 (2005): 1099–1104; R. F. Schoeni et al., *Making Americans Healthier: Social and Economic Policy As Health Policy* (New York: Russell Sage Foundation, 2010).

86. E. Page, *Localism and Centralism in Europe: The Political and Legal Bases of Local Self-Government*, Comparative European Politics (Oxford and New York: Oxford University Press, 1991), 186.

87. Ibid.

88. Interview #40.

89. R. B. Saltman and S. E. Bergman, "Renovating the Commons: Swedish Health Care Reforms in Perspective," *Journal of Health Politics, Policy, and Law* 30, no. 1–2 (2005): 253–75.

90. Interview #32.

91. E. Colmorten, T. Clausen, and S. Bengtsson, *Providing Integrated Health and Social Care for Older People in Denmark* (Copenhagen, Denmark: Danish National Institute of Social Research, 2003), 7, 17, 18.

92. See http://www.tips-info.com/, accessed June 2013. See also W. T. Hegelstad et al. "Long-Term Follow-Up of TIPS Early Detection in Psychosis Study: Effects on 10-Year Outcome." *American Journal of Psychiatry* 169, no. 4 (April 2012): 379-380.

93. Interview #67.

94. For more-detailed analysis of the policy reforms implemented in the last decades as well as related outcomes, see M. I. Harrison and J. Calltorp, "The Reorientation of Market -Oriented Reforms in Swedish Health-care," *Health Policy* (Elsevier) 50, no. 3 (2000), 219–40; S.-E. Bergman, "Swedish Models of Health Care Reform: A Review and Assessment," *International Journal of Health Planning and Management* 13 (1998): 91–106, doi: 10.1002/(SICI)1099–1751(199804/06)13:2<91:AID-HPM509>3.0.CO;2-C; R. Andersen, B. Smedby, and D. Vågerö, "Cost Containment, Solidarity and Cautious Experimentation: Swedish Dilemmas," *Social Science & Medicine* 52, no. 8 (1982, 2001): 1195–1204; Magnussen, Vrangbaek, and Saltman, *Nordic Health Care Systems*.

95. A. H. Glenngård et al., *Health Systems in Transition: Sweden* (Copenhagen, Denmark: WHO Regional Office for Europe on Behalf of the European Observatory on Health Systems and Policies, 2005).

96. OECD, "Waiting Times," in *Health at a Glance 2011: OECD Indicators* (Paris, France: OECD Publishing, 2011).

97. C. Guibourg, "Private Health Insurance in Sweden: A Clash of Cultures," *The Local* (Sweden), October 10, 2011.

98. "139 Days Waiting in the Health Line," in *Health Care Reality in Norway*, August 14, 2009, accessed June 1, 2013, http://therichestcountry.blogspot.com/.

99. OECD, *Country Statistical Profiles: Sweden, Denmark, and Norway* (Paris, France: OECD StatExtracts, 2012), accessed May 31, 2013, http://www.stats.oecd.org.

100. This experience is in contrast to former waves of immigration to Scandinavia. For instance, in the 1960s, the region's long-standing minority groups (people of Jewish or Roma backgrounds) were joined by an influx of people from Eastern Europe. At the time, the social response to immigration was largely to assimilate minority groups into the Scandinavian identity through teaching of language and cultural norms, and the provision of the full range of social and health services due to every citizen.

101. D. Zimmerman, "Better Protection of National Minorities and Minority Languages in Sweden? Sweden's Act on National Minorities and National Minority Languages of 2010," *International Law Observer*, 2010, accessed May 31, 2013, http://www.internationallawobserver .eu/2010/02/16/better-protection-of-national-minorities-and-minority-languages-in-sweden/.

102. Ibid.

103. Interview #65.

104. R. Cohen, "For 'New Danes,' Differences Create a Divide," in *New York Times*, December 18, 2000, World section; E. Haavio-Mannila and K. Stenius, "Mental Health Problems of Immigrants in Sweden," *Acta Sociologica* 17, no. 4 (1976): 367–92.

105. Interview #32.

106. Interview #69.

107. "Special Report: The Ins and the Outs: Immigration and Growing Inequality Are Making the Nordics Less Homogeneous," *The Economist*, February 2, 2013, Special Reports.

108. Interview #67.

109. Interview #32.

110. N. Kindal and S. Kuhnle, *Normative Foundations of the Welfare State* (London: Routledge, 2005).

111. Interview #69.

112. Magnussen, Vrangbaek, and Saltman, *Nordic Health Care Systems*; Saltman and Bergman, "Renovating the Commons"; R. Andersen, B. Smedby, and D. Vågerö, "Cost Containment, Solidarity and Cautious Experimentation: Swedish Dilemmas," *Social Science & Medicine* 52, no. 8 (1982, 2001): 1195–1204; P. Pierson, *The New Politics of the Welfare State* (New York: Oxford University Press, 2001).

113. "Special Report: The Secret of Their Success: The Nordic Countries Are Probably the Best-Governed in the World," *The Economist*, February 2, 2013, Special Reports.

114. Colmorten, Clausen, and Bengtsson, *Providing Integrated Health and Social Care*.

CHAPTER 5: HOME-GROWN INNOVATIONS

1. B. Obama, "State of the Union Address," accessed May 25, 2013, www.whitehouse.gov /the-press-office/2011/01/25/remarks-president-state-union-address.

2. H. Moses III et al., "Financial Anatomy of Biomedical Research," *JAMA* 294, no. 11 (2005): 1333–42; M. Bronstein, "Are We Willing to Relinquish Our Global Leadership?" (Alexandria, VA: Research America, September 2012), accessed May 26, 2013, http://www .researchamerica.org/uploads/healthdollar11.pdf.

3. "Total quality management" (TQM) is a management approach to long-term success through achieving customer satisfaction. In a TQM effort, all members of an organization participate in improving processes, products, services, and the culture in which they work. http://asq.org/learn-about-quality/total-quality-management/overview/overview.html.

"Six Sigma" at many organizations simply means a measure of quality that strives for near perfection. Six Sigma is a disciplined, data-driven approach and methodology for eliminating defects in any process—from manufacturing to transactional and from product to service. http://www.isixsigma.com/new-to-six-sigma/getting-started/what-six-sigma/.

"Toyota Lean" describes a philosophy that incorporates a collection of tools and techniques into the business processes to optimize time, human resources, assets, and productivity, while improving the quality level of products and services to their customers. http:// www.sae.org/manufacturing/lean/column/leanjun01.htm.

Some of these, particularly TQM and Toyota Lean, originated in Japan. For more reading in this area, see W. E. Deming, *Out of the Crisis* (Cambridge, MA: MIT Press, 1986); K. Ishikawa, *What Is Total Quality Control? The Japanese Way* (Upper Saddle River, NJ: Prentice Hall, 1985); A. V. Feigenbaum, *Total Quality Control* (New York: McGraw-Hill, 1991); J. M. Juran, *Juran on Leadership for Quality: An Executive Handbook* (Detroit, MI: Free Press, 1989).

4. J. M., Rodrigues, "DRGs: Origin and Dissemination Throughout Europe," in *Diagnosis Related Groups in Europe*, eds. M. Casas and M. Wiley (Berlin/Heidelberg, Germany: Springer -Verlag, 1993), 17–29; N. Proudlove, C. Moxham, and R. Boaden, "Lessons for Lean in Healthcare from Using Six Sigma in the NHS," *Public Money and Management* 28, no. 1 (2008): 27–34; M. Roland, "Linking Physicians' Pay to the Quality of Care—A Major Experiment in the United Kingdom," *New England Journal of Medicine* 351, no. 14 (2004): 1448–54.

5. A. Gawande, "The Velluvial Matrix," in "Commencement Address to the Stanford School of Medicine," *New Yorker*, June 26, 2010, http://www.newyorker.com/online/blogs /newsdesk/2010/06/gawande-stanford-speech.html.

6. Interviews included selected front-line, program-management, and executive-level staff. Interviews were audio recorded and transcribed after informed consent. (See Appendix A.)

7. Interview #56.

8. Ibid.

9. Ibid.

10. Ibid.

11. Ibid.

12. Ibid.

13. Ibid.

14. Ibid.

15. Ibid.

16. Ibid.

17. Source: unpublished data from LA PALESTRA client records.

18. Interview #3.

19. Ibid.

20. Ibid.

21. Interview #12.

22. Ibid.

23. Interview #3.

24. Ibid.

25. J. A. Barber et al., "Monitoring the Dissemination of Peer Support in the VA Health-care System," *Community Mental Health Journal* 44, no. 6 (2008): 433–41; S. Resnick and R. Rosenheck, "Integrating Peer-Provided Services: A Quasi-Experimental Study of Recovery Orientation, Confidence, and Empowerment," *Psychiatric Services* 59, no. 11 (2008): 1307–14; S. G. Resnick et al., "A Model of Consumer-Provider Partnership: Vet-to-Vet," *Psychiatric Rehabilitation Journal* 28, no. 2 (2004): 185–87.

26. L. Harkness, *Profile of Laurie Harkness, PhD*, Smith College, http://www.smith.edu /ssw/docs/LaurieHarkness.pdf.

27. Interview #26.

28. Ibid.

29. NAEH, *What Is Housing First?* Solutions Brief (Washington, DC: National Alliance to End Homelessness, 2006), http://www.endhomelessness.org/library/entry/what-is-housing -first.

30. LAHSA, *Greater Los Angeles Homeless Count Report* (Los Angeles: Los Angeles Homeless Services Authority, 2011).

31. NAEH, *SOH 2012: Chapter One—Homelessness Counts* (Washington, DC: National Alliance to End Homelessness, 2012).

32. M. R. Burt, *Homelessness: Programs and the People They Serve* (Darby, PA: Diane Publishing Company, 1999).

33. M. Gladwell, "Million-Dollar Murray," *New Yorker*, February 13, 2006, http://www .gladwell.com/2006/2006_02_13_a_murray.html.

34. M. E. Larimer et al., "Health Care and Public Service Use and Costs Before and After Provision of Housing for Chronically Homeless Persons with Severe Alcohol Problems," *JAMA* 301, no. 13 (2009): 1349–57; R. Kuhn and D. P. Culhane, "Applying Cluster Analysis to Test a Typology of Homelessness by Pattern of Shelter Utilization: Results from the Analysis of Administrative Data," *American Journal of Community Psychology* 26, no. 2 (1998): 207–32; M. R. Burt, C. Wilkins, and D. Mauch, "Medicaid and Permanent Supportive Housing for Chronically Homeless Individuals: Literature Synthesis and Environmental Scan," (Washington, DC: US Department of Health and Human Services, 2011), accessed June 9, 2011, http://aspe.hhs.gov/daltcp/reports/2011/ChrHomlr.htm#intro; L. Gulcur et al., "Housing, Hospitalization, and Cost Outcomes for Homeless Individuals with Psychiatric Disabilities Participating in Continuum of Care and Housing First Programmes," *Journal of Community & Applied Social Psychology* 13, no. 2 (2003): 171–86.

35. Interview #26.

36. Ibid.

37. Ibid.

38. Interview #28.

39. Interview #26.

40. Ibid.

41. Interview, Mary Luthy, February 21, 2012.

42. Interview #27; additional statement accessed May 29, 2013, http://www.youtube.com /watch?v=bJYGBz809L4&feature=youtu.be; similar effects have been seen nationally by

the National Health Care for the Homeless Council, http://www.nhchc.org/wp-content/uploads/2011/09/RespiteCostFinal.pdf.

43. Interview #26.

44. Interview #71.

45. J. Berthold, "Take the C-Train: Hospital-Funded Transitions-of-Care Program Targets Underserved Patients," *ACP Hospitalist*, March 2012, http://www.acphospitalist.org/archives/2012/03/ctrain.htm.

46. Interview #71.

47. Ibid.

48. M. M. Davis et al., "'Did I Do As Best As the System Would Let Me?' Healthcare Professional Views on Hospital to Home Care Transitions," *Journal of General Internal Medicine* 27, no. 12 (2012): 1649–56.

49. Interview #71.

50. Interview #76.

51. Ibid.

52. H. Englander and D. Kansagara, "Planning and Designing The Care Transitions Innovation (C-Train) for Uninsured and Medicaid Patients," *Journal of Hospital Medicine* 7, no. 7 (2012): 524–29.

53. Interview #71.

54. Interview #76.

55. Interview #71.

56. Interview #73.

57. Ibid.

58. Interview #76.

59. Interview #71.

60. Interview #74.

61. Ibid.

62. Interview #76.

63. Ibid.

64. Ibid.

65. J. K. Iglehart, "The Uncertain Future of Medicare and Graduate Medical Education," *New England Journal of Medicine* 365, no. 14 (2011): 1340–45; D. D. Maeng et al., "Can a Patient-Centered Medical Home Lead to Better Patient Outcomes? The Quality Implications of Geisinger's Proven Health Navigator," *American Journal of Medical Quality* 27, no. 3 (2012): 210–16.

66. Gawande, "The Velluvial Matrix."

CHAPTER 6: AN AMERICAN WAY FORWARD

1. G. Rosen, "Public Health: Then and Now. The First Neighborhood Health Center Movement—Its Rise and Fall," *American Journal of Public Health* 61, no. 8 (1971): 1620–37.

2. Much of what follows derives from the work of Alice Sardell, professor of urban studies at Queens College, City University of New York, in her book *The U.S. Experiment in Social Medicine: The Community Health Center Program, 1965–1986*, Contemporary Community Health (Pittsburgh: University of Pittsburgh Press, 1988), x, 278.

3. B. Lefkowitz, *Community Health Centers: A Movement and the People Who Made It Happen* (New Brunswick, NJ: Rutgers University Press, 2007).

4. Sardell, *The U.S. Experiment in Social Medicine*; P. Starr, *The Social Transformation of American Medicine* (New York: Basic Books, 1982), xiv, 514.

5. The funding for the neighborhood health centers, including their infrastructure, overhead, and reimbursement for uninsured care, came from government grants. Specifically, the funding came from the OEO and was bundled with other of President Johnson's Great Society programs. The Department of Health, Education, and Welfare (DHEW) funded most traditional domestic health programs and worked closely with the medical profession represented by the AMA.

6. I. Marcus, *Dollars for Reform: The OEO Neighborhood Health Centers* (Lanham, MD: Lexington Books, 1981); Sardell, *The U.S. Experiment in Social Medicine*.

7. More detail is provided on the political dynamics and consequences of this challenge in Sardell, *The U.S. Experiment in Social Medicine*.

8. Sardell, *The U.S. Experiment in Social Medicine*, x, 278.

9. President Johnson in 1967 argued with Congress that the neighborhood health centers should not be confused with the other OEO programs, as they were run "by professionals" and were free from corruption. Furthermore, he is cited as arguing, "[Neighborhood health centers] were not socialism . . . [they] were just the good old American process of trying to give some people who didn't have something, something." Sardell, *The U.S. Experiment in Social Medicine*, 67.

10. See Chapters 3 and 4 of Sardell, *The U.S. Experiment in Social Medicine*, for more detailed development of this act and its consequences.

11. J. W. Wilson, "Indian Health Service," *JAMA* 231, no. 12 (1975): 1228; J. P. Rife, *Caring and Curing: A History of the Indian Health Service* (Landover, MA: PHS Commissioned Officers Foundation for the Advancement of Public Health, 2009).

12. The model has been considered highly effective in its impact on health outcomes, as argued by Luisa Buada: "Studies showed that the health center model reduced health disparities, lowered infant mortality rates, and reduced chronic disease. Health centers created jobs and other investments in hard pressed communities, and produced cost-savings for the health care system by reducing the need for acute care at hospital emergency rooms." From L. Buada, *The Community Health Center Movement* (East Palo Alto, CA: Ravenswood Family Health Center, 2012), February 28, 2012, http://www.ravenswoodfhc.org/images/pdf/History-of-community-Health-Center-Movement.pdf.

13. Sardell, *The U.S. Experiment in Social Medicine*.

14. R. Nixon, "Veto Message on the Labor-HEW-OEO Appropriations Bill," 1970, The American Presidency Project, 1970, http://www.presidency.ucsb.edu/ws/?pid=2491.

15. Sardell, *The U.S. Experiment in Social Medicine*; Congress, *Public Law 94–63* (Public Health Service Act), 42 U.S.C. § 2689 (1975).

16. NACHC, *United States Health Center Fact Sheet* (Bethesda, MD: National Association of Community Health Centers, 2011).

17. For more detail, see Sardell, *The U.S. Experiment in Social Medicine*; J. C. Donovan, *The Politics of Poverty* (New York: Pegasus, 1967); F. F. Piven and R. A. Cloward, *Poor People's Movements: Why They Succeed, How They Fail* (New York: Vintage, 1967); L. Friedman, "The Social and Political Context of the War on Poverty: An Overview," in *A Decade of Federal Antipoverty Programs: Achievements, Failures, and Lessons*, ed. R. H. Haveman (Philadelphia, PA: Academic Press, 1977), 26; Starr, *The Social Transformation of American Medicine*.

18. R. Nixon, "Special Message to the Congress Proposing a National Health Strategy," The American Presidency Project, 1971, accessed February 12, 2013, http://www.presidency.ucsb.edu/ws/index.php?pid=3311.

19. P. M. Ellwood Jr. et al., "Health Maintenance Strategy," *Medical Care* 9, no. 3 (1971): 291–98.

20. HMO development activities included establishing a physician group or structure for accepting payment, developing payment contracts, creating guidelines for utilization and quality reviews, and other activities to establish a new entity.

21. G. Claxton et al., *Employer Health Benefits: 2012 Annual Survey* no. 5 (Menlo Park, CA: The Kaiser Family Foundation and Health Research & Educational Trust, 2012) 65–70.

22. AMA, *Code of Medical Ethics: Managed Care* (Chicago: American Medical Association, 1996).

23. M. A. Faria, "The AMA, Medical Liability Tort Reform, and HMO Lawsuits," in *Medical Sentinel* (n.p.: Hacienda Publishing, 2002).

24. OECD, *Health Policies and Data: OECD Health Data 2012–Frequently Requested Data* (Paris, France: OECD Publishing, 2012).

25. As an example, in 1995, the Connecticut legislature amended regulations of the Department of Insurance in Connecticut to require HMOs to cover at least two nights in the hospital for childbirth, at a time when HMOs were experimenting with what the press called "drive-through deliveries," where only one night of hospital stay was covered for childbirth, in D. E. Kuper, "Newborns' and Mothers' Health Protection Act: Putting the Brakes on Drive-Through Deliveries," *Marquette Law Review* 80 (1996): 667. 26. J. Csellak, "US Healthcare Spending as Percentage of GDP," *Econographics: Exploring Data Visually*, September 28, 2012, accessed 5/30/2012, http://econographics.wordpress.com/2012/09/28 /u-s-healthcare-spending-as-percentage-of-gdp/.

27. Claxton et al., *Employer Health Benefits*; MCOL, *Managed Care Fact Sheets: National HMO Enrollment Graph 1987–2011*, accessed March 28, 2013, http://www.mcol.com/factsheet _hmo_enrollment_graph.

28. Whether this finding is due to their skimming off the healthier patients (who do not need or use as many services) is debated, and has been most thoroughly documented for Medicare HMOs. Please see M. Gold, M. Sparer, and K. Chu, "Medicaid Managed Care: Lessons from Five States," *Health Affairs* (Millwood) 15, no. 3 (1996): 153–66; N. K. Sekhri, "Managed Care: The US Experience," *Bulletin of the World Health Organization* 78 (2000): 830–44; V. S. Staines, "Potential Impact of Managed Care on National Health Spending," *Health Affairs* 12, suppl. 1 (1993): 248–57; R. H. Miller and H. S. Luft, "Does Managed Care Lead to Better or Worse Quality of Care?," *Health Affairs* 16, no. 5 (1997): 7–25; B. E. Landon et al., "Analysis of Medicare Advantage HMOs Compared with Traditional Medicare Shows Lower Use of Many Services During 2003–09," *Health Affairs* 31, no. 12 (2012): 2609–17; R. S. Brown et al., "Do Health Maintenance Organizations Work for Medicare?," *Health Care Financing Review* 15, no. 1 (1993): 7–23; B. H. Gray, "Trust and Trustworthy Care in the Managed Care Era," *Health Affairs* 16, no. 1 (1997): 34–49.

29. "A Gagged Physician Cannot Fully Serve the Patient: If the Offending HMOs Persist, New Laws May Be Needed," *Los Angeles Times*, April 21, 1996, accessed May 30, 2013, http://articles.latimes.com/1996-04-21/opinion/op-61021_1_patient-care.

30. Gray, "Trust and Trustworthy Care"; A. C. Kao et al., "The Relationship Between Method of Physician Payment and Patient Trust," *JAMA* 280, no. 19 (1998): 1708–14.

31. Nixon, "Special Message to the Congress."

32. P. M. Lantz, R.L. Lichtenstein, and H. A. Pollack, "Health Policy Approaches to Population Health: The Limits of Medicalization," *Health Affairs* (Millwood) 26, no. 5 (2007): 1253–57.

33. R. C. Fox, "The Medicalization and Demedicalization of American Society," *Daedalus* 106, no. 1 (1977): 9–22; I. Illich, A. Cochrane, and R. Williams, *Medical Nemesis* (Sydney, NSW: Australian Broadcasting Commission, Science Programmes Unit, 1975); H. Waitzkin and J. D. Stoeckle, "Information Control and the Micropolitics of Health Care: Summary of an Ongoing Research Project," *Social Science & Medicine* (1967) 10, no. 6 (1976): 263–76; H. Waitzkin and B. Waterman, "Social Theory and Medicine," *International Journal of Health Services* 6, no. 1 (1976): 9–23; P. Conrad, *Identifying Hyperactive Children: The Medicalization of Deviant Behavior* (Lexington, MA: Lexington Books, 1976), xvi, 122.

34. H. M. Krumholz, "Post-Hospital Syndrome—An Acquired, Transient Condition of Generalized Risk," *New England Journal of Medicine* 368, no. 2 (2013): 100–102.

35. Paul Starr refers to the cultural authority of physicians, highlighting their ability to frame reality for patients. Starr suggests that when a physician tells patients they have an illness, patients are likely to believe the physician regardless of how they may feel. See Starr, *The Social Transformation of American Medicine*, xiv, 514.

36. S. Brownlee, "Shannon Brownlee, Acting Director, Health Policy Program," 2012, May 30, 2013, http://newamerica.net/user/218; S. Brownlee, "Escape Fire: The Fight to Save American Health Care," 2013, accessed May 30, 2013, http://transcripts.cnn.com/TRAN SCRIPTS/1303/10/se.01.html.

37. A. Kaplan, *The Conduct of Inquiry: Methodology for Behavioral Science* (San Francisco: Chandler Publishing Company, 1964).

38. M. I. Roemer, "Bed Supply and Hospital Utilization: A Natural Experiment," *Hospitals* 35 (1961): 36; the idea of cultural authority is further developed in Starr, *The Social Transformation of American Medicine*, xiv, 13–15.

39. Roemer, "Bed Supply and Hospital Utilization."

40. D. L. Crooks, "American Children at Risk: Poverty and Its Consequences for Children's Health, Growth, and School Achievement," *American Journal of Physical Anthropology* 38, suppl. 21 (1995): 57–86; E. Brunner, "Socioeconomic Determinants of Health—Stress and the Biology of Inequality," *BMJ* 314, no. 7092 (1997): 1472–76; M. R. Cullen, C. Cummins, and V. R. Fuchs, "Geographic and Racial Variation in Premature Mortality in the U.S.: Analyzing the Disparities," *PloS One* 7, no. 4 (2012): e32930; E. A. Platz et al., "Proportion of Colon Cancer Risk That Might Be Preventable in a Cohort of Middle-Aged US Men," *Cancer Causes & Control* 11, no. 7 (2000): 579–88; M. J. Stampfer et al., "Primary Prevention of Coronary Heart Disease in Women Through Diet and Lifestyle," *New England Journal of Medicine* 343, no. 1 (2000): 16–22; R. G. Wilkinson and M. Marmot, *The Solid Facts: Social Determinants of Health* (Copenhagen, Denmark: World Health Organization, 2003); D. R. Williams and P. B. Jackson, "Social Sources of Racial Disparities in Health," *Health Affairs* 24, no. 2 (2005): 325–34; J. M. McGinnis, P. Williams-Russo, and J. R. Knickman, "The Case for More Active Policy Attention to Health Promotion," *Health Affairs* 21, no. 2 (2002): 78–93; M. Marmot, "Social Determinants of Health Inequalities," *Lancet* 365, no. 9464 (2005): 1099–1104; R. F. Schoeni et al., *Making Americans Healthier: Social and Economic Policy As Health Policy* (New York: Russell Sage Foundation, 2010); Rebecca Onie, Paul Farmer, and Heidi Behforouz, "Realigning Health with Care," *Stanford Social Innovation Review* (Summer 2012).

41. "Mississippi Governor Signs 'Anti-Bloomberg' Bill," ABC News, March 19, 2013, accessed May 30, 2013, http://abcnews.go.com/Health/mississippi-governor-signs-anti-bloomberg-bill/story?id=18731896.

42. C. Buckley, "Cheering a Setback to the City's Drink Limits," *New York Times*, March 12, 2013.

43. F. Newport, "For First Time, Majority in U.S. Supports Public Smoking Ban" (Princeton, NJ: Gallup, 2011).

44. CDC, "Overweight and Obesity: Adult Obesity Facts," 2012, accessed February 1, 2013, http://www.cdc.gov/obesity/data/adult.html.

45. S. Begley, "The Costs of Obesity," Reuters, April 30, 2012, http://www.huffingtonpost.com/2012/04/30/obesity-costs-dollars-cents_n_1463763.html.

46. G. Rubenstein, "New Health Rankings: Of 17 Nations, US Is Dead Last," Atlantic, January 10, 2013, accessed May 30, 2013, http://www.theatlantic.com/health/archive/2013/01/new-health-rankings-of-17-nations-us-is-dead-last/267045/.

47. F. S. Fitzgerald, "The Crack-Up," *Esquire*, February–April 1936.

48. B. Herman, "7 States Establishing Medicaid ACOs," *Becker's Hospital Review*, August 16, 2012, accessed February 12, 2013, http://www.beckershospitalreview.com/hospital-physician-relationships/7-states-establishing-medicaid-acos.html.

49. D. Muhlestein et al., *Growth and Dispersion of Accountable Care Organizations: June 2012 Update* (Salt Lake City, UT: Leavitt Partners, Center for Accountable Care Intelligence, 2012).

50. D. M. Berwick, T. W. Nolan, and J. Whittington, "The Triple Aim: Care, Health, and Cost," *Health Affairs* (Millwood) 27, no. 3 (2008): 759–69.

51. Examples of the measures include whether patients thought there was adequate access to specialists, whether the doctor communicated well, and whether they were readmitted to the hospital within thirty days. ACO performance is also rewarded for using an electronic health record, for reconciling medications the patients were taking at the time of hospital admission with those prescribed as patients are discharged, and for targeted screening and prevention activities.

52. As highlighted by Dr. Marc Gourevitch and colleagues in the *American Journal of Public Health*, ACOs would have most incentive to invest in neighborhood-level resources

and services if the individuals whose care the ACOs were responsible for were defined by geography. That is not the case currently, as individuals are assigned to ACOs based on where they received the plurality of their primary care, as documented by billing records. We agree with this point, although we focus more heavily on establishing the best performance measures to reward health-promoting activities. M. N. Gourevitch et al., "The Challenge of Attribution: Responsibility for Population Health in the Context of Accountable Care," *American Journal of Public Health* 102, suppl. 3 (2012): S322–24.

53. A. S. Brett, "'American Values'—A Smoke Screen in the Debate on Health Care Reform," *New England Journal of Medicine* 361, no. 5 (2009): 440–41.

54. Paula Lantz and colleagues refer to this as the "medicalization" of health policy, noting that lack of access to health care is not the most important reason for poor health: P. M. Lantz, R. L. Lichtenstein, and H. A. Pollack, "Health Policy Approaches to Population Health: The Limits of Medicalization," *Health Affairs* (Millwood) 26, no. 5 (2007): 1253–57.

CHAPTER 7: CONTINUING THE DISCOURSE

1. S. H. Woolf and L. Aron, eds. *U.S. Health in International Perspective: Shorter Lives, Poorer Health* (Washington, DC: National Academies Press, 2013).

2. Ibid.

3. J. M. McGinnis, P. Williams-Russo, and J. R. Knickman, "The Case for More Active Policy Attention to Health Promotion," *Health Affairs* 21, no. 2 (2002): 78–93; B. D. Smedley and S. L. Syme, *Promoting Health: Intervention Strategies from Social and Behavioral Research* (Washington, DC: National Academies Press, 2000); D. R. Williams, M. B. McClellan, and A. M. Rivlin, "Beyond the Affordable Care Act: Achieving Real Improvements in Americans' Health," *Health Affairs* 29, no. 8 (2010): 1481–88.

4. D. M. Cutler and A. Lleras-Muney, *Education and Health: Evaluating Theories and Evidence* (Cambridge, MA: National Bureau of Economic Research, 2006); for extensive review of the academic literature on the influence of education, housing, welfare, income transfers, and civil rights on health, see R. F. Schoeni et al., *Making Americans Healthier: Social and Economic Policy As Health Policy* (New York: Russell Sage Foundation, 2010).

5. The literature in this area is broad and deep; for more detail, see Smedley and Syme, *Promoting Health*; D. R. Williams and P. B. Jackson, "Social Sources of Racial Disparities in Health," *Health Affairs* 24, no. 2 (2005): 325–34; M. Marmot, "Social Determinants of Health Inequalities," *Lancet* 365, no. 9464 (2005): 1099–1104; A. L. B. Pavão et al., "Social Determinants of the Use of Health Services Among Public University Workers," *Revista De Saúde Pública* 46, no. 1 (2012): 98–103; Schoeni et al., *Making Americans Healthier*; S. H. Woolf and P. Braveman, "Where Health Disparities Begin: The Role of Social and Economic Determinants—and Why Current Policies May Make Matters Worse," *Health Affairs* 30, no. 10 (2011): 1852–59.

6. Williams and Jackson, "Social Sources of Racial Disparities in Health"; Schoeni et al., *Making Americans Healthier*; H. Thomson, M. Petticrew, and D. Morrison, "Health Effects of Housing Improvement: Systematic Review of Intervention Studies," *BMJ* 323, no. 7306 (2001): 187; C. M. Olson, "Nutrition and Health Outcomes Associated with Food Insecurity and Hunger," *Journal of Nutrition* 129, no. 2 (1999): 521S–24S; M. R. Frone, M. Russell, and M. L. Cooper, "Relation of Work-Family Conflict to Health Outcomes: A Four-Year Longitudinal Study of Employed Parents," *Journal of Occupational and Organizational Psychology* 70, no. 4 (1997): 325–35; M.-Y. Chen, E. K. Wang, and Y.-J. Jeng, "Adequate Sleep Among Adolescents Is Positively Associated with Health Status and Health-Related Behaviors," *BMC Public Health* 6, no. 1 (2006): 59.

7. Please note that these sources apply to the text from the bottom paragraph on page 185 through the first paragraph on page 187. W. T. Gallo, E. H. Bradley, M. Siegel, and S. V. Kasl, "Health Effects of Involuntary Job Loss Among Older Workers: Findings from the Health and Retirement Survey," *Journals of Gerontology: Social Sciences* 55B (2000): S131–140; W. T. Gallo et al., "Findings from the Health and Retirement Survey," *American Journal of Industrial Medicine* 45 (2004): 408–16; W. T. Gallo et al.,

"The Impact of Late-Career Job Loss on Myocardial Infarction and Stroke: A 10-Year Follow-up Using the Health and Retirement Survey," *Occupational and Environmental Medicine* 63 (2006): 683–87; R. Auster, I. Levesson, and D. Saracheck, "The Production of Health: An Exploratory Study," *Journal of Human Resources* 4 (1969): 431–36; M. Grossman, *The Demand for Health: A Theoretical and Empirical Investigation* (New York: Columbia University Press, 1972); M. Grossman and R. Kaestner, "Effects of Education on Health," in *Social Benefits of Education*, ed. Jere R. Behrman and Nevzer Stacey (Ann Arbor: University of Michigan Press, 1997); V. R. Fuchs, *Time Preference and Health: An Exploratory Study* (Chicago: University of Chicago Press, 1982); M. Yoo, "Does Increased Education Lower Health Care Spending? Findings for Self-Managed Health Conditions" (New Brunswick, NJ: Rutgers University, Department of Economics, November 2011); Robert Wood Johnson Foundation report and study by Bridget Booske Catlin of University of Wisconsin, Population Health Institute, cited in Sabrina Tavernise, "Longevity Up in US, but Education Creates Disparity Study Says," *New York Times*, April 3, 2012; N. Kaye, S. C. Harris, and J. Rosenthal, "Chronic Homelessness and Higher Users of Health Services: Report from a Meeting to Explore a Strategy for Reducing Medicaid Spending While Improving Care," *Common Ground* (Portland, ME, and Washington, DC: National Academy for State Health Policy, 2008); M. E. Larimer et al., "Health Care and Public Service Use and Costs Before and After Provision of Housing for Chronically Homeless Persons with Severe Alcohol Problems," *JAMA* 301, no. 13 (2009): 1349–57; L. Gulcur et al., "Housing, Hospitalization, and Cost Outcomes for Homeless Individuals with Psychiatric Disabilities Participating In Continuum of Care and Housing First Programmes," *Journal of Community & Applied Social Psychology* 13 (2003): 171–86; D. P. Culhane, S. Metraux, and T. Hadley, "Public Service Reductions Associated with Placement of Homeless Persons with Severe Mental Illness in Supportive Housing," *Housing Policy Debate* 13, no. 1 (2002); M. Cunningham, "Targeting Chronically Homeless Veterans with HUD-VASH" (Washington, DC: The Urban Institute, August 1, 2009), accessed May 31, 2013, http://www.urban.org/poverty/consequences ofpoverty.cfm; J. Ludwig et al., "Neighborhoods, Obesity, and Diabetes: A Randomized Social Experiment," *New England Journal of Medicine* 365, no. 16 (2011): 1509–19.

8. D. Sullivan and T. von Wachter, "Job Displacement and Mortality: An Analysis Using Administrative Data," *Quarterly Journal of Economics* 124, no. 3 (2009): 1265–1306.

9. A. Reeves et al., "Increase in State Suicide Rate in the USA During Economic Recession," *The Lancet*, November 5, 2012, http://dx.doi.org/10.1016/ S0140-6736(12)61910-2.

10. G. Hardin, "The Cybernetics of Competition: A Biologist's View of Society," *Perspectives in Biology and Medicine* 7 (1963): 58.

11. J. Gleick, *Chaos: Making a New Science* (New York: Open Road, 2011); for an in-depth discussion of complex adaptive systems, see D. H. Meadows, *Thinking in Systems: A Primer* (White River Junction, VT: Chelsea Green Publishing Company, 2008).

12. L. A. Curry, I. M. Nembhard, and E. H. Bradley, "Qualitative and Mixed Methods Provide Unique Contributions to Outcomes Research," *Circulation* 119, no. 10 (2009): 1442–52; E. H. Bradley, L. A. Curry, and K. J. Devers, "Qualitative Data Analysis for Health Services Research: Developing Taxonomy, Themes, and Theory," *Health Services Research* 42, no. 4 (2007): 1758–72; M. Q. Patton, *Qualitative Research & Evaluation Methods* (Thousand Oaks, CA: SAGE Publications, 2002).

13. Interview #80.

14. Interview #72.

15. R. D. Putnam, "Bowling Alone: America's Declining Social Capital," *Journal of Democracy* 6, no. 1 (1995): 65–78.

16. R. D. Putnam, *Bowling Alone: The Collapse and Revival of American Community* (New York: Simon & Schuster, 2001). Lisa Berkman and colleagues have also conducted decades of research to demonstrate the positive health effects of one's social support and social network; see L. F. Berkman and I. Kawachi, Social Epidemiology (New York: Oxford University Press: 2000).

17. K. Bolin et al., "Investments in Social Capital—Implications of Social Interactions for the Production of Health," *Social Science & Medicine* 56, no. 12 (2003): 2379–90.

18. C. Åslund, B. Starrin, and K. Nilsson, "Social Capital in Relation to Depression, Musculoskeletal Pain, and Psychosomatic Symptoms: A Cross-Sectional Study of a Large Population-Based Cohort of Swedish Adolescents," *BMC Public Health* 10, no. 1 (2010): 715.

19. The IOM Report of 2009, *For the Public's Health: Investing in America's Future*, highlighted the woefully inadequate investment in public health and recommended doubling the investment and stabilizing Congress's financial commitment to public health services. The United States devotes less than half of 1 percent of the $2.5 trillion spent on health care per year to public health efforts. The sentiment we describe is noted in Theodore Brown's history of public health, which describes the national support for public health as occurring only in times of crisis and fear of epidemics, bioterrorism, and the like, rather than as a constant source of support for a healthy population. E. Fee and T. M. Brown, "The Unfulfilled Promise of Public Health: Déjà Vu All Over Again," *Health Affairs*, 21, no. 6 (2002): 31–43.

20. Interview #59.

21. D. J. Simons, and C. F. Chabris, "Gorillas in Our Midst: Sustained Inattentional Blindness for Dynamic Events," *Perception* (London) 28, no. 9 (1999): 1059–74.

22. Meadows, *Thinking in Systems*.

23. Nursing Online Education Database, "25 Shocking Facts About the Pharmaceutical Industry," 2008, accessed March 29, 2013, http://noedb.org/library/features/25-shocking -facts-about-the-pharmaceutical-industry; M. Angell, *The Truth About the Drug Companies: How They Deceive Us and What to Do About It* (New York: Random House, 2005).

24. R. Siegel, "U.S. Health Care Workforce Larger Than Ever," on All Things Considered with Tony Carnevale, National Public Radio, March 19, 2012, accessed May 31, 2013, http://cew.georgetown.edu/media/MediaNPR031912.pdf.

INDEX

Elizabeth H. Bradley is the president of Vassar College, professor of science, technology, and society, and professor of political science. She has been a recipient of a Bill & Melinda Gates Foundation grant, and was previously the founder and faculty director of the Global Health Leadership Institute at Yale University and served as hospital administrator at Massachusetts General Hospital. She is a member of the National Academy of Medicine and lives in Poughkeepsie, New York.

Lauren A. Taylor is a Presidential Scholar at Harvard Divinity School where she studies the interactions between science, religion, and culture. She is a research fellow at the Harvard Global Health Institute and was formerly on staff at the Yale Global Health Leadership Institute, where she led a team in building a model of scale-up for public health innovations for the Bill & Melinda Gates Foundation. She completed a master's in public health at Yale University in 2009. She now lives in Boston.

PublicAffairs is a publishing house founded in 1997. It is a tribute to the standards, values, and flair of three persons who have served as mentors to countless reporters, writers, editors, and book people of all kinds, including me.

I. F. STONE, proprietor of *I. F. Stone's Weekly*, combined a commitment to the First Amendment with entrepreneurial zeal and reporting skill and became one of the great independent journalists in American history. At the age of eighty, Izzy published *The Trial of Socrates*, which was a national bestseller. He wrote the book after he taught himself ancient Greek.

BENJAMIN C. BRADLEE was for nearly thirty years the charismatic editorial leader of *The Washington Post*. It was Ben who gave the *Post* the range and courage to pursue such historic issues as Watergate. He supported his reporters with a tenacity that made them fearless and it is no accident that so many became authors of influential, best-selling books.

ROBERT L. BERNSTEIN, the chief executive of Random House for more than a quarter century, guided one of the nation's premier publishing houses. Bob was personally responsible for many books of political dissent and argument that challenged tyranny around the globe. He is also the founder and longtime chair of Human Rights Watch, one of the most respected human rights organizations in the world.

·　　·　　·

For fifty years, the banner of Public Affairs Press was carried by its owner Morris B. Schnapper, who published Gandhi, Nasser, Toynbee, Truman, and about 1,500 other authors. In 1983, Schnapper was described by *The Washington Post* as "a redoubtable gadfly." His legacy will endure in the books to come.

Peter Osnos, *Founder and Editor-at-Large*